"Morley Swingle is a rarity among lawyers, and almost unique among prosecutors: a man who loves the books as much as the courtroom, and who writes as well as he dissects witnesses on the stand. Swingle presents the life of a country prosecutor with verve and wit. Scoundrels is a highly enjoyable romp through crime and punishment. If Tom Wolfe's *Bonfire of the Vanities* captured the essence of criminal practice in a major metropolis, then *Scoundrels* surely captures the essence of that practice in small town and rural America."

—**Robert H. Dierker, Circuit Judge, St. Louis, Missouri**

• • •

"Morley Swingle, a career prosecutor with a fine sense of humor and an appreciation of the English language, has produced an often funny, sometimes moving, but always interesting account of his 25 years as a prosecutor. The reader will gain an understanding of the importance of the prosecutor in our criminal justice system and the nature of decisions a prosecutor must make. Such an understanding is easy to acquire when the presentation is spiced with humor. The reader will also learn that Missouri has its share—maybe more than its share—of weird and sometimes dangerous scoundrels."

—**Edward H. Hunvald, Professor of Law, University of Missouri**

• • •

"Through true tales from his career, Morley Swingle offers an insightful look into the life of a small-town prosecutor. From the bright lights of *Oprah* to the gritty details of crimes, Swingle deftly details both the comic foibles of lawbreakers and the sometimes-tragic consequences of their criminal behavior. Along the way, the reader gains an appreciative feel for the wide range of issues prosecutors must address and the often-difficult decisions they must make."

—**Gary P. Toohey, Editor, *Journal of the Missouri Bar***

Scoundrels
to the
HOOSEGOW

Scoundrels to the HOOSEGOW

Perry Mason Moments
and Entertaining Cases
from the Files of a
Prosecuting Attorney . . .

Morley Swingle

University of Missouri Press
Columbia and London

Library of Congress Cataloging-in-Publication Data

Swingle, Morley.
  Scoundrels to the hoosegow : Perry Mason moments and
entertaining cases from the files of a prosecuting attorney / by
Morley Swingle.
     p. cm.
  Summary: "Morley Swingle, veteran prosecuting attorney,
combines true crime and legal analysis with a healthy dose of
humor as he re-creates more than thirty stories of villains,
heroes, and ordinary citizens, taking readers from the crime
scene to the courtroom and sharing the occasional 'Perry Mason
moment'"—Provided by publisher.
  Includes index.
  ISBN 978-0-8262-1717-2 (hard cover : alk. paper)—ISBN
978-0-8262-1722-6 (pbk. : alk. paper)
  1. Swingle, Morley. 2. Public prosecutors--Missouri--Cape
Girardeau County--Biography. I. Title.
  KF373.S95A3 2007
  364.102'07—dc22   2006100944

Design and Composition: Kristie Lee
Printer and binder: Thomson-Shore, Inc.
Typeface: Berkeley Book

This book is dedicated, with love,
to Olivia . . .

Even Mark Twain would grudgingly admit
that your beauty, intelligence, and
kindness rival those same attributes
of your namesake.

Contents . . .

The highwayman is worth money to the man who
denounces him, to those who arrest him, to
the jailer who guards him, to the judge who
condemns him, and to the hangman who executes
him. In short, if there were no thieves, lock-
smiths would die of hunger.

—Voltaire

The difference between the almost right word
and the right word is really a large matter—
'tis the difference between the lightning bug
and the lightning.

—Mark Twain

Mark Twain is my favorite writer, hands down. If I could share dinner and conversation with anyone who ever lived, this remarkable author and humorist would be the one I would choose. His story-telling talent is unmatched. His ability to find just the right word is inspirational. His voice is inimitable. His humor is infectious and enduring. Even though I have been a prosecutor for most of my adult life, I agree with Twain's observation about mankind: "I haven't a particle of confidence in a man who has no redeeming petty vices whatever." As prosecutor, I have seen my share of vices, both petty and enormous. The need for my line of work would be greatly reduced if more people lived by another Mark Twain maxim: "Let us endeavor so to live that when we come to die even the undertaker will be sorry."

My goal in writing this book is ambitious. I want to do for the occupation of public prosecutor in this generation what Mark Twain did in his era for river-boat piloting in *Life on the Mississippi* and for gold prospecting and frontier reportage in *Roughing It*. I want to tell you about my job, and I want you to laugh now and then as I tell you.

I realize I am setting myself up as an easy target for ridicule and calumny. I can picture former senator Lloyd Bentson standing at a podium, his Texas drawl dripping with disdain, as he fixes me with an icy glare and drills me with the piercing truth of his Quayle-inspired observation: "Mr. Prosecutor, I knew Mark Twain. Mark Twain was a friend of mine. Sir, you are no Mark Twain!"

Okay. I admit it. I'm no Mark Twain. I am merely the elected prosecuting attorney of Cape Girardeau County, Missouri. I practice law next to the Mississippi River about two hundred miles south of the sleepy hamlet where Mark Twain grew up. The town where I live rests on the banks of the Mississippi equidistant between St. Louis and Memphis. Mark Twain called Cape Girardeau "The Athens of the Mississippi" in *Life on the Mississippi,* but I see it with somewhat more jaded eyes.

After several years as a prosecutor, your community, no matter where it is, becomes for you a montage of crime scenes. The Super 8 Motel at 2011 North Kingshighway is not just a clean and inexpensive place to spend the night, but also the battlefield where a drug-crazed killer died in a gunfight with local police officers; the Abe Stuber Track and Field Complex is not just the site where the local university's track team practices, but also the field of shattered dreams where a fraternity pledge was beaten to death in a hazing ritual memorialized on the television shows *Dateline* and *Oprah;* the Humane Society headquarters at 2536 Boutin Drive is not just a fenced-in pet sanctuary, but also a fortress whose walls were comically scaled by a drunken burglar intent on setting free the dogs; the white house at 815 Themis is not just a quaint old home in the historic part of town, but also happens to contain the window from which an aging attorney proudly flashed his worn genitalia at a young waitress who lived across the street; and the since-replaced bridge spanning the Mississippi at Cape Girardeau was not just a 1,342-foot-long "Gateway to the Ozarks," but always remained for me the springboard from which an adventurous thief escaped pursuing police by leaping into the river, only to telephone them later to let them know he had survived.

The list goes on and on.

The story of my job is for neither the squeamish nor the prudish. No matter how attractive the community, the prosecutor sees its underbelly. He sees the murderers, the rapists, the robbers, the drug dealers, the burglars, the wife beaters and the child molesters. As a retiring judge from a criminal court once said, "In my courtroom, day after day, I have seen the dregs of the community—and some of their clients, too."

Just kidding, esteemed members of the defense bar. For the most part.

Which brings me to another warning.

Part of my philosophy of life is to find humor where I can, even in certain aspects of otherwise gruesome and tragic events. This is common in law enforcement, more as a defense mechanism than from callousness. Okay, maybe there is *some* callousness. But certainly, if a prosecutor could not detach himself emotionally from the horrible things he sees daily in police reports, photographs, and courtrooms, he could not remain a prosecutor very long.

The stories I am about to tell thus contain much black humor. I don't mean "black" in the racial sense, but in its meaning of finding comedy in things that are profoundly sad. I cannot begin to relate all of the thousands of cases I have prosecuted during a career that has covered more than two decades. The stories I've chosen are the tales I'd tell Mark Twain if I had that chance to swap yarns with him over the dinner table. Most are included for their humor, some for their oddity, and some because they so clearly portray what it means to be a prosecutor. I'd like to think I could hold up my end of the conversation with Mr. Clemens.

If my attempts to draw a laugh fall flat or appear insensitive, I hereby plead guilty and apologize. Don't send me hate mail. The truth is, I like to laugh. Life is too short to be serious all the time. My intention is to give *you* a chuckle or two.

Every story described in this book really happened. The scoundrels are real. Their misdeeds occurred. In several instances, however, I have changed their names. While each deserved a measure of punishment from the court system, in many cases having his or her stupidity and amorality forever preserved in the pages of a prosecutor's book exceeded the scope of justifiable punishment for the crime. In general, I have used real names of homicide defendants and those convicted criminals whose cases evolved into published appellate court decisions but altered the names of the rest. In a sense I am indebted to each scoundrel for providing me with both a vocation and fodder for these pages.

A certain amount of ego is required to write a book that is, to a great extent, autobiographical. To that charge I also enter a guilty plea and throw myself upon the mercy of the reader. If I did not consider myself a good prosecutor, I would have hung up the spurs long ago. So grant me some leeway should I tend to boast.

Most of all, while I entertain you, I hope to show you what it is like to be a prosecutor in America. Not many career prosecutors have taken the time to tell their stories. Nor have many biographies been written about them, except for those individuals who used the role of prosecutor as a stepping-stone to a judgeship or a seat in Congress, in which cases their stints as public prosecutors usually received minor treatment in their biographies. Did you know, for example, that United States Supreme Court Chief Justice Earl Warren (often castigated during his judicial tenure as being soft on crime) actually served for nearly seventeen years as the elected district attorney of Oakland, California? Or that Thomas E. Dewey, famously defeated by Harry Truman in the presidential election of 1948, earned his national fame as the "Gangbuster" who successfully prosecuted New York City mobsters like Lucky Luciano? Did you know those two former prosecutors made up the Republican ticket for president and vice president in 1948? See, you might even learn a thing or two from reading this book.

So, settle down with me to listen to my side of a conversation with Mark Twain. Feel free to laugh out loud.

I hope you do.

Scoundrels
to the
HOOSEGOW

The American prosecutor enjoys an independence
and a wealth of discretionary power unmatched in
the world. With few exceptions, he is a locally
elected official and the chief law enforcement
official of his community. He represents a local
jurisdiction, is selected for the position by the
voting public and his office is endowed with
unreviewable discretionary authority. Nowhere
else in the world does this combination of features define prosecution.

—Joan E. Jacoby, "The American Prosecutor
in Historical Context" (1997)

"Hoosegow, (hoos gou), n. *Slang*. a jail."

—The Random House Dictionary of
the English Language (1967)

Perry Mason Moment

Every criminal trial is a man-hunt where the
object of the pack is to get the prey. The
purpose of the defense is to effect his escape.
—Clarence Darrow

To be a prosecutor is to accept the responsibility of being the only thing standing between the
defendant and the jailhouse door.
—Christopher Darden

Hamilton Burger was the prosecutor in the Perry Mason mysteries by Erle Stanley Gardner. In the hit television series based on the novels, his record against Mason was roughly 0 wins and 271 losses. William Talman, the actor who played Burger, perfected a look of baffled amazement, an expression worn weekly as the stunned and hapless prosecutor fell victim to yet another sensational courtroom stunt sprung by Perry Mason to prove that his client, whom Burger thought guilty, was actually innocent.

It is a wonder this punching bag of a prosecutor could face going into a courtroom, the place where he had suffered more shocks than Pavlov's dog on a busy week at the laboratory. It is even more amazing that Burger never found a reason to assign an assistant prosecutor to handle cases against Perry Mason. Talking tough but delegating the case to someone else is the practice of more than one head prosecutor.

In real life, it would take an utterly incompetent prosecuting attorney, with remarkably bad judgment, to build such a pathetic track record. An elected prosecutor could not do it and keep getting elected. An assistant prosecutor could not do it and keep getting trial assignments. For one thing, no prosecutor files cases that are likely to be lost. Time is better spent on those that have a reasonable likelihood of yielding guilty verdicts. More important, under ethical canons, a prosecutor cannot file a charge unless he believes it is supported by the evidence. If, after filing, he develops a reasonable doubt about a person's guilt, he is obligated to dismiss the charge. A prosecutor simply could not be totally wrong in his analysis of the strength of his case 271 consecutive times.

Furthermore, through the procedure called discovery, the prosecutor will usually find out about any weaknesses in his case prior to trial. In Missouri, each side is required to supply the other with the names and addresses of all witnesses they intend to call, plus any statements those witnesses have given. Thus, a prosecutor usually knows what is coming when he or she walks into the courtroom. The days of trial by ambush are long gone. In this day and age, a true "Perry Mason moment" is a rare thing for prosecutors and defense attorneys alike.

By "Perry Mason moment," I mean that climactic instant during a trial when you have just done something fantastic and everyone in the courtroom knows it. Your brilliant question or some stunning admission you coerced from a witness has left the opposing lawyer reeling, his mouth agape, and jurors amazed and entertained. The case is won; the rest of the trial is a formality. Your friends and colleagues are itching to congratulate you as soon as a recess is called. Only a supreme effort of will on your part, coupled with the knowledge that the judge and jurors are watching, keeps you from high-fiving everyone in sight.

Perry Mason moments have become especially few and far between in an age when both sides know in advance what the witnesses are going to say. Yet, every now and then, one comes along.

I will tell you about my personal favorite. The case was *State v. Delores Luton*.

⚖

Delores Luton was notorious even before she tried to murder her husband. By all accounts, she had been a gorgeous young woman. Men who had known her when she was a young head-turner nostalgically recalled that she had borne a striking resemblance to Elizabeth Taylor. Harry Naeter, the former publisher of Cape Girardeau's local newspaper, the *Southeast Missourian*, recalled one hot summer when the staff at the paper noticed that the shapely

Delores, who lived just a few blocks from the newspaper's office, always washed her car in her driveway on Thursday afternoons. More important, she always wore a revealing black bathing suit for the occasion. Male reporters soon found reasons to leave the office on Thursday afternoons to cruise by her house. The weekly ritual continued until one of them crashed his car into a telephone pole while gawking at her.

Over the years, lurid rumors circulated about Delores Luton. True or not, they surrounded her with an aura of titillating scandal. She was a woman people noticed and talked about.

Along with her beauty, Delores Luton had keen business sense. She amassed a fortune in rental property in downtown Cape Girardeau, and at various times, she owned every kind of business, from a bar, to a clothing store, to a pet store. She was said to be worth more than a million dollars, and she jealously guarded every one of them. The familiar vice of greed caused her downfall.

Delores Luton was fifty-nine years old when she decided to hire a hit man to kill her husband. By that time, quite frankly, she looked a bit more like Margaret Thatcher than Elizabeth Taylor. Yet, people respected and feared her. She had a reputation for getting what she wanted. Her immediate problem in turning her husband into a corpse was the difficulty faced by homicidal spouses for centuries: it is hard to find a reliable, discreet hit man. These guys do not advertise in the yellow pages.

She finally determined that a good way to find a killer was to seek a reference from another killer. One of her former paramours was currently imprisoned for murder. His own incarceration rendered him unavailable for the chore, but he kindly provided her with the name of a friend who just might be willing to do it: Henry Clapp. Henry lived in Portageville, a small town in the Missouri bootheel, just sixty miles from Cape Girardeau.

To his credit, Henry high-tailed it straight to the Missouri Highway Patrol after his first meeting with her and spilled his guts. Henry Clapp may not have led an exemplary life, but he was no killer.

Henry was a small, wiry man, and he was hairy. His appearance was one part Woody Allen and two parts hillbilly bad guy from the movie *Deliverance*. Henry, because of his admirable scruples about murder, was shortly to prove to be something of an award-winning actor himself.

A few days after ratting out Delores Luton to the highway patrol, Henry met her at a restaurant parking lot in Cape Girardeau to work out the details of the killing. As the aging sexpot bustled from her car to Henry's pickup

truck and climbed inside, she was being photographed by Sheriff Norm
Copeland and other officers hiding in a nearby surveillance van. Henry was
wearing a tape recorder supplied by Sergeant Donnie Smith of the Missouri
State Highway Patrol, ready to record for posterity every incriminating word.

Henry, performing well in his role as ice water-in-the-veins hit man, drove
slowly through Cape Girardeau as Delores gave him directions to her home.
She explained to him that she wanted her husband, Wilber, killed on an
upcoming Sunday afternoon. She and Wilber would leave for brunch. She
would make sure the back door was unlocked. While they were out, Henry
was to sneak into the house. She would leave a crowbar and a pair of gloves
lying on the steps inside the back door. Henry was to don the gloves, grab the
crowbar, and wait at the top of the stairs. She would send her husband home
for a pair of shoes around 2:00 P.M. When Wilber got to the top of the steps,
Henry was to whomp him upside the head with the crowbar.

"He won't know what hit him," she said.

"How big a man is he?" Henry asked.

"Two hundred pounds, but he's dying. He suffers like crazy."

"Well, we're just doing him a favor then."

Delores laughed. "I kinda feel that way. He's got nervical cranial syndrome
on the brain, but don't let that faze you. Man, just take him like he's a tiger."

"There's not a doubt in your mind, then?" Henry said. "You want the man
dead?"

"There's not a doubt in my mind."

When they drove by her house, a large home just three blocks from the
Mississippi River, she pointed to the door he was to enter.

"You go in that door and wait at the top of the steps. He'll be walking up
the steps. His head will be down as he's coming up them."

"Do you want me to make it look like an accident?"

"No. It doesn't matter. Whatever is the easiest, the fastest and the quickest.
The insurance company will pay either way."

Knowing her chilling words were being captured on tape, Henry asked a
very logical and extremely incriminating question: "Why don't you just
divorce the guy?"

Delores snorted. "If I divorce him, he gets half of everything. This way, I
get it all."

As Henry drove the would-be widow back to her car, she ranted about
how unfair it was for her husband to get half of the money she had made

through her own hard work. He was lazy, she said. She was the one who had worked her tail off to make that money!

Before they parted, they also discussed the terms of the contract. Delores was to pay Henry a total of $20,000. She paid $2,500 on the spot. She would pay another $2,500 on the day after the murder. The rest would be delivered once the two-million-dollar life insurance policy paid off.

The police decided to nab Delores Luton right before the murder was scheduled to take place. That Sunday morning they watched as she and her husband went to brunch. When she left him to return home alone to open the house for Henry, Patrolman Mark Majoros pulled her over not far from her house. Looking through the driver's window, he could see a crowbar and a pair of gloves. He arrested her.

I charged her with conspiracy to commit murder. A murder conspiracy is absolutely my favorite kind of case. It involves all of the drama and excitement of a murder trial without the inconvenience, unpleasantness, and tragedy of a dead body.

The Delores Luton case did not appear to be a likely vehicle for a Perry Mason moment. It was incredibly strong. We had the tapes. We had Henry as a witness. We had the crowbar and the gloves. We had the $2,500 down payment for the hit. We had the insurance policy she had taken out on her husband's life without his knowledge and proof that she had forged his signature on the application. We had a husband who, once he found out his wife wanted him dead, became a very cooperative state's witness. I did not need any more evidence. I was good to go. That's what puzzled me most about what happened next.

I was at my desk working on other cases one afternoon when my secretary announced a visitor at the front desk. His name was Beck Jolly. He claimed to be a witness in the upcoming Delores Luton trial. Normally, an unexpected witness would meet with my investigator rather than with me since a prosecutor should avoid becoming a potential witness. The person who takes a witness's statement can be called as a witness should the person giving the statement later change his story. But my investigator was out. I was intrigued, and rather than let the opportunity slip through my fingers, I ushered Jolly into my office.

He was a big man, heavyset, with black hair and beard. Once I checked the file, I saw that the defense had indeed listed him as a potential witness but had never disclosed to me what he would be saying.

Over the next hour or so, he told me that Delores Luton was trying to bribe him to lie on the witness stand. She was offering him $5,000, a set of drums, and a diamond ring to commit perjury. All he had to do was take the stand and claim that she had been with him in Sikeston on the day Henry Clapp said he had first met her in Portageville. Her plan was to make it look like Henry had invented the whole thing. She was going to claim she had never had any intention of killing her husband. Her story would be that she had merely played along on the tapes because Henry had approached her with the idea of killing dear Wilber, and she had been suspicious and afraid of this scary killer.

As Beck Jolly told me his story, my mind was racing. On the one hand, my case was already strong. I really did not need another witness, particularly one I had no reason to trust. Perhaps this homicidal woman was sending him to me to try to lure me into doing something stupid. Yet, testimony about an attempt to bribe a witness is admissible in court since it shows an awareness of guilt. Perhaps I *would* want to use him as a witness.

"Are you willing to put everything you told me in writing?" I asked.

Jolly nodded.

I handed him a statement form, and he wrote for several minutes. His statement was short, just two pages. But it was dynamite.

"I don't know yet what I am going to do with this," I told him, "but thank you for coming in. If you're called as a witness by either side, just tell the truth. They probably won't call you once they know what you're going to say, but if I need you I'll subpoena you."

Jolly left, and I pondered the ethics of the situation.

Discovery rules require the prosecutor to supply the defense with a list of *his* witnesses, plus any written statements from those witnesses. A constitutional requirement called the "Brady Rule" also forces a prosecutor to give the defense notice of any exculpatory information, meaning anything tending to show the innocence of the defendant. Jolly's statement did not fall into either category. It was not a statement from one of my witnesses, since Jolly was a defense witness. Nor was it exculpatory, since it did not show her innocence, but rather piled on even more proof of her guilt.

I spent four hours in the law library researching the issue. The bottom line was that if I were going to call Jolly as my own witness, I needed to disclose the statement to the defense; otherwise, I was not required to disclose it.

I decided not to call him. My case was strong enough without him. Besides, I did not completely trust Beck Jolly, even though he struck me as honest. I decided to just carry on with the business of presenting my own case. If the defense called him, I would be armed with the written statement. If he testified to what he had written in his statement, it would be great for the prosecution. If he testified to anything else, I could cross-examine him with his written statement, which would also be great for the prosecution. Either way, the case would not be hurt, and might be helped, by his testimony. I would leave it to providence to determine what would happen.

Several weeks later, the case proceeded to trial in front of Circuit Judge Stephen N. Limbaugh, Jr., an excellent trial judge who was one of my predecessors as the elected prosecutor for Cape Girardeau County. Limbaugh became a judge at the tender age of thirty-five. He proved impossible to stereotype. The first cousin of conservative radio talk-show host Rush Limbaugh, he undoubtedly harbored his share of conservative beliefs, but he was also a card-carrying member of the American Civil Liberties Union before donning his judicial robe. Although he ran his courtroom with stern formality, off the bench his lively sense of humor and talent at the piano entertained everyone around him. He was strictly professional during the Luton trial, though.

The prosecution's case went smoothly. Henry made a decent witness, despite being vigorously cross-examined by Ken Shrum, the former prosecuting attorney for Bollinger County, who happened to be one of the best trial lawyers in southeast Missouri. Henry's own past was less than stellar, and Shrum explored every wart and character flaw. The tapes, though, were sinking the Luton ship. After Henry identified them, I played the damning conversation on a sound system with speakers large enough for every juror to hear every word. Just to make sure they understood what they were hearing, I supplied each juror with a transcript to review while listening to Luton's cold and practically gleeful voice. The case could not have gone much better. The state rested during the second day of the trial.

The defense began its case that same afternoon. Nothing remarkable happened until Ken Shrum announced, "The defense calls Beck Jolly."

Chills literally shot down my spine. I did not know exactly what would happen next, but I knew whatever it was, it would be dramatic. I pulled out Jolly's written statement and watched as the burly man took the oath to tell the truth.

After having Jolly describe how he had known Delores Luton for four years because he had played music in her bar at one time and rented an apartment from her, Shrum got to the gist of Beck Jolly's testimony.

"Did you happen to be at my client's business on Monday, April 4th?"

"Yeah."

"Do you have any recollection that morning of Delores getting a telephone call that you became involved in?"

"She got a phone call, but, being under oath as I am, I can't say that I was really involved in it."

"Well, did you overhear any of the conversation?"

"No, I didn't listen to any of it."

"Did you then talk to her about it?"

"I don't believe I did."

"Later on that week, did you go with her any time any place?"

"No."

A blush crept up the back of Shrum's neck and spread across the back of his balding head. Fury crossed his scalp like a red wave.

He finally exhaled in disgust.

"I have no other questions, Judge."

I gripped Beck Jolly's written statement and rose to my feet. I walked slowly toward him, holding the statement where he could see it. Chills were still coursing up and down my spine. I had never felt quite the same sensation before nor have I since.

"Beck, isn't it true that Delores Luton offered you $5,000, a ring, and a set of drums to lie on the witness stand today?" I asked slowly, pointing to Delores Luton.

The silence in the courtroom lasted only a second or two, but it seemed like an eternity before he gave his answer.

"Yes, sir," Jolly said softly.

"Would you tell the jury exactly what it was she wanted you to say?"

"She wanted me to say that I overheard—I got up beside the phone and listened while the guy made the conversation with her that her husband wanted to kill her, so he thought Delores better talk to him before he did anything about it."

"Was there anything else that she wanted you to testify to that wasn't true?"

"That I went to Sikeston with her and waited for her at the Holiday Inn while she went down and talked to Henry Clapp to set up the meeting, or whatever they were going to do; and, if she wasn't back in two hours, I was supposed to send a State Patrol after her 'cause she was in some kind of trouble."

"And was any of that true?"

"No, sir. She came up with this idea."

"And how were you supposed to remember what to say?"

"She wrote it out on a legal pad, yellow legal pad, long paper; it was two pages of it."

"And then what did she have you do?"

"Go home and rehearse it like I was rehearsing a script for a TV show or whatever."

"And what exactly was it that Delores Luton said she'd pay you today for lying on the witness stand?"

"Five thousand dollars, a gold diamond ring, with about maybe a couple carats altogether, and a set of drums that I was trying to buy from her. And if she got off, I believe it was ten thousand if she got off."

My gaze traveled from Beck Jolly past the jury and finally rested on Delores Luton, who was staring daggers at her witness.

"No further questions."

Perry Mason moment complete, I walked back to my chair.

Of course, the trial was not officially over. It went into a third day, when Delores Luton testified to her innocence and I cross-examined her. Both the prosecutor and the defense lawyer gave impassioned closing arguments. The jury fulfilled its oath by deliberating until the members reached a unanimous verdict. But the suspense had been over from the moment Beck Jolly answered my questions. No way the jury would let her walk after finding out how she had tried to bamboozle them with perjured testimony.

The jury found Delores Luton guilty of conspiracy to commit murder and recommended the maximum sentence available under the law: fifteen years in prison. Judge Limbaugh later imposed the full sentence. A special prosecutor, Tom Dittmeier from St. Louis, was appointed to prosecute her for suborning perjury. I could not prosecute the case myself since I was a potential witness. She subsequently pled guilty to that offense and received an additional four years in prison.

Many years have passed since that trial. I have enjoyed other exhilarating moments in the courtroom. I have tried bigger and more important cases. I have obtained much longer sentences. But I have never since experienced a courtroom moment quite so scintillating as the instant I heard Ken Shrum call the name of the witness who would provide me with my own personal and unforgettable Perry Mason moment.

Thank you, Beck Jolly.

Dog on Death Row

> Probably the least publicly visible aspect of prosecutorial discretion is the charging decision.
>
> —Burton Atkins and Mark Pogrebin

> The freedom to make a choice among possible courses of action or inaction—unreviewable prosecutorial discretion—was, in the end, what truly set the American prosecuting attorney apart from all members of the criminal justice system.
>
> —Joan E. Jacoby

When Jim Smiley stood before Associate Circuit Judge Benjamin F. Lewis and heard that he was being placed on probation, he probably heaved a sigh of relief. Instead of a jail sentence for his misdemeanor offense of driving while intoxicated, he received probation with several specific conditions. They included the usual things like obeying all laws, undergoing alcohol counseling, and performing community service. It was the community service that ultimately did him in.

Jim most likely assumed he would pay his debt to society by picking up trash along the side of a highway or sweeping floors in a public library. He drew a more unusual assignment. He was to spend eight hours at the humane society.

Humane society, he must have thought. *Sounds okay to me. I like dogs. It'll sure beat cleaning toilets at some park.*

Maybe. Maybe not.

Any excitement Jim felt at the opportunity to spend his community service hours in the company of man's best friends undoubtedly evaporated when he reported for duty and learned the true nature of his assignment. His eight hours were to be spent helping euthanize dogs.

Sadly, the humane society cannot possibly find homes for most of the hundreds of dogs it receives each year, so the bulk must be executed. The local humane society goes through more lethal injections in one day than the State of Texas administers to its human death-row population in a decade. Jim Smiley's eight-hour shift as a canine killer proved to be community service of the most gruesome and repulsive sort, particularly for someone with a fondness for dogs.

At the end of his long day, Jim returned to his home, exhausted and deeply depressed. He dragged his tail to his couch and replayed in his mind the events of his humane society sojourn, recalling the sad eyes, the floppy ears, and the tails that would wag no more. He soon realized he was thirsty. He remembered the cold beer in his refrigerator. Sure, one of the conditions of his probation was to consume no alcohol. But here in the privacy of his own home, who was to know?

As it usually does, one beer led to another, and then another. As he dulled the pain of his lethally vivid day, he descended into an alcoholic fog. He kept thinking of the dogs: live dogs, dead dogs, frisky dogs, tired dogs, dogs he helped kill, dogs still in cages awaiting the needle. Particularly acute in his memory bank was a pit bull, a loner much like Jim, sitting so forlornly in its cell on death row. The pit bull was doomed to die because of a humane society policy that pit bulls were never put up for adoption. Once a pit bull came to the shelter its fate was sealed. Unless reclaimed by its owner, any pit bull would ultimately receive a lethal injection.

As Jim Smiley contemplated the dog and its impending doom, he continued drinking. Jim was a man who could hold his booze, but the beers piled up to the point where even *his* judgment was affected. Gradually, a plan formed in his alcohol-addled mind: he would break into the humane society and free the dogs. Yes, it could be done, and he was just the man to do it.

That night, under cover of darkness, Jim stealthily made his way to the humane society. He broke into the canine calaboose. Working quickly, he released each dog from its cage. When he got to the pit bull, he picked it up and held it in his arms. Within minutes, the dogs were all outside, happily departing the premises for places unknown. The pit bull—later to be known as state's exhibit 1—went home with Jim.

Unfortunately for Jim Smiley, a drunk does not do an efficient job of covering up his crime. Within forty-eight hours, the neatly typed and extremely thorough police reports from the Cape Girardeau County Sheriff's Department reached my desk. By setting free the dogs, Jim had committed the felonies of burglary and stealing. Jim was in big trouble. Felonies carry potential prison time.

One of the important functions of a prosecutor is to determine whether charges should be filed in a particular case, and, if so, which precise charges. Charging decisions are extremely important. A judge or jury cannot find a person guilty of murder, for example, if the prosecutor only filed the case as manslaughter. Deciding what charges to file is seldom as simple as connecting the dots. The *National Prosecution Standards* established by the National District Attorneys Association list several factors to consider in determining whether to file a charge:

1. The probability of conviction
2. The nature of the offense
3. The characteristics of the offender (dangerousness; criminal history)
4. Possible deterrent value of prosecution to the offender and society in general
5. Likelihood of prosecution by another criminal justice agency
6. The willingness of the offender to cooperate with law enforcement
7. Aid to other criminal justice goals through non-prosecution
8. The interests of the victim
9. Possible improper motives of a victim or witness
10. The availability of adequate civil remedies
11. The age of the offense
12. Undue hardship caused to the accused
13. Excessive cost of prosecution in relation to the seriousness of the offense
14. Any mitigating circumstances

Burglary is committed when the person unlawfully enters someone else's building for the purpose of committing a crime. Jim had clearly committed a burglary, which carries up to seven years in prison. He had also committed felony stealing, good for another seven years in prison. Thus, it was up to me to decide whether to seek up to fourteen years in prison for Jim Smiley for setting free the dogs. That's why they pay me the big bucks.

I studied the police reports, conscious of the impact my decision would have not only upon Jim Smiley's life but also upon the humane society and upon other would-be dognappers and dog-freers. Charging decisions are not made in a vacuum. The prosecutor stalks his prey in open court with the public watching. The ramifications can be far-reaching.

I employed not only the factors suggested by the *National Prosecution Standards,* but also my own highly scientific and carefully refined test for determining whether to file a criminal charge in a particular case. I call it the "Where's the Beef?" test. This test may require explanation for minds untrained by countless hours spent in law school classes and law libraries. Understanding it also requires some knowledge of pop culture.

In the eighties, the Wendy's restaurant chain came up with a clever television ad in which a little old lady buys a hamburger at a competitor's fast-food joint. She opens up the bun, gawks at the puny smidgen of meat, and in a deep gravelly voice loudly squawks, "Where's the beef?" The ad campaign was a huge hit, and the line was famously and effectively employed by President Ronald Reagan in a televised debate with his challenger, Senator Fritz Mondale. Reagan proclaimed that he had studied Mondale's proposed ideas, and his reaction was, "Where's the beef?"

That was the genesis of my "Where's the Beef?" prosecutorial discretion test. To use it, I picture myself standing in front of a jury, giving my closing argument. I envision myself asking the jury to punish this individual for this offense. If I cannot see myself arguing the case to the jury, it does not pass the "Where's the Beef?" test. If it fails the test, I don't file the charge.

Is this a terrible thing, a prosecutor deliberately choosing not to file a charge when a crime has technically been committed? What about the rule of law? Is it a miscarriage of justice? I think not. I consider it bringing a human and commonsense touch to justice.

One of the most satisfying differences between being a prosecutor and being a defense attorney or a lawyer in private practice is that as a prosecutor you never find yourself arguing anything to a judge or jury that you do not believe in your own heart. As prosecutor, your first obligation is to do justice, not simply to win a particular case. This was eloquently explained by Robert H. Jackson, who served as attorney general for Franklin Roosevelt and later as a Supreme Court justice and eventually as the lead prosecutor for the United States at the Nuremberg trials of Nazi war criminals. To an audience of federal prosecutors in 1940 he said, "A spirit of fair play and decency should animate the prosecutor. Your positions are of such independence and importance that while you are being diligent, strict and vigorous in law enforcement you can also afford to be just. Although the government technically loses its case, it has really won if justice has been done."

Part of the prosecutor's job in dispensing justice is to use his discretion in deciding how to charge a case. Sometimes justice is best served by declining to seek a conviction, rather than by getting it.

I read and reread the police reports in Jim Smiley's case. I pictured him setting free the dogs. I imagined myself arguing to a jury that he should be sent to jail. I applied the "Where's the Beef?" test. I did not overlook the notion that if people who learned about the case saw that he received no punishment, break-ins at the pound might become monthly events. After a great deal of thought, however, I reached my decision: Jim Smiley would not be charged with burglary and stealing. Nor would I charge him even with the misdemeanor of trespass.

Instead, I filed a written probation violation report with Judge Lewis. I notified the judge that Jim Smiley had violated the terms of his probation both by consuming alcohol and by committing this burglary of the humane society. Jim ended up confessing his probation violation to Judge Lewis. The judge made him serve some weekends in the county jail and added twenty more hours of community service as additional conditions of his continued probation.

I have not kept tabs on Jim Smiley. I do know, however, that the humane society is still going strong. My refusal to file the felony charges against Smiley did not produce a rush of canine breakouts. The organization later changed its policy about never putting pit bulls up for adoption. I believe it had something to do with canine profiling.

Like most criminals, Jim Smiley possessed certain redeeming features. Not the least was his love of dogs. Perhaps he was familiar with the story of another Missourian, Senator George Graham Vest.

Vest served as a United States senator for twenty-four years, from 1879 to 1903, but he is best remembered for originating the phrase "man's best friend" in a closing argument to a jury in 1870. A trial lawyer at the time, Vest was representing Charles Burden in a lawsuit for damages against his neighbor, Leonidas Hornsby, who had shot Burden's dog, Old Drum, when it ventured onto the neighbor's property, perhaps with sheep-killing in mind. Vest won the case, and Hornsby had to pay damages for killing the dog. Vest's closing argument in this almost insignificant case brought him immortality. A bronze statue honoring Old Drum and Vest was later erected in Warrensburg, Missouri, where the trial took place. Over the years, portions of the closing argument have been printed in a number of anthologies as well as in the Congressional Record in 1990 as a part of a speech delivered by Senator Robert C. Byrd.

Jim Smiley, legal historian or not, undoubtedly shared the sentiments so eloquently expressed by the rural trial lawyer from Missouri on September 23, 1870:

> Gentlemen of the jury. The best friend a man has in the world may turn against him and become his enemy. His son or daughter whom he has reared with loving care may prove ungrateful. Those who are nearest and dearest to us, those whom we trust with our happiness and our good name, may become traitors to their faith. The money that a man has he may lose. It flies away from him perhaps when he needs it most. A man's reputation may be sacrificed in a moment of ill-considered action. The people who are prone to fall on their knees to do us honor when success is with us may be the first to throw the stone of malice when failure settles its cloud upon our heads. The one absolutely unselfish friend that a man can have in this selfish world, the one that never deserts him, the one that never proves ungrateful or treacherous, is the dog.
>
> Gentlemen of the jury, a man's dog stands by him in prosperity and in poverty, in health and in sickness. He will sleep on the cold ground when the wintry winds blow and the snow drives fiercely, if only he can be near his master's side. He will kiss the hand that has no food to offer, he will lick the wounds and sores that come in encounter with the roughness of the world. He guards the sheep of his pauper master as if he were a prince.
>
> When all other friends desert, he remains. When riches take wings and reputation falls to pieces, he is as constant in his love as the sun in its journey through the heavens. If fortune drives the master forth an outcast into the world, friendless and homeless, the faithful dog asks no higher privilege than that of accompanying him, to guard him against danger, to fight against his enemies. And when the last scene of all comes, and death takes his master in its embrace and his body is laid in the cold ground, no matter if all other friends pursue their way, there by his graveside will the noble dog be found, his head between his paws and his eyes sad but open, in alert watchfulness, faithful and true, even unto death.

Jim Smiley might not have been familiar with Vest's summation to the jury in that old civil case, but I was. I had no intention of filing a case where an alert defense lawyer could summon up the ghost of George Graham Vest to trump me in closing argument!

Far-Flung Firearm

A lawyer learns most of his law at the expense of
his clients. No matter what his preparation is,
he isn't much when he starts practicing, and he
either learns or he doesn't learn from then on.
                            —Robert H. Jackson

I now had a license to practice law, but no one
had called me to practice on him.
                            —Clarence Darrow

As a young lawyer, future Supreme Court justice Robert H. Jackson realized the importance of preparation. An opposing lawyer said of him: "He never neglected the most painstaking preparation. He never made the mistake I have seen so many brilliant lawyers make of relying on his wit to win." Preparation and experience are essential to becoming an effective trial lawyer. Although experience is the best teacher, a good training seminar conducted by experienced litigators can speed up the learning curve.

Early in my career, I attended a seminar for trial lawyers in Washington, D.C. One of the speakers was an accomplished Texas attorney named Bob Gibbons.

Gibbons told the audience about one of his sensational trials as a criminal defense lawyer. It was a case where the local prosecuting attorney had been murdered. The killer pulled a gun on the prosecutor inside the prosecutor's office, chased him outside, and gunned him down on the courthouse lawn in front of fifty eyewitnesses.

Gibbons was appointed to represent the killer. With fifty eyewitnesses, the case was a professional challenge for even the most talented of defense lawyers. He did not give himself much of a chance of winning it.

The trial was moved to a different county on a change of venue. As the trial date approached, Gibbons began receiving anonymous death threats. The prosecutor had been a popular guy. Letters to Gibbons questioned how he could possibly represent a monster capable of such a cold-blooded killing. The volume of hate mail began making him nervous. A lot of vitriol was being directed specifically at him. Eventually, he bought a gun to take along when he traveled to the other county—just in case.

On the day before he was to leave for the trial, he was talking with the senior partner in his law firm—the wily, old Texas lawyer who had founded the firm. Gibbons mentioned his recent firearm purchase and the fact that he was taking it with him on his trip.

"That's interesting," said the senior partner. "You've got a lot of experience with guns, I suppose?"

"No," said Bob. "But I've taken it out to the firing range once or twice."

"I see. That's good, very good. Commendable, even. By the way, did you file the metal sight off of the end of the barrel yet?"

Bob was confused. The man at the gun shop had not mentioned doing any such thing.

"Well, no. Why would I do that?"

The wise old lawyer grinned.

"So when some big fellow takes that gun away from you and sticks it up your ass, it won't hurt quite so bad."

Based upon that eloquent advice, Bob Gibbons decided not to take the gun with him on his trip out of town. Gibbons lost the case, as he had expected. He made it home safely without the help of a gun.

⚖

I am reminded of Bob Gibbons's experience with his handgun when I think about "The Case of the Far-Flung Firearm." It involved the execution of a search warrant.

Prosecutors are not encouraged to accompany police officers when they enter someone's home to execute a search warrant. It is generally a bad idea for the prosecutor to tag along. Not only is it dangerous, but the prosecutor might see or hear something important that would make him a witness. A prosecutor cannot be both the public's lawyer and a witness in a case.

So, when the police need a search warrant, the prosecutor meets with the officer and types up the paperwork: the application for the search warrant, the probable-cause affidavit, and the search warrant itself. But once a judge signs the warrant, the prosecutor's immediate role is ended. The police dash off to execute the warrant, and the prosecutor usually heads home to go back to bed, as the calls for warrants most often come in the middle of the night.

A search warrant gives the police the authority to enter someone's home to search for contraband or evidence of a crime. The judge, a neutral and detached magistrate, reads the affidavit and decides whether the facts presented amount to probable cause that some evidence of a crime is located inside the building. In this context, probable cause means a "fair probability" that contraband or evidence will be found when the police conduct the search. If the judge decides probable cause exists, he or she signs the warrant and the police carry out the search. Although police are usually required to knock before entering, the search warrant gives them the power to bash down the door if the person won't open it, but only if "knocking and announcing" would be dangerous or imprac-tical. Crooks need to hurry when cops come knocking. The Supreme Court requires police to wait only fifteen to twenty seconds for a suspect to open the door of an apartment or small house.

At the Cape Girardeau County Prosecuting Attorney's Office, we have a policy allowing a new assistant prosecutor to accompany the police *one time* when they execute a search warrant. This is a useful educational experience for the prosecutor. It gives the attorney a better sense of what is involved in executing the warrant, which can be helpful background information for handling suppression hearings down the road, in situations where a defen-dant is trying to have evidence thrown out, sometimes because of the manner in which the warrant was executed. A prosecutor who has ridden along for the serving of a search warrant can better understand what the officers and the people at the scene were experiencing and can better handle these cases in the courtroom.

The night I went along on the execution of a search warrant is one I will never forget. The targeted house belonged to Kenny Nasby, a known drug dealer. An informant had just bought marijuana from Nasby inside the house, so probable cause existed to believe that more marijuana would be in the dealer's home. We got the search warrant from Judge Stanley A. Grimm. Judge Grimm was a scholarly and conscientious judge, who always meticu-lously studied the affidavits presented to him, often suggesting places where additional facts should be added to strengthen the probable cause.

At the time, I was a young assistant to Prosecuting Attorney Larry H. Ferrell. The other assistant prosecutor was Jim Hahn. Neither Larry, Jim, nor I had ever accompanied the police on an execution of a search warrant.

We decided this case would be an opportune time for that extra bit of education.

My first clue that we might have misjudged the situation came at the police station at 2:00 A.M., when the officers were strapping on bulletproof vests and loading shotguns as they prepared for the trip to Kenny Nasby's house. Seeing those shotguns, hearing the metallic pumps as they were loaded, and watching the officers don those vests drove home the point that this was not fun and games, but a very dangerous business where someone might well get hurt.

At this point there ran through my mind the thought shared by many people over the past centuries during their last moments upon this earth: *Well, I've already said I would do this stupid thing, and I'd look like a chicken if I backed out now.*

I glanced at Larry and Jim. From their faces it appeared their thoughts mirrored mine. All of us kept silent, though.

Our group took three cars to Nasby's house. The first two squad cars were packed with officers and weapons, and in one was a battering ram that looked like a huge hotdog with handles. It was approximately four feet long. The final car contained the three nervous prosecutors and our driver. He must have been the cop who drew the short straw.

As the convoy of police cars sped into Nasby's neighborhood, the drivers shut off their headlights. This came as a shock to me, but upon reflection it made sense. You cannot exactly surprise a drug dealer by driving up to his house with your lights flashing. Needless to say, no sirens were used, even though we were most definitely speeding.

The cars pulled to a stop directly in front of Nasby's white frame house in the 1200 block of Spanish Street. The officers bolted from the cars and took up their assigned positions. Some sprinted to the back door. Others rushed to the front door. We three prosecutors lingered near our car. We were standing on the grass near the curb, right smack in the dealer's front yard. The moon bathed everything in an eerie light.

Brad Moore was one of the officers who went to Nasby's front door. He knocked loudly. I was surprised how loudly. The sound reverberated throughout the neighborhood.

"Police officers! Search warrant! Open up!"

He peered through a small window at the top of the front door and watched as Kenny Nasby approached the door, realized who was on the other side, turned, and fled up some steps.

"Uh, oh!" thought Brad Moore, "he's about to flush his stash of drugs down the toilet!"

The battering ram hit the door with a crash. It flew open. The officers poured into the house.

From the safety of the front yard, we three prosecutors watched, our mouths agape, our eyes wide. Wow! Seeing a door battered down in person is much different from reading about it in a police report. It was much more violent than we had imagined.

We listened to the shouting coming from inside the house. I could not make out all the words, but someone was definitely being told to get down on the floor. We waited, wondering what would happen next. We were still standing by the curb, next to the police car. I thought about those shotguns and about the bulletproof vests. I hoped I would not hear the sound of gunfire.

Suddenly, a loud crash filled the night. Looking up, we saw an upstairs window shatter and glass shower down. Something metallic banged loudly against the side of the police car not five feet from where I stood.

Grenade! I thought.

In hindsight, I do not know why I thought it was a grenade. From the routine drug investigation of Kenny Nasby, I had no reason to suspect that this particular person would be armed with grenades. Nor would he have a logical reason for lobbing a grenade into the midst of the three prosecutors loitering in his front yard while his house was filling with police. But the crazed killer who shot down the Texas prosecutor in the courthouse square in front of fifty witnesses had not been acting logically, either.

For some reason, I was sure the object thunking against the side of the car was a grenade. The vivid memory is burned into my mind.

Grenade! Get down!

Jim Hahn and I experienced the exact same epiphany at the exact same moment. Both of us threw ourselves to the pavement behind the squad car and covered our heads. Our boss, Larry Ferrell, a better athlete, was already quite a remarkable distance down the road, his arms and legs churning in a full sprint.

There was no explosion.

A few minutes later, we screwed up enough courage to get up from the pavement and go examine the object that had struck the car. We were, by the way, smart enough not to touch it. It was a handgun. It turned out to be a stolen gun. Nasby had thrown it through his window in an effort to avoid being caught possessing it. Little did he dream he would almost hit three prosecutors hanging around in his front yard at 2:00 A.M.

Once Nasby and the two other dopers in the house were handcuffed and the building was secure, the police officers invited us into the scene of the crime. They had found the marijuana and were photographing it. They thought we might like to watch their search procedures.

When I entered the living room, the men were seated shirtless on the couch, their hands cuffed behind them. They faced the television. The movie *The Groove Tube* was playing. A writer of fiction would be hissed for attempting such irony. I had seen that movie in college. It was a comedy. Among other things, it glorified illegal drug use. The three drug suspects were not smiling as they watched *The Groove Tube* while their house was being searched by the police.

Upstairs, in Kenny Nasby's bedroom, I noticed something else that surprised me. Nasby was twenty-five years old, long out of high school, but hanging on his wall was a Presidential Physical Fitness Award certificate from his school years. Up until that moment, it had never occurred to me that a drug dealer might have won any sort of award. I certainly had not expected a dealer to be a good athlete. I know now that this was a very naive view. I have since prosecuted many star athletes for selling drugs, including college-level basketball and football players. But still, at that moment in time, it came as a surprise to me that "The Pusher" so demonized by the band *Steppenwolf* could end up being a young guy who still proudly displayed his physical fitness certificate on his bedroom wall.

The house was dirty. It stank of unwashed clothes and marijuana smoke. I was glad to get out of there.

Kenny Nasby was one more scoundrel hauled off to the hoosegow. We were about the same age. I went home that night. He went to jail. He was ultimately convicted of the felonies of possession of marijuana and possession of methaqualone. He first received probation but later went to prison, when his probation was revoked. We never charged him with possession of the stolen gun since that particular count might have required the testimony of at least one of the prosecutors. None of us wanted to tell the story in public. Besides, we had enough charges against him, anyway.

As far as I know, Kenny Nasby still does not realize that when he flung that semiautomatic pistol through the second-story window of his house, he almost hit three prosecutors. It had been a long toss, through solid glass, clear over his front yard, and all the way to the car parked at the curb. But then, Kenny Nasby was an award-winning athlete.

Shuddering Door

> The prosecutor has more control over life,
> liberty and reputation than any other person
> in America.
>
> > —Robert H. Jackson

> The charging decision is not an exact science.
> > —*National Prosecution Standards*

One blazing summer the national news was abuzz with warnings that a serial killer named Rafael Resendez-Ramirez, aka Angel Resendez, was on a cross-country rampage, murdering complete strangers in their own homes. The FBI placed him on its "Ten Most Wanted Fugitives" list. *People* magazine called him "the most wanted man in America." CNN reported that he had already been charged with two murders and was a suspect in twelve others. His modus operandi was to force his way into a victim's home and beat the victim senseless with whatever household object was at hand. He murdered victims with everything from sledgehammers to tire irons. His victims often lived near railroad tracks, so the media dubbed him the "Railroad Killer" and warned people living near train tracks to be especially careful. The FBI press release proclaimed him "armed and extremely dangerous."

The Cape Girardeau community was thrown into paroxysms of paranoia in late June when an elderly couple were bludgeoned to death in their home in Gorham, Illinois. The next day their red pickup truck was found in Cairo, Illinois, just thirty miles from Cape Girardeau. Ramirez's fingerprints were found in the truck.

The three local television stations devoted considerable airtime to warning viewers of the danger. The Cape Girardeau CBS affiliate, KFVS-12, carried 108 minutes of news stories about Ramirez over an eight-day period. The *Southeast Missourian* also ran front-page stories sounding the warning that this serial killer had struck right across the river. The stories described his pattern of breaking into his victims' homes and battering them to death. Prompted by calls from concerned viewers, a television reporter for KFVS-TV, Lisa Crane, was working on a story about how much force the law allowed a homeowner to use in protecting himself if Ramirez showed up at his door.

Roger Hightower, thirty-three, worked for the Missouri Department of Natural Resources as a naturalist at the Trail of Tears State Park in Cape Girardeau County. He lived with his girlfriend, Jenna, in a small house near the train tracks. They had been following the news. What's more, Roger and other employees at the park had not only discussed Ramirez, but had also searched the quarry and the area along the railroad tracks that ran through the 3,415-acre park to make sure Ramirez was not lurking in the wooded hills.

One Wednesday at about midnight, Hightower was in the shower. His girl-friend was sewing patches onto one of his shirts. The door to their home was locked. Suddenly, someone began pounding on the door.

Jenna hurried to the door.

"Who is it?" she called.

No one answered, but the violent pounding continued. The door rocked against its hinges but did not give way.

"Roger!" Jenna screamed. "Somebody's trying to break in!"

Hightower scrambled out of the shower, pulled on a pair of shorts, and grabbed his nine-millimeter semiautomatic handgun from the bedroom. He ran into the living room.

Meanwhile, Jenna dialed 9-1-1.

"Someone is trying to break into our home!" she told the dispatcher. "Someone's at the door!"

The dispatcher notified patrol officers that a burglary was in progress and sent them to the Hightower residence.

"Hurry!" Jenna urged. "Please hurry!"

While Jenna was talking to the dispatcher, Hightower was watching in horror as the person outside kept slamming against the door. The door was not solid. The bottom half was wood, but the top half consisted of a window covered by miniblinds.

"Who is it?" he yelled.

No answer.

Again the door shook in its frame as the person on the other side tried to force it open. The blurry shadow of the would-be intruder loomed ominously on the opaque blinds, rendered larger than life by the streetlight outside.

"Who's that?" he shouted.

Again, no answer.

"Go away or I'll shoot!" he yelled.

Still, the determined figure crashed over and over into the door. The thin barrier rattled in its frame and flexed inward as it was pushed from the other side. Someone was obviously lunging against it, trying to get in.

Hightower held off firing until the door seemed about to break free of the doorframe, then he rapidly fired four shots through the door, aiming high, hoping to scare the person away. All four shots were fired within five seconds.

The assault on the door stopped abruptly. It became completely quiet outside—*deathly* quiet.

Roger and Jenna waited until police arrived before working up the nerve to venture outside. In fact, they wouldn't open the door until Patrolman Aaron Brown repeatedly confirmed for them that he was a police officer. When they opened the door, they saw a horrifying sight: the body of a blonde-haired woman, Debra Ann Poch. One of Roger's shots had struck her in the head.

"Oh my God! I shot someone!" he gasped. His eyes filled with tears when he realized what he had done.

Most of the incident had been captured on the 9-1-1 tape, including the popping sound of the gunfire.

The police investigation revealed that Debra Ann Poch, forty-four, was one of Roger and Jenna's neighbors. She had been out drinking that night. By the end of the evening, her blood-alcohol level was .26, over three times the legal level in Missouri. She was so drunk the bartender had refused to keep serving her. Wisely, she had elected not to drive home, and her friends had called a cab for her and loaded her into it. Unfortunately, one of her friends had kept her purse so she wouldn't lose it. The purse contained the key to her house.

When the cabbie got her home, he noticed that she was "falling-down drunk." He helped her walk to her front door. He watched as she tried unsuccessfully to open the door with what she thought was her key. (It was actually a quarter.) He helped her sit down on her front porch and left to take another call. She was sitting on her front porch when the cabbie last saw her. In her drunken stupor, Debra must have arisen and gone to the wrong door and begun trying to break into what she thought was her own home.

Of the four shots Roger Hightower fired through the door, only one struck Debra, but it killed her almost instantly.

The officers examined the door and found that even a normal knock upon it would cause it to rattle in its frame. A hard knock made the door shudder and the blinds bounce.

When the investigation was complete, the police reports came to me. It was my responsibility to determine what charges, if any, should be filed against Roger Hightower.

Sometimes a prosecutor finds it necessary to do some legal research before filing a criminal charge. This was one of those times. If Roger Hightower had knowingly killed Debra Ann Poch, he had committed second-degree murder. If he had recklessly killed her, he had committed involuntary manslaughter. If he had acted in self-defense, *reasonably* believing that his life was in danger, the shooting was justified. I expected to be filing a charge of involuntary manslaughter against him, but first I wanted to do further research on an obscure statutory defense I had read about but never encountered: defense of premises.

I hit the books hard, spending many hours in the law library. I read every defense-of-premises case ever decided in Missouri. What I learned surprised me.

Under Missouri law, if you reasonably believe that another person is trying to cross the threshold of your home to commit a burglary (or to commit another crime inside your house, such as rape, assault, or theft) you can use deadly force to prevent that person from getting inside. You do *not* need to believe your life is in danger, only that the intruder is trying to get inside your home to commit a crime. In fact, once the issue is raised, the burden of proof is on the prosecutor to show beyond a reasonable doubt that the defendant did not act in lawful defense of premises.

This was significantly different from the normal law of self-defense, which had come up in many of my earlier cases. Under traditional self-defense analysis, you can only use deadly force when you reasonably believe you are in danger of death or serious physical injury. You cannot use deadly force in self-defense merely to protect yourself from a slap or a kick or to protect your possessions as opposed to your life.

Ironically, under the juxtaposition of the two defenses, you could shoot a burglar to stop him from climbing through your window, but once he made it inside, the traditional law of self-defense would apply; then you could only shoot him if you reasonably believed your life was in danger. The old adage "if you shot someone in your yard you should drag him into your house" was not quite accurate. Rather, you should drape him half-in and half-out of your window, as if he had been shot coming in.

Suddenly, things did not look quite so bleak for Roger Hightower. His shooting of Debra Ann Poch, while a tragic mistake, had not been a crime.

I wrote a letter to Police Chief Rick Hetzel explaining why no criminal charge would be filed against Hightower. I supplied copies to Hightower, to the surviving family members of Debra Ann Poch, and to the media (omitting Hightower's name). The newspaper carried a detailed story about the case, quoting extensively from my discussion about the law of defense of premises.

A few weeks later, I was reading the *St. Louis Post-Dispatch*. I turned to page E2 of the metro section, and to my surprise, I found a full-page story devoted to my decision not to file the homicide charge against Hightower. A glance at the story showed it to be full of quotes from Professor Edward Hunvald of the University of Missouri School of Law.

The Hun!

Hunvald had taught my evidence and criminal law and my criminal procedure classes at Mizzou. I was in awe of him when I was in law school and that feeling had never faded. With his undergraduate degree from Princeton and his law degree from Harvard, he had become an institution at the University of Missouri–Columbia School of Law. He had also been the head of the committee that wrote Missouri's criminal code in the late 1970s. He taught by the Socratic Method, meaning that the law students were assigned cases to read, and when they came to class he would select that day's victims and question them vigorously about the facts and holdings of the cases. The public skewering of daily sacrificial lambs proved educational and entertaining for the rest of the class, but the entertainment value was always diminished by the worry that you might be next. His style of teaching prepared one well for dealing with cantankerous judges later in one's career, even if it did make for a stressful law-school experience.

The Hun, with his black hair and his pointy goatee, could have stepped into the role of Satan in *Damn Yankees* with no additional makeup.

When I saw that the *St. Louis Post-Dispatch* had tracked down The Hun to grill me personally, I suddenly felt as though I was back in law school, getting ready to take my verbal flogging.

As I read the article, relief gradually began coursing through my body. Hunvald explained the law of defense of premises quite clearly. It was not difficult for him. He had, after all, written the statute. He finally concluded, "If Swingle believed Hightower's story was true, then he made the right decision not to charge him."

I let out the breath I'd been holding. It would have been hard enough on my ego to be criticized by *any* legal expert, but it would have been excruciating to receive a public slapping-around from someone I admired as much as I did Hunvald.

A month after Roger Hightower shot Debra Ann Poch, Ramirez was finally captured by the Texas Rangers. The FBI said he had murdered as many as eighteen people in several midwestern states. He was later tried in Houston, Texas, for murder and was sentenced to death.

I have never personally spoken to Roger Hightower. My heart goes out to him, though. I would not be surprised if he still has nightmares about the pounding at his front door. He has to live with the awful fact that he shot someone to death, knowing that if he had just had the courage to wait a moment longer for the door to give way and swing open, he might never have fired that fatal shot. An act lasting less than five seconds ended the life of Debra Ann Poch and changed Roger's life forever.

At least Roger Hightower can be thankful that he was never required to face the nightmare of being arrested, handcuffed, jailed, and charged with homicide, nor forced to stand trial before a judge and jury with his very freedom at stake. Roger Hightower has probably never heard of Justice Robert H. Jackson, but he has certainly heard of Morley Swingle, who chose not to charge him with manslaughter. I'm sure he would agree with Justice Jackson's observation, made during a much-quoted speech to federal prosecutors in 1940: "The prosecutor has more control over life, liberty and reputation than any other person in America." During at least one crisis in his life, Roger Hightower lived the truth of those words.

5. The Case of the . . .

Spiked Milkshake

> What are lawyers really? To me a lawyer is
> basically the person that knows the rules of
> the country. We're all throwing the dice, play-
> ing the game, moving our pieces around the
> board, but if there's a problem, the lawyer is
> the only person that has actually read the
> inside of the top of the box.
>
> —Jerry Seinfeld

The Hun was not the only professor terrorizing first-year law students during my time at Mizzou. Another intimidating figure was the venerable Willard L. Eckhardt.

Eckhardt taught Property I. He was in his sixties when my class matriculated. He was a dignified man, with a gray moustache, and thinning hair above a wide forehead. He was always immaculately dressed in a dark suit, and he always wore spectacles. He reminded me of an overweight owl. Yet, if he was the owl, we were his mice. He made that point perfectly clear right from the start.

On the first hour of the first day of my first week of law school, I sat in Property I at 7:40 A.M., along with approximately seventy-five other first-year students. Eckhardt was explaining certain rules about how his class would operate.

"I will assign you cases to read from your casebook," he said. "You *will* read them before coming to my class. I will call upon a certain number of you during the class period, and question you about the cases. If I ever call your name and find that you have not read the cases, you will be kicked out of the class."

He surveyed our expressions. I expect our faces showed the appropriate level of apprehension.

"Three times a semester," he continued, "you may approach me before class and give me a note that you are unprepared. If you give me the note in advance, I will not call upon you. But you may do this only three times. *Only three times. Does everyone understand?*"

We all nodded. No one made a sound. Eckhardt then cleared his throat regally and launched into a discussion of property law, introducing us to some feudal England stuff. Not the sort of things a criminal prosecutor uses on a day-to-day basis, but hey, I could remember it if you put a gun to my head.

I tell you all this because of an unfortunate incident that happened to Dan Decker, another first-year law student in my class. Dan was a clean-cut, athletic guy. He had been on his college golf team as an undergraduate.

The class of 150 law students was divided into two sections of 75 students each. You attended all of your first-year classes with those same 75 students. The first semester consisted of Property I, Contracts I, Torts I, Introduction to Law, Civil Procedure I, and Legal Research and Writing.

Dan Decker was not in my section, so he had not been in Professor Eckhardt's Property I class with the rest of us. Dan's section had Professor William Fratcher for Property I. Compared to Eckhardt, the mild-mannered Fratcher had been a pussycat. For some reason, Dan switched sections after Christmas break, and ended up in Eckhardt's class for Property II in January. Unfortunately for Dan, he had missed Eckhardt's "big warning" on the first day of class.

The sun was shining brightly through the tall classroom windows shortly before 8:00 A.M. on that memorable day in February when Eckhardt called on Dan Decker. I do not recall Eckhardt's exact question (it had something to do with property law, I suspect), but I will never forget Dan's answer.

"I'm sorry, sir, I didn't have time to read that case last night."

Oh. My. God. A collective gasp sucked the air out of the high-ceilinged room. Then the class sat in stunned silence. Dan was the only person in the entire classroom with no inkling of what was going to happen next. Those of us in the know (which constituted the other seventy-five people in the classroom) held our breath.

Eckhardt fixed him with a steely glare. I am sure Dan felt uncomfortable, but he refrained from groveling, whining, or coming up with some elaborate excuse. He simply sat in polite silence.

Finally, Eckhardt issued his verdict.

"You are excused!" he thundered.

Dan Decker just sat in his seat, glancing occasionally at his neighboring students. He told me later that he thought Eckhardt was dismissing the entire class, but it surprised him because the class was only half over. He was waiting for other students to get up and leave before he, too, would stand up. Eckhardt continued to glare at him.

Still, Dan remained in his seat. *Oblivious* would be the precisely correct word for his state of mind.

Finally, Eckhardt erupted like a volcano. "I said you are excused, Mr. Decker! Leave this classroom and go to the library and do *not* come back to *my* class until you have *read* the assigned cases!"

Dan's face reddened. He glanced around again and realized that the rest of us were staring at him like Romans gawking at a Christian in the lion pits. He gathered his books, rose, and slunk from the classroom.

Dan went on to build a successful law practice somewhere in Texas. As the philosopher Friedrich Nietzsche said, "What does not kill us makes us stronger."

⚖

I did not know Dan Decker all that well in law school, but I think of him often because of that memorable moment. Likewise, I don't know Cape Girardeau Police Department dispatcher Paul Johnson very well, but I think of him often because of his role in "The Case of the Spiked Milkshake." Paul was the recipient of a spiked milkshake—the spike-ee, so to speak.

It was 8:50 on a Saturday night. Paul Johnson was working the 3:00 to 11:00 shift. The dispatcher, as one might guess, is the person at the department who answers the telephone and handles the 9-1-1 calls. He is basically chained to the telephone for his entire shift. On this night, with just a couple of hours left in his workday, Paul Johnson asked Patrolman Bill Bohnert to run out and pick up a chocolate milkshake for him.

Bohnert, in uniform, left the station and drove a marked patrol car through the drive-through at a convenience store and ordered the shake. Bohnert frowned when he recognized the person who handed him the milkshake through the window. It was Tom Quartz, someone he had arrested in the past. What was Quartz doing out of jail? It seemed like just yesterday the young hooligan had been sent to prison. Bohnert paid for the shake and headed back to the station, where he delivered it to Paul Johnson.

Few things in life compare with a good chocolate milkshake. Milk is good. Ice cream is good. Chocolate syrup is good. Whoever got the idea to put all three together deserves a Nobel Prize.

Yet, a chocolate milkshake is much more enjoyable when it does not contain unrecognizable, partially dissolved little pills in the bottom of the cup. Finding unknown pills lurking in the last 10 percent of a milkshake can really suck the pleasure right out of an otherwise pleasant dessert beverage experience.

Paul Johnson was horrified when he saw the pill remnants in the bottom of his shake. So was everyone else at the department. What were the pills? LSD? Cocaine? Speed? At 9:40 P.M. the dispatcher, now feeling somewhat queasy, was rushed to Southeast Hospital. There doctors gave him a drug screen and a dose of Epicac to induce vomiting. Once the Epicac kicked in, Paul Johnson was wishing he had never seen a milkshake in his life. Meanwhile, Dr. Robert C. Briner from the Southeast Missouri Regional Crime Lab was called in to analyze the pills.

While all that frenzied activity was going on, Bill Bohnert and Sergeant Brad Moore went to the convenience store to get to the bottom of the spiked-milkshake caper.

Besides Tom Quartz, the only other employee on duty was Dan Slote. Both Quartz, age twenty, and Slote, age eighteen, were already convicted felons. Both were under the supervision of the Missouri Board of Probation and Parole. Quartz had only been out of jail for three weeks. Of course, Quartz and Slote first claimed to have no idea how the pills could possibly have gotten into the milkshake. They had no clue what those pills might be. They professed to be as puzzled as anyone else.

The officers called the owner of the store, who interrupted his Saturday night to come to his business. Once he arrived, the mystery gradually unfolded.

"I've got a video camera above the cash register," he told the officers. "It's to keep the employees from stealing from the cash register. They all know about it, so it's legal. You're welcome to rewind it and see exactly what happened when you ordered the shake." Quartz and Slote began sweating. They had forgotten about the recording equipment.

The videotape told a cautionary tale for anyone in law enforcement who frequents public restaurants. When Bohnert ordered the shake, one of the dynamic duo waiting on him said, "It's a cop!"

The other snickered.

"The last time a cop drove through here I spit on his hot dog."

They laughed like hyenas.

"Oh, that's good. That's real good. Hey, let's give this one an Ex-Lax shake!"

"What?"

"Put Ex-Lax in his shake. I'll go get it!"

Snorting and guffawing, the two felons dumped the super-strength laxative pills into the chocolate milkshake before handing it out the window.

Case solved. The videotape was collected as evidence. Both Quartz and Slote were arrested.

The next day their paperwork arrived at my office. Assistant Prosecuting Attorney Ian Sutherland had the job of deciding how to charge the culprits. After due consideration, and after failing to find a criminal charge specifically mentioning laxatives in milkshakes, he charged each miscreant with third-degree assault. A person commits this least serious form of assault when he recklessly causes a physical injury to another person; "physical injury" includes any "physical pain, illness, or any impairment of physical condition." Paul Johnson's unpleasant evening at the emergency room certainly met the test. There is nothing wrong with a bit of creativity in the prosecutor's charging decision, as long as he or she can prove the elements of the crime in court.

Three weeks later, Slote pled guilty to the misdemeanor charge. His probation (on an earlier offense of felony stealing) was revoked, and he was sent to prison. Quartz (whose parole was also for a stealing offense) later pled guilty and was returned to prison, too.

I have often wished I could have been a fly on the wall when those two guys were delivered to prison. I picture some beefy, mean-looking criminal, perhaps convicted of murder, rape, or robbery, sidling up to them, sizing them up, and saying, "So, what are *you* in here for?" I will bet they did not mention the Ex-Lax.

Paul Johnson later told me that after Tom Quartz got out of prison, the young felon remained a frequent flyer at the police department. The dispatcher always made it a practice to saunter into the booking room after Quartz had been brought in and ask the arresting officer, "Think he wants a milkshake? I'll pay for it." Quartz not only declined all offers of a free milkshake, but he has steadfastly refused to eat any jail food while in custody at the Cape Girardeau Police Department. His guilty conscience must be affecting his appetite.

Camera-Shy Car Thief

> I could win all of my cases if it weren't for
> the clients.
>
> —Horace Rumpole

> Well, I was drunk the day my Mom got out
> of prison,
> And I went to pick her up in the rain,
> But before I could get to the station in
> my pickup truck,
> She got runned over by a damned old train.
>
> —Steve Goodman

According to an old saying, if it weren't for bad luck, some people would have no luck at all. So it was for a car thief named Billy Clagget. His story is the stuff of which great country-western songs are made. It also shows that criminals create problems for themselves when they fail to keep abreast of developments in modern technology.

The hugely popular television drama *CSI* glamorizes the dedicated officers who investigate crime scenes. Although it is possible that some evidence technician somewhere in the United States looks something like the alluring Marg Helgenberger, real-life crime-scene technicians often tend to be the nerds of the department—the ones who are a bit small to participate in the street fights or the ones who actually *liked* chemistry and physics classes in high school and college. Good folks, certainly, and dedicated public servants, but generally nothing like glamorous television icons.

A show like *CSI* is good for the police community in that it shows the very real dedication these officers feel toward their work, but it also causes problems for law enforcement, one being that it creates unrealistic expectations in the minds of jurors about what they are going to see in a real-life courtroom. Most routine criminal cases involve little or no scientific evidence. The shoplifting, domestic assault, and bad-check cases simply do not involve things like DNA analysis, global tracking devices, or other high-tech bells and whistles. In fact, more times than not, a person does not even leave a fingerprint when he touches something. This would surprise jurors steeped in the forensic techniques of *CSI,* who often report for jury service expecting to be dazzled by DNA and captivated by chemistry, only to find the prosecution presenting mundane, old-fashioned eyewitness testimony. So, *CSI* has not been an entirely good thing for the criminal justice system.

That being said, a prosecutor loves it when the police bring over a case involving some new sort of scientific evidence. I vividly remember one such case—my first case involving OnStar—a global tracking device placed by General Motors into many new cars.

A car equipped with OnStar contains a chip that allows a satellite to track the vehicle. This eye in the sky can tell where a particular car is located at any given time. This can be a wonderful thing for both the car's owner and the police when the car is stolen.

At 9:30 one July morning, Tom Reinagel realized that his red Chevrolet Tahoe had been stolen from the driveway outside his son's college apartment. He immediately called the Cape Girardeau Police Department. Patrolman Daryl Ferris responded.

"I've got OnStar," Reinagel said. "Supposedly all we need to do is call them and they can tell us where it is."

"Let's do it," Ferris said.

Moments later, the OnStar operator was telling them exactly where the Tahoe was—on County Road 301, just off Highway 60 about three miles east of Van Buren, Missouri.

"That's in Carter County, about one hundred miles from Cape," Ferris said. "I'll call their sheriff's department."

Within minutes, Carter County Deputy Sheriff Chip Brewer located the stolen Tahoe. Standing right next to it was Billy Clagget, age nineteen. He was well dressed but a bit scruffy-looking.

"Some guy just pulled up and jumped out and ran into the woods!" Clagget claimed. "He went that way. You'd better go get him!"

A woman who lived in a nearby house came outside, however, and told Deputy Brewer that Clagget was the one who had arrived in the Tahoe. Brewer slapped the cuffs on Clagget.

I was delighted when the police reports came to me. It is always fun to prosecute a case with a new twist.

A few weeks later, when the case was scheduled for its preliminary hearing, I called the Cape Girardeau television station to let them know that our first OnStar case was going to court. I had a feeling they would be interested.

The preliminary hearing is the stage in a felony case when the prosecutor is required to call enough witnesses for a judge to make a finding that there is probable cause that a felony was committed and that the defendant is the person who committed it. The prosecution does not need to prove its case beyond a reasonable doubt. Usually, probable cause can be shown with testimony from a witness or two. Most preliminary hearings last less than an hour. They are held in open court, though, and are public events. The news media likes the chance to cover a preliminary hearing in a newsworthy case. KFVS-12 was glad to get the tip about the county's first OnStar case.

On the morning of the preliminary hearing, Billy Clagget and his lawyer, an assistant public defender, sat in the courtroom and listened as the television reporter tried to get permission from Associate Circuit Judge Gary A. Kamp to allow cameras in the courtroom. Although criminal trials are always public events, and reporters cannot be barred from attending the proceedings, whether cameras will be allowed in a Missouri courtroom is always up to the judge.

"What's the TV station doing here?" Clagget asked.

"Well," his lawyer said, "apparently you're the first person in Cape Girardeau County history to be caught by OnStar. They're going to put you on TV."

Clagget groaned.

"I can't be on TV! My grandmother doesn't know I did this!"

A few minutes later, the defense waived the preliminary hearing, meaning that it conceded that the prosecution had sufficient evidence for the case to be bound over to the circuit court level. It would not require the state to call any witnesses. The television station was thus deprived of its chance to hear and report all of the interesting details. It appeared, for a time, that Billy Clagget had cleverly avoided being on the nightly news, after all.

The KFVS-12 reporter was undaunted, however. A savvy newshound, he hurried outside and lay in wait for Clagget. He knew that since Clagget was in custody at the county jail, the deputies would eventually walk him the half block back to the jail. The reporter's cunning and patience were rewarded a bit later when Deputy David Taylor emerged through the back door of the courthouse with prisoner Billy Clagget in tow.

Clagget was dressed for success in his extremely photogenic bright orange jail-issue jumpsuit, accessorized with shiny stainless steel handcuffs. Deputy Taylor wore a stylish sport coat and tie. As they approached the cameraman, the domed courthouse made a perfect backdrop behind them.

The cameraman had to be happy about the way the day was shaping up. As he backpedaled, pointing the camera at his quarry all the while, he made sure the courthouse could be seen over Clagget's shoulder.

The camera work was really quite artistic. The shot started with a long-distance view of the courthouse, then zoomed in on Billy Clagget and the deputy sheriff, and finally closed with a close-up of Clagget's scowling face.

The cameraman moved closer, getting some good sound to go with his pictures. Clagget's colorful language would need some editing before it could run on the evening news, of course, but there might be some words that would survive the bleeping.

Then, Billy Clagget, the defendant who had not wanted to be on television, who had waived his preliminary hearing specifically so he would *not* be on television, looked directly into the camera and uttered a phrase that not only guaranteed he would be on the news, but pretty well assured he would be the lead story.

Frowning ruefully, he muttered, "OnStar! Don't mess with OnStar!"

I videotaped the news that night. The next day I mailed a copy of the newscast to Chet Huber, the president of OnStar, whose office was in Detroit. I sent along a cover letter telling him about the case.

A couple of weeks later I heard back from Huber. He replied that he had not only shown the tape at an office meeting, but also had played it for every single OnStar employee. He concluded, "As far as we know, this is the most public endorsement of our product by a criminal."

Another amusing twist to the OnStar saga revealed itself on the morning of the aborted preliminary hearing. I was meeting with Tom Reinagel, the Tahoe's owner, preparing for the hearing, when he told me that some clothing was missing from the Tahoe.

"My son is a college student who likes to wear those name-brand clothes," he said. "He had a blue-striped Nautica shirt in the car, as well as a pair of American Eagle pants. When we picked up the Tahoe from the impound lot, those clothes were missing. Instead, we found some old grungy clothing all wadded up in the backseat."

"Well," I said. "Let's just check Billy Clagget's booking photo from the Carter County Sheriff's Department."

Sure enough, when Deputy Brewer arrived for court, he brought with him the Carter County booking photo. In it, Billy Clagget could be seen wearing the blue-striped Nautica shirt. Both the shirt and the American Eagle pants had been collected from him to be held in storage until his release from jail. I had them transferred from his property storage locker to the evidence storage locker. If the case went to trial, the clothing would become state's exhibits 1 and 2.

Billy Clagget's case did not go to trial. He had already been on felony probation for burglary and stealing. In fact, he had only been out of jail six days before he confiscated the Tahoe. It was a no-brainer for Judge David Dolan; he sent Billy Clagget right back to prison.

I am assuming that one way or another, Clagget's grandmother eventually learned that he had committed these offenses. To my knowledge, though, OnStar has not yet used his image in any sort of advertisement. If they want to contact him to get permission to use his face, however, they know where to find him. He is enjoying free room and board in the Missouri Department of Corrections.

Cross-Eyed Juror

When the peremptory challenges were all
exhausted, a jury of twelve men was empaneled—
a jury who swore they had neither heard, read,
talked about nor expressed an opinion concerning a murder which the very cattle in the
corrals, the Indians in the sagebrush and the
stones in the streets were cognizant of! It was
a jury composed of two desperadoes, two low
beer-house politicians, three barkeepers, two
ranchmen who could not read, and three dull,
stupid, human donkeys! It actually came out
afterward, that one of these latter thought
that incest and arson were the same thing. The
verdict rendered by this jury was, Not Guilty.
What else could one expect? The jury system
puts a ban upon intelligence and honesty, and a
premium upon ignorance, stupidity and perjury.
—Mark Twain

In my opinion, the greatly restricted scope
of permissible questions on voir dire reduces
jury selection to at best one-third art and
skill and two-thirds guesswork.
—Vincent Bugliosi

T he most extraordinary moment I ever experienced in a courthouse occurred during a manslaughter trial in St. Louis. Although I do not share Mark Twain's dim view of juries, the case shows how difficult it can be to select a good jury in a criminal case. A mistake I made during jury selection almost proved disastrous. As it turned out, I was saved only by dumb luck.

The trial was no laughing matter. A group of college fraternity boys had accidentally killed a pledge during initiation hazing. The pledge, Michael Davis, was a college senior who wanted to add fraternity membership to his resume. He would soon be graduating with a degree in journalism from Southeast Missouri State University, and he thought being a member of the Kappa Alpha Psi fraternity might help him land a good job.

The hazing lasted an entire week. Each night the five young men who were pledging met with fraternity members at a different location, where the frat boys made them recite memorized fraternity secrets and history. The frat members also inflicted various sorts of physical punishment upon the pledges, including punching them on their chests, hitting their bare feet with canes, and slamming the "Book of Knowledge" (a fat encyclopedia) on their backs.

The beatings were so painful that two of the university's varsity football players dropped out before the last night, saying that the hazing hurt worse than anything they had encountered on the football field. Michael Davis and the two others remained to suffer through the entire ordeal.

At midnight on the last night, several fraternity members took the three pledges to a grassy field near the Abe Stuber Track and Field Complex on the grounds of Southeast Missouri State University. Seven frat brothers assumed positions, or stations, in a large circle. The pledges were required to run from station to station. At each station, a fraternity member would inflict some type of abuse upon the pledge, then the pledge would go to the next station. At some stations, the frat member would punch the pledge; at others, he would kick or slap him. Two frat brothers "body-slammed" the pledges. They actually lifted each pledge into the air and then threw him to the ground. All the while, the pledges were guzzling beer.

At some point during the early morning hours, Michael Davis staggered and collapsed to the ground. The fraternity boys figured that he had passed out from the alcohol or that he was faking. They carried his limp form to his car and took him home. On the way to his apartment, they went through a Taco Bell drive-through and picked up food while Michael Davis slumped unconscious in the backseat of his car. Ironically, the Taco Bell was right across the street from a hospital.

What nobody knew was that Michael Davis was dying. One of the blows he had taken that night had torn a blood vessel in his brain. Blood was pouring through the vein into his skull cavity. As the bleeding continued, the pressure inside his skull forced oxygenated blood out of his brain, starving his brain cells, and the subdural hematoma grew. Sometime after Michael lost consciousness, he lost the functioning of the part of his brain controlling his breathing, and he died.

Unaware of what was happening, the fraternity members put him to bed in his own apartment and delegated another pledge to spend the night with him to make sure he was okay in the morning. Then they all went home.

The next morning, Michael Davis was dead.

At first the panicked fraternity brothers tried to cover up their crime. They cleaned his apartment and hid evidence of the hazing in a nearby dumpster. Finally, they called 9-1-1. At the hospital, they told medical staff that Michael had been injured playing football. In spite of their efforts to get away with it, a thorough investigation by the major case squad solved the homicide within hours. As prosecuting attorney, I then had to assess the case against the young men involved in the killing of Michael Davis.

The decision of how to charge the fraternity brothers was a difficult one. It was impossible to tell which of the many blows inflicted upon Michael Davis had killed him. Most likely it was one of the body-slams, but Dr. Michael Zaricor, the medical examiner, was not absolutely certain. What was certain was that seven individuals had each punched, hit, kicked, or body-slammed Michael Davis during that fateful night. One or more of their blows had caused his death. All were acting in concert. I charged all seven with involuntary manslaughter for recklessly causing his death.

According to Dr. Zaricor, if the fraternity brothers, whom Michael had so hoped to join, had simply taken him to the hospital the night of the beating, a routine CAT scan would have revealed the subdural hematoma. A tiny hole could have been bored into his skull to release the pressure and save his life. Their decision to take him home and put him to bed had sealed his fate.

The defendant for whom I felt the most sympathy was Carlos Turner. He had been one of the college students who kicked Michael Davis that fatal night, and he was the one who called 9-1-1 when Michael died. When Carlos talked to the doctors at the hospital, he told them that Michael had been injured playing football, but after going home to St. Louis and talking with

his parents, Carlos returned to Cape Girardeau and went to the police station
to tell the truth about what had happened, no matter what the consequences
might be for himself.

Over the ensuing months, three of the seven fraternity members charged
with manslaughter pled guilty and agreed to testify against any of the others
who chose to take their cases to trial. Carlos Turner was one of those who
agreed to testify.

Fraternity president Laimmoire Taylor was one of those who chose to take
his case to trial. His lawyers requested and were granted a change of venue.
The trial was moved to St. Louis.

Trying a case in the city of St. Louis proved different from my usual experience. I was accustomed to juries pulled from the population of Cape
Girardeau County, a community of sixty thousand people, with less than 5
percent unemployment. Cape is a college town, with a large number of
teachers, farmers, businessmen, blue-collar workers, and professionals
who generally like and respect law enforcement officers. We get cop-
friendly juries in Cape Girardeau County. In St. Louis, I found myself picking from a panel in which half the members admitted distrusting police
officers, and a significant number were unemployed. The defense lawyers,
Elbert Dorsey and Gaylard Williams, had specifically suggested St. Louis as
the site of the trial. Kappa Alpha Psi was a black fraternity, and all of the
defendants were African American. The defense lawyers thought a jury
with a high percentage of African Americans would not convict their client.
I agreed to St. Louis because I felt confident that race would not play a role
in the trial. I was sure jurors of any color would unanimously agree that the
fraternity members had acted recklessly in killing Michael Davis. Race had
nothing to do with this tragedy.

I vividly remember the first day of jury selection in the courtroom of Circuit Judge David Mason. The bailiff called, "All rise!" Judge Mason, a big man
weighing every bit of three hundred pounds, lumbered to his place at the
bench and greeted the packed courtroom.

"Good morning," he thundered, his voice deep and booming.

Most people responded quietly, but one prospective juror in the front row
shouted out, "Good morning!"

I glanced at the juror, number twelve. He was tall, perhaps six feet, four
inches. He was cross-eyed and wore his hair in a sixties Afro. He sported
large muttonchop whiskers covering his jowls. I glanced at the jury information sheet, a bare-bones document listing only age, marital status, address,

educational background, and occupation. He was an unmarried dishwasher, who worked at one of the downtown hotels. I decided that I might later use one of my preemptory strikes to remove this guy from the jury because of his general squirrellyness.

In a routine felony case in Missouri, each side gets six preemptory strikes, meaning that of the fifty or so people who report for jury service, your side can eliminate any six you choose for any reason. The idea is that those who remain unstruck by either the prosecution or the defense will be those to whom neither side has a significant objection. The purpose is to find twelve impartial people who can be fair to both sides by getting rid of the folks most likely to be unfair to one side or the other.

Picking the jury is called the voir dire process. I have heard it pronounced "vor dire" and I have heard it pronounced "vwah deer." The breakdown in the number of people using either pronunciation is roughly equivalent to the breakdown of those who pronounce Missouri "Mis-sir-eee" as opposed to those who say "Mis-ir-rah." No matter how you say it, voir dire is the time when the jury is picked.

The voir dire process is by far the most seat-of-the-pants part of a trial. A lot of gut instinct is involved. It is impossible to look at a potential juror and *know* whether that person will sympathize with your side of the case or have a visceral negative reaction to one of your witnesses. Along with the little bit of information you know from the jury information sheets, you can assume potential jurors are not convicted felons because felons are ineligible for jury service. But people with misdemeanor convictions can end up being on the jury. The panel, drawn primarily from voter lists and driving records, is truly a cross section of society.

I usually meet in advance with local law enforcement officers in the community where the case is being tried and get them to look over the list of potential jurors. They often know some of them personally and can be an invaluable asset by alerting me to possible "bad eggs."

When famed Texas criminal defense attorney Richard "Racehorse" Haynes was representing T. Cullen Davis, a millionaire charged with murdering his wife's lover, the investigator for the defense lawyer took photographs of the homes of every juror on the panel in an effort to know each juror better. Some trial lawyers with unlimited budgets hire jury consultants. These are usually psychologists who pore over each juror's background and study body language to glean clues about which panelists should be struck. Personally, I do not think the taxpayers of my county want their prosecutor or his investigator taking pictures of their homes, nor do I think they want taxpayer money being spent on jury-selection specialists, who in my book are only slightly more scientific than practitioners of voodoo or astrology. Deciding which jurors to strike is a job for the trial lawyer. I am sufficiently vain to think that my insights are as good as any psychologist's.

That being said, I did not do such a great job of picking the jury in that hazing trial in St. Louis. Oh, my instincts were right. I just did not execute one particular preemptive strike very well.

During the voir dire process, first the prosecutor and then the defense lawyer questions members of the jury panel. At the end of the questioning, the jury pool is temporarily dismissed from the courtroom, and each side asks the judge to strike certain jurors for cause. Those who admit to knowing one of the parties personally, to having already formed an opinion about the case, or to feeling they cannot be unbiased for any reason are struck for cause. Of those remaining, each side uses preemptive strikes to exclude six.

It is not exactly accurate to say that the prosecutor may strike six for any reason whatsoever. In 1986, in the case of *Batson v. Kentucky,* the United States Supreme Court ruled that neither side may strike a potential juror because of that juror's race. Under *Batson,* when one side or the other makes its preemptive strikes, opposing counsel may object to a particular strike on the grounds that it must have been based on race. The lawyer wishing to strike that juror must then state for the record a race-neutral reason for striking the juror. If the judge is satisfied that the strike was not made for racial reasons, the strike may stand. Otherwise, the attorney must withdraw the strike of that particular juror and strike someone else. The challenged juror remains on the panel.

The cross-eyed dishwasher was one of my six strikes for cause. During the questioning of the jury, he had continued to shout his answers. I felt something was wrong with him. Furthermore, I could never tell where he was looking, and it bothered me.

The defense immediately made a *Batson* challenge to my strike of the cross-eyed juror. Judge Mason made the proper response: "Mr. Swingle, what are your race-neutral reasons for that strike?"

In the heat of the moment one is sometimes not as articulate as one would hope to be. I should have elaborated about his shouting of his answers. I should have talked in terms of "inappropriate demeanor." Instead, the words

I heard coming out of my mouth sounded lame, even to me: "He's cross-eyed and goofy-looking. I'd always strike such a goofy-looking guy, whether black or white."

I knew when I said the words that I'd failed in my mission to remove the peculiar juror. I did not yet fully appreciate, however, the true extent of my failure.

"I don't believe you've made an adequate record," Judge Mason responded calmly. "The objection will be sustained, and the juror will remain a part of the panel."

We finished jury selection that morning and seated the twelve regular jurors, plus three alternates. In the afternoon, we gave opening statements, and I began calling the state's witnesses. The cross-eyed juror was sitting in the front row of the jury box, charged with the same responsibility as the rest of the jurors: to listen to the evidence and consider the jury instructions and apply the facts and the law to decide what should happen to this college student who had accidentally taken the life of a fellow human being. Laimmoire Taylor was facing up to seven years in prison. His future, to some extent, was in the hands of this cross-eyed dishwasher from the big city hotel.

We broke off that day, and every day, at 4:30 P.M. so the jurors could catch the bus home. This was quite a contrast to trying a case in Cape Girardeau County, where the trial might rumble on until after midnight because jurors would typically rather serve one very long day than come back the next day. What would have been a three-day trial in Cape Girardeau County turned into a two-week trial in St. Louis.

The big surprise came first thing in the morning on the third day of the trial. One of the alternate jurors, a woman in her thirties, approached the judge with obvious apprehension, saying she needed to speak with him in private. He ordered the prosecutor, the defense lawyers, and his court reporter to join the two of them back in his chambers.

When the court reporter was set up, ready to record the proceedings, Judge Mason said, "I understand there's something you need to tell me about this case?"

"Yes, sir," she said.

"Go on."

"You know that cross-eyed juror?"

"Yes."

"Well, yesterday, on the bus on the way home from the courthouse, he sat on a seat in front of me."

She paused.

"Go on," said the judge.

"Well, he was sitting on his seat, having a long, loud, animated conversation, with the *empty seat* next to him."

"Hmmm," intoned Judge Mason.

"Then he went to the window, pulled it down, and started yelling obscenities at complete strangers on the street until the bus driver finally pulled over and kicked him off the bus."

"I see." The judge nodded. "Anything else?"

"No, that's about it. I thought you should know."

He thanked her and excused her from the room.

"Well, gentlemen," he said. "Do you have anything to say?"

This time I said the right thing.

"Judge, it's clear to me that this juror does not have the mental capacity to sit as a juror in this case. I move to strike him and replace him with one of the alternate jurors."

"Objection!" said Gaylard Williams, one of the defense lawyers. "We want him!"

Judge Mason turned to his bailiff, a burly deputy sheriff.

"Go get juror number twelve," he ordered.

A few minutes later the cross-eyed juror was ushered into the judge's office. He took a seat with the rest of us in front of the judge's large desk. Judge Mason smiled at him like a benevolent uncle.

"I don't mean to offend you," the judge said, "but I have a few questions for you."

"Sure," said the juror.

"I understand that, ah, you were in some kind of altercation on the bus on the way home yesterday."

The juror bristled.

"No, absolutely not! There was a question about *where* I would get off, but I wouldn't call it an altercation."

"Hmmm," said the judge. He paused a few moments before continuing. "Again, I don't want to offend you, but I feel it's necessary to ask: Have you ever been diagnosed with any sort of mental disease or defect or have you ever received any sort of mental health counseling from a psychologist or psychiatrist?"

"No!" exclaimed the cross-eyed juror, quite loudly. He was clearly insulted.

"I see," said the judge. He frowned as he mulled over his next questions.

Suddenly the cross-eyed juror leaned forward.

"I know who's behind this," he whispered loudly.

"You do?" asked the judge.

"Yes!" exclaimed the dishwasher from the downtown hotel. "*Joe Torre* is behind this! When Whitey Herzog was the manager of the St. Louis Cardinals, I was the mastermind behind that team. I called *all* the shots. Whitey consulted me about everything. Since Joe Torre has been with the Cardinals, though, I haven't lifted a finger to help *him*. Joe Torre's behind this, isn't he?"

Judge Mason looked straight into the wild eyes.

"Yes," he agreed. "Joe Torre *is* behind this. You are excused as a juror."

The judge nodded to the bailiff, who escorted the juror from the room.

As the defense lawyers and I made small talk, the judge was still frowning. When the bailiff came back, he gave him additional instructions.

"You know, I don't want that guy getting an Uzi and coming back to the courthouse or going down to Busch Stadium gunning for Joe Torre. Go find the guy and tell him it was that prosecutor from Cape Girardeau who wanted him off the jury."

Judge Mason glanced at me, his eyes twinkling.

"There," he said. "You wanted him off. He's off."

In the end, the jury found Laimmoire Taylor guilty of the felony of involuntary manslaughter and five counts of misdemeanor hazing. Judge Mason sentenced him to one year in jail on the manslaughter charge, plus six months in jail on each of the hazing counts. He ordered that the hazing counts would run concurrently, but consecutive to the manslaughter count, meaning that Laimmoire Taylor was sentenced to spend a year and a half in jail. Unfortunately, due to overcrowding, the St. Louis Sheriff's Department let him out on an electronic shackle after he had served just fourteen days. He ended up serving most of his sentence in the comfort of his own home.

Ever since the Laimmoire Taylor trial, I have added another question to my standard voir dire questions. I now always ask: "Have any of you ever been diagnosed with any sort of mental illness, or have you ever had any sort of counseling from a psychologist or a psychiatrist?" I tell the jurors that if the answer to the question would embarrass them, they may discuss the matter with the judge and the attorneys outside the hearing of the other jury panel members. I don't know if asking this question would have made any difference in my case in St. Louis, but I should have asked it.

Joe Torre compiled a record of 351 wins and 354 losses during his stint as manager of the St. Louis Cardinals. After he switched to the New York Yankees, he got a lot smarter, as he likes to say. He has since led the Yankees to one World Series victory after another. Most people think Joe Torre improved as a manager due to age and experience. Others attribute his increased success to the high payroll of the Yankees. Yet, it is just remotely possible that his change in fortune came after a certain cross-eyed dishwasher from a downtown St. Louis hotel thawed out and began giving him those nuggets of wisdom previously supplied only to Whitey Herzog. Joe Torre has never gone on the record to deny it.

Oprah Appearance

The qualities of a good prosecutor are as
elusive and as impossible to define as those
which make a good gentleman. And those who need
to be told would not understand it anyway. A
sensitiveness to fair play and sportsmanship is
perhaps the best protection against the abuse
of power, and the citizen's safety lies in the
prosecutor who tempers zeal with human kindness, who seeks truth and not victims, who
serves the law and not factional purposes, and
who approaches his task with
humility.

—Robert H. Jackson

Morley Swingle was the prosecuting attorney who
got seven convictions for Michael's death.

—Oprah Winfrey

I have tried many cases more sensational than the Michael Davis hazing case. I have prosecuted more important crimes as well as cases that drew more publicity. But the Michael Davis case is the only one that ever drew the attention of Oprah Winfrey.

All seven defendants charged with involuntary manslaughter for the death of Michael Davis ended up pleading guilty or being found guilty by a jury. Not one got away with the crime. Five others were convicted of misdemeanor hazing for events occurring during the week-long hazing ritual. The appellate decision for one of the defendants established the constitutionality of Missouri's hazing statute.

The trials were long over when I got a telephone call from Jim Brady, a producer with the Oprah Winfrey television show in Chicago.

"Oprah is doing a show about dangerous hazing initiation rituals," he said. "We'd like to have you come on the show."

As we spoke, I thought about the pros and cons of going on *Oprah*. A prosecutor is barred by ethical rules from talking about the details of a case before it goes to trial, but the case was completely over, so talking about it publicly would not be improper. As always, I was extremely busy with upcoming cases, but still, making the trip to Chicago for the taping would only involve a couple of days. I knew the family members of Michael Davis would approve of the publicity because they were hoping that Michael's death might serve as an example to help stop fraternity hazing nationwide. What better chance of having an impact than being on a show watched daily by nine million people?

"Our plan is to have you tell the facts of the case at the beginning of the segment," Brady was saying. "It will be an important show."

I recalled the strength of character Carlos Turner had shown by coming forward to admit to what had happened. The judge had ordered him to spend five hundred hours doing community service. To the extent possible his work was to be geared toward giving speeches about hazing prevention.

"You ought to contact Carlos Turner," I suggested. "He was one of the defendants, but I was impressed by him." I told Brady about Carlos admitting what had happened, even while knowing that what he said would probably get him arrested.

"You also ought to contact Michael Davis's mother, Edith Davis, and his sister, Marisa Hilliard," I added. "Both of them are extremely articulate and dedicated to making something positive come out of Michael's death."

Brady agreed that adding these additional guests would make the show even better. He also confirmed that Oprah would pay for my plane ticket and my hotel room in Chicago while I was there for the taping.

In one of life's little coincidences, my oldest daughter, Olivia, had read a biography of Oprah just a month or two earlier. She was thinking she might want to grow up to be a journalist.

"One other thing," I said. "My daughter just read a book about Oprah. She's ten. May I bring her along? I'll pay for her plane ticket, of course."

"Sure," Brady said.

A few minutes later he called me back.

"Good news," he said. "I found a two-for-one special on the plane tickets, so your daughter's ticket is free."

⚖

When the day arrived, Olivia and I flew to Chicago for my big *Oprah* appearance. After we got off the plane, we spotted a limousine driver awaiting us. Clad in black, he held up a handwritten sign bearing our last name. It was a heady experience, marred only slightly by the fact my name was misspelled: *Swindle.*

We rode in the lap of luxury to the Omni Hotel in downtown Chicago, where we stayed on Oprah's tab until the taping the next day. The hotel was so fancy it even had real books on the bookshelves in the room.

The next morning the long, black limousine picked us up to take us to Harpo Studios. Harpo is Oprah spelled backward. This was news to me, although millions of Oprah's fans probably knew the story. Years before, Oprah had bought an entire block and remodeled its towering old buildings to create her company's offices and the studio where she filmed her show. It was impressive. The security was more thorough than that at any courthouse I had ever visited. Each visitor walked through a metal detector, then stood as security guards double-checked clothing with handheld wands. All packages and cameras were confiscated, to be returned only when you left. Olivia was disappointed about losing her camera because she had been hoping to have her picture taken with Oprah.

After clearing security, we were escorted to the "greenroom," where guests on the show waited. The show had more than one greenroom. We shared ours with Edith Davis, Marisa Hilliard, and some other members of the Davis family. Thoughtfully, the show had placed Carlos Turner (who, after all, had participated in killing Edith Davis's son) in a different room.

A young woman who worked for Oprah as a makeup artist approached me in a very businesslike manner.

"I need to get you ready," she said.

"I don't wear makeup."

"Oh, everybody needs makeup for the show."

Who was I to argue? I was just a visitor.

I sat patiently as she applied something to my face.

"You must have an interesting job," I said.

"Very! Oprah is great to work for!"

Suddenly, she was applying some sort of goop to my hair. I had not put anything on my hair since my grade school butch wax days.

"Hey!" I said. "What are you doing?"

"This will make your hair look better on TV."

It had not occurred to me that my looks were all that important to Oprah, especially considering the content of this particular show, but I shut up. After all, everyone wants to look better.

Soon, I sported makeup on my face and gel on my hair. It was time for me to be escorted to my spot on the stage.

It turned out, however, that since Olivia was under sixteen, she would not be allowed to sit in the audience during the taping. She had to wait in the greenroom. It had a television, though, so she would be able to watch the show live.

The room where the show was taped was amazing. It was much like a theater, with Oprah's stage in the middle, and audience seats on risers on three sides. The most interesting feature was the ceiling. It was a honeycomb of bright lights, each separately dimmable to get the lighting just right. The audience was already seated by the time the other guests and I were led into the room.

When I arrived at my seat I got a bit of disappointing news. When Oprah took my advice and added Carlos Turner and Edith Davis to the show, she decided to place herself between Carlos Turner and Edith Davis. She wanted to play up the show as the first time since the trial that the mother of the hazing victim had actually confronted one of the young men who killed her son. I had inadvertently bumped myself off the stage. Although we were physically in Chicago, this was still Hollywood. I was relegated to the front row of the audience. I was equipped with a microphone and told to be ready to field an occasional question from Oprah.

I had never seen the *Oprah* show before being a guest. As I sat with the others, awaiting Oprah, it occurred to me that perhaps I should have watched her show a few times, just to be familiar with its format. After all, I often take witnesses into the courtroom to build up their comfort level before they testify. Maybe I should have done a bit more homework in preparation for this appearance. I was not nervous, though. Unlike my times in a courtroom, the stakes here did not involve winning or losing a criminal prosecution. It was far less pressure than a murder trial. No comparison. In fact, it dawned on me that I was actually having fun. That realization made me feel a bit guilty, since the death of Michael Davis was a serious matter.

Meanwhile, Oprah was on her way down a hallway, preparing to make her grand entrance. Her route took her past the greenroom. She spotted Olivia.

Now, I had never spoken with Oprah personally. All of my contact with her show had been through Jim Brady. Brady, though, had obviously told Oprah about my daughter, Olivia, the little girl from Missouri who had read Oprah's biography and was considering a career in journalism.

While the audience and I waited for Oprah to emerge onto the stage, to tape a show that would be watched by nine million people, Oprah detoured into the greenroom for a visit with Olivia Swingle. They chatted several minutes, Oprah telling Olivia how nice it was to meet her and how wonderful it was that her father had brought her along with him. Then Oprah was off to tape the show.

The audience cheered wildly as Oprah bounded into the room and took center stage. She quickly launched into the theme of the show, "dangerous initiation rituals." As she recited the facts of the Michael Davis case, I grew more and more impressed by her. She had memorized the facts like a good lawyer delivering an opening statement. In fact, it pretty much *was* my opening statement, which I had sent to Jim Brady. As far as I could tell, Oprah was delivering it without notes or cue cards. At key times, pictures of the victim flashed on a big screen behind her. Pretty soon, she had much of the audience in tears. I was about as necessary to the proceedings as football cleats at a scholar bowl.

After her wonderful opening statement, Oprah then led Michael's mother and sister into a moving discussion about the loss of a beloved son and brother. By the time they were through, the audience was clearly ready to hang Carlos Turner by his heels. I felt sorry for him. The hatred of the audience was palpable. The poor guy had agreed to be on the show at my suggestion. I felt like the scout who encouraged Custer to chase that inconsequential band of Indians toward the Little Big Horn. I decided that no matter what question I was asked, I would point out that Carlos Turner had done the right thing by coming forward and was trying to do his part to end hazing.

Sure enough, Oprah eventually threw a question my way.

"Morley Swingle was the prosecuting attorney who got seven convictions for Michael's death. Morley, why were the sentences so light? Minimal jail and community service. Why?"

Ooof. That was not exactly the question I had been anticipating and certainly not one I would have chosen. I did, however, manage to work some praise of Carlos Turner into my answer:

"In this case we had seven people who had been involved in a reckless beating, but we couldn't say, through the medical examiner, which blow had caused which injury. As Carlos indicated, he knew he had kicked Michael, but the kick was not what caused his death. He had broken ribs, he had a lacerated spleen, he had a lacerated liver, and he died of a subdural hematoma caused by his brain being shaken. The medical examiner said he didn't know which of the blows thrown by different individuals caused that subdural hematoma. It was most likely something called 'body-slamming,' which was picking the victims, the pledges, up in the air and throwing them down to the soft, grassy field, causing the brain to begin a slow bleed. The problem with the case was we could not say for sure which of the individuals threw *the* blow that killed him, so I charged all seven people that were involved in throwing any kind of blow that night with manslaughter for recklessly causing a death. Two of them went to jury trial and juries gave one of them a year in jail and the other a year and a half. The others pled guilty. Carlos, as a couple of others did, served thirty days behind bars, and got five years probation with five hundred hours community service, which was to be geared toward giving talks about hazing. As I understand it Carlos has already used up his five hundred hours and is here today because he does want to do something to help end hazing."

The rest of the show flew by. Before I knew it, the taping was over and I was back in the greenroom. My fifteen minutes of fame had consisted of answering one question. You could read it aloud yourself to get a sense of exactly how long I was on camera with Oprah. Still, it had been quite an experience.

Back in the greenroom, Olivia peered closely at my head.

"Why is your hair so stiff, Dad?"

"They put something on it." I looked into the mirror and tentatively touched my hardened, goop-encrusted hair.

Jim Brady, the producer of our segment, approached us.

"Oprah wants to visit some more with Olivia," he said.

"Great!" I said, fully prepared to tag along.

"Not you," Brady said. "She just wants Olivia."

"Oh."

I cooled my heels there in the greenroom while my daughter hobnobbed with Oprah. Oprah gave her a personal tour of the production room and talked with her about her life and her future. Before parting, she gave Olivia a big bear hug. When Olivia returned, she was glowing.

To this day, I have never had a conversation with Oprah Winfrey other than to answer the one question she asked me during her show. I learned all

I needed to know about her, though, from the wonderful way she treated my daughter. Oprah Winfrey is a class act. I will even give her the ultimate compliment a trial lawyer can bestow upon another human being: Had Oprah Winfrey chosen to be a courtroom lawyer, she could have been the Clarence Darrow of our generation.

Unlucky Forger

It's better to be tried by twelve than carried
by six.
                —Popular law enforcement aphorism

Roger Fields is one of my favorite police officers. He is a big, powerful, strapping guy, 6', 2", 225 pounds, tough and athletic. He is also incredibly funny. He maintains a large network of entertaining friends and acquaintances who regularly supply him with jokes and stories, so he is always good for a laugh or two when you run into him. Two of my best anecdotes, however, involve Roger Fields himself.

One summer day he was patrolling Cape Girardeau, looking for a fugitive wanted by another county. When the fugitive was pointed out by a helpful citizen, Roger approached the suspect.

"I understand you're Harlan Huggins?" he asked.

"No. You got the wrong guy."

Before Roger could even ask another question, Huggins sucker punched him on the side of his head. Roger recovered quickly, grabbed his assailant, and the two men tussled on the street for a few seconds. Huggins eventually broke away and did what successful fugitives are wont to do—he took off running.

Roger sprinted after him, brimming with the supreme confidence of an athlete who does not yet fully appreciate the sad truth that the prime years of his athletic prowess are now in the rearview mirror. Roger Fields had been a varsity letterman in high school. He had played basketball and baseball and would have played football had his school fielded a team. Like most student athletes, he took justifiable pride in his athleticism. Thus, it came as a rude shock to discover that scrawny little Harlan Huggins was gradually pulling away from him.

How was this possible? Realization struck Roger like a kick in the gut from a Bollinger County mule.

"I'm getting too old for this," he grunted. He was, at the time, twenty-seven years old. The fugitive was several years younger.

The fugitive, too, wore Reebok running shoes. Roger was wearing heavy boots (as well as a bulletproof vest).

They tore across backyards for two or three blocks. Arms churning, Harlan Huggins opened up a fifty-yard lead on Fields. Roger realized with bitter indignation that he was losing ground on the rail-thin punk with every passing second. Oh, this was going to be embarrassing when he got back to the station! He would never live it down!

Jeez, he was even developing a side stitch. Ouch!

Harlan Huggins glanced over his shoulder, smiled grimly, and quickly returned to the business of outrunning Roger Fields. They were now racing across a grassy field. Roger was struck by sudden inspiration.

"Stop or I'll shoot!" he yelled.

Now, Roger was well aware that in 1985 the United States Supreme Court had ruled in *Tennessee v. Garner* that a police officer could not lawfully shoot a fleeing suspect unless he had reasonable grounds to believe that the suspect posed a danger to public safety. Danger to property was not enough. In other words, a person running from a police officer had a constitutional right not to be shot in the back unless the officer reasonably thought the suspect was a murderer, rapist, or other extremely bad actor likely to physically hurt someone if he got away. Fields was well-trained. He knew that gunning down Harlan Huggins would get him sued, fired, roasted in the media, and quite possibly charged with manslaughter.

He was hoping, however, that Harlan Huggins was not up to speed on his constitutional law. The fugitive clearly believed that Roger *might* gun him down; the moment Roger mentioned shooting, Huggins began weaving as he ran.

"Stop or I'll shoot!" Roger yelled again.

Huggins kept bobbing and weaving and seemed to move even faster.

Keeping his gun in its holster, Roger formed his thumb and index finger in the shape of a pistol and pointed at the fleeing suspect.

"I mean it!" he yelled as he galloped across the field. "Stop or I'll shoot!"

Harlan Huggins did not stop. If anything, he picked up speed. Perhaps he was spurred on by the notion of receiving a bullet in the back.

Exasperated, Roger bellowed one tremendously loud word.

"Bang!"

Harlan Huggins, who had been running at a full sprint, hit the ground and rolled, sending grass and dirt flying up around him. At that speed, it could not have felt good. He was moaning and complaining about being shot as Roger cuffed him. He pleaded to be taken to the hospital.

"Where are you hit?" Roger asked.

"I don't know," Huggins groaned. "I hurt all over."

"I guess it's these high-caliber bullets," Roger said. He blew imaginary smoke from the tip of his index finger and winked.

"Gotcha," he said.

At least, that is how Roger tells the story now.

⚖

The best "Roger Fields Amazing and Extraordinary Arrest" saga, however, took place in "The Case of the Unlucky Forger."

Calvin Higbie had just gotten out of prison, but he was already wanted as a parole absconder. He was twenty-one years old and came fully equipped with a loaded resume packing five felony convictions. He had no job, no prospects, and, apparently, no brain.

As Higbie strolled down a Cape Girardeau street one sunny March afternoon, he ran into a "dude" who had some checks for sale. The "dude" informed him that this particular book of twenty-five checks was a bargain at twenty-five dollars, because these hot little numbers had not yet been reported stolen and could easily be passed for big bucks. In fact, another satisfied customer had already cashed some earlier in the day and had not been arrested. Hooked by the lure of easy money, Higbie made the purchase.

He proceeded immediately to a local pawnshop, where he intended to forge one of the checks. Oh, life was good!

In general, pawnshop employees are not rocket scientists, but most regularly read the local newspaper. The employee working behind the counter that day quickly developed more than a sneaking suspicion that the rough-looking, scarred, muscle-bound, threadbare customer presenting a check supposedly signed by State Senator Peter Kinder had not come by the check lawfully.

The check was from Peter Kinder's personal account, so the word *senator* did not appear on the checks; however, Kinder was not only well known as the local state senator, he was also the associate publisher of the *Southeast*

Missourian newspaper. His smiling face appeared two or three times per week above the title of his regular column. His face bore no resemblance whatsoever to the mug of Calvin Higbie. The two men were not even the same race. It was an extremely unfortunate roll of the dice for Calvin Higbie.

The alert pawnshop employee maintained a poker face for Higbie and eventually came up with a reason to visit the back room. He made a hasty call to Senator Kinder's office and reached the senator personally. It is amazing how quickly a person can get past a secretary screening calls with the simple statement: "There's a man standing in my business trying to pass one of your boss's personal checks!" Kinder quickly verified that the checks had been stolen from his home during a burglary three days earlier and that Higbie did not have permission to be cashing a two-hundred-dollar check. The senator said he would call the police immediately and send them to the pawnshop.

"Stall him," Kinder suggested.

The pawnshop employee hung up, took a deep breath, and hurried back to the front of the store. A smart criminal might have been spooked by the delay, but Higbie was still in the shop, proving that he was both unlucky and criminally incautious.

"So, nice weather, isn't it?" the pawnshop employee began.

As luck would have it, Roger Fields was the closest officer to the scene of the crime. He arrived within minutes. At precisely 1:30 in the afternoon, he strolled into the shop like John Wayne sauntering through the swinging doors of a saloon full of desperadoes. He put his hands on his hips, nodded at Calvin Higbie, and said in his friendliest voice, "Good afternoon. How are you today, *Senator Kinder*?"

Calvin Higbie, while not the smartest scoundrel in the world, nevertheless realized that, in the lingo of the lawless, the jig was up. What he lacked in smarts, he made up for in ferocity. He charged Fields. Roger, appalled by Higbie's unexpected inability to take a joke, valiantly fought back against the sudden attack.

It was a fierce fight. The officer had the advantage in training, intelligence, and size. The felon had the advantage in desperation and meanness.

They grappled with each other. During the thrashing and body-slamming, they managed to smash virtually every glass cabinet in the store. They were the proverbial bulls in the china shop.

Roger's level of concern ratcheted up several notches when he realized that Calvin Higbie was trying to pull the service weapon from his holster. Now, he thought to himself, his attempt at humor had admittedly fallen flat with this audience—even the pawnshop employee had not laughed—but getting shot for a bad joke, that seemed a bit extreme.

Positioning his elbow on his holster to prevent Higbie from getting control of the gun, Roger wrapped the struggling man in a headlock and put his mace canister to Higbie's face.

Cayenne pepper spray is a great invention for law enforcement. In the old days—the old days being the 1980s—police officers still carried black wooden billy clubs. They often needed them in situations like this, where someone desperate and large has decided that this particular officer is not man enough to bring him in. Not everyone, you see, meekly submits when told he is under arrest. In the billy-club days, the suspect who resisted often ended up with lumps on his head and wounds requiring stitches. The medical bills often proved expensive for law enforcement agencies, and for the county jail, which held the prisoners after their arrest. Hence, the invention of pepper spray.

One short burst of the spray into the face of a typical suspect will usually end the fight immediately. The thug will quickly lose interest in fighting. His eyes, nose, and mouth will experience such excruciating, burning pain that he will fall to his knees, the only thought in his mind being something like *"Aaaggggghhhaaa!! Someone get these burning hot embers out of my eyes, nose and mouth! Aaaggggghhhaaa!!"*

At least, that is how it is supposed to work. Officers who have been sprayed themselves—either during official training sessions or accidentally by some "moron" of a colleague aiming for someone else—all report the same vivid sensations.

Calvin Higbie, however, must have had his own prior experience with pepper spray. When he spotted Fields bringing the small canister near his face, he clenched his jaw and squeezed his eyes shut. His cheeks puffed out like those of a chipmunk as he held his breath. His fingers, crablike, kept clawing at Fields's holster.

Fields waited patiently for Higbie to run out of breath, at least as patiently as possible for one locked in a violent struggle with another man. Finally, Higbie exhaled, and as he sucked in another breath Fields zapped him with the pepper spray.

"Mommy!" Higbie shouted. (Truth be told, the word was not "Mommy," but rather a polysyllabic epithet having something to do with mothers.)

The fight was over. Fields had made his arrest.

After hearing Roger Fields's account of the case, I charged Calvin Higbie with the felonies of forgery and resisting arrest. I was hoping the case might go to trial. You don't always get to call a senator as your crime victim. What jury appeal! Higbie, however, must have come to the same conclusion. He opted to plead guilty and receive a six-year prison sentence, three for the forgery and three for resisting arrest, with the sentences to run consecutively.

So that's how Roger Fields and I made the world safe for senators whose checkbooks are stolen. Peter Kinder quickly recovered from the trauma of being a crime victim. His political star continued to rise, and a few years later he was elected lieutenant governor of the State of Missouri.

As for Calvin Higbie, one hopes he learned a valuable lesson about the importance of reading the newspaper. Had he been a regular reader of the *Southeast Missourian,* he would have quickly fathomed the fatal flaw in his hastily planned criminal enterprise. It would have been well worth the paltry subscription price. As it was, his poor reading habits and careless victim selection cost him six years.

Combat Prosecutor

The [Prosecuting] Attorney is the representative not of an ordinary party to a controversy, but of a sovereignty whose obligation to govern impartially is as compelling as its obligation to govern at all; and whose interest, therefore, in a criminal prosecution is not that it shall win a case, but that justice shall be done. As such, he is in a peculiar and very definite sense the servant of the law, the twofold aim of which is that guilt shall not escape or innocence suffer. He may prosecute with earnestness and vigor—indeed, he should do so. But, while he may strike hard blows, he is not at liberty to strike foul ones. It is as much his duty to refrain from improper methods calculated to produce a wrongful conviction as it is to use every legitimate means to bring about a just one.

—Justice George Sutherland

No man should be in public office who can't make more money in private life.

—Thomas E. Dewey

By far the most fascinating person to ever work at my office was Assistant Prosecuting Attorney Ian D. W. Sutherland. Ian was a remarkable person who fit three successful careers into one lifetime.

First, Ian was a soldier. He served three tours of duty in Vietnam and rose to the rank of lieutenant colonel. He served in the United States Army Special Forces, the elite unit known as the Green Berets. He was in the thick of combat in Vietnam. He trained and led the local Montagnards into battle against the North Vietnamese and was heavily involved in efforts to rescue American prisoners of war. Later, he served at the American Embassy in Iran, and was somehow affiliated with the CIA during that time, although you could never get any details about that from him. I only found out about it when I wanted to put a photograph and short biography of each assistant prosecutor on the Web page for my office, and Ian kept stalling. It eventually came out that there were still people in Iran who would want him dead. Ian finally decided "what the heck" and let me use his photograph.

When he returned from Vietnam, Ian earned his master's degree from the John F. Kennedy School of Government at Harvard. Former presidential candidate Michael Dukakis was his favorite professor. Although their worldviews must have been strikingly different, they developed a friendship and corresponded frequently over the years.

After getting his master's, Ian wrote a book, *Special Forces of the United States: 1952–1982,* that ran seven hundred pages. No less an authority than General Colin Powell wrote him a fan letter, praising his book as "the authoritative work in the field." Had I received a letter like that, I first would have made sure the media knew about it, and I then would have framed it and hung it on a wall in a prominent place. Ian just took it home and stuck it in a file cabinet.

After writing his book, Ian went to law school. He was fifty-three when he graduated, and the bigger law firms were not interested in hiring him. He took a job as an assistant city attorney in Cape Girardeau.

He so impressed me at our first meeting that I swore I'd steal him away from the city attorney's office the first chance I got. So I did.

When Ian joined my office, he was old enough to be my father, but as lawyers go, he was a "baby lawyer" with no experience whatsoever, while I was the veteran trial lawyer with over eighteen years of experience and fifty jury trials under my belt. While one might have thought it would be difficult for someone with Ian's background, pride, credentials, and world experience to take orders from a younger man, it turned out to be quite the contrary. I was Ian's teacher and mentor in the field of trial practice and criminal prose-cution. He became my right-hand man and a pillar of strength for our office for fifteen years.

On Ian's first day at my office, I happened to be driving to Scott County for the sentencing of a biker caught possessing a mortar shell. The precise crim-inal charge was the felony of possession of an explosive weapon. He was a somewhat dangerous fellow. A murderer had once confessed that when he chopped up his victim with a hatchet, this biker was the person he called to help bury the pieces. We never could make a case against the biker for help-ing dispose of the body, though, because the hatchet-murderer was too afraid of him to testify. Besides, I wasn't willing to make a sweetheart deal with a killer merely to get his testimony against a thug whose only involvement in the murder had been after the fact. But the fact that this biker was someone a murderer would call when he needed help disposing of a corpse told you basically all you needed to know about the man.

The biker was a big, mean fellow with a reason to dislike me. I was, after all, the first prosecutor who had ever tagged him with a felony. The biker also had a pack of biker friends. I felt a little uneasy driving off to rural Scott County alone for the sentencing, so an unpaid part-time investigator for my office had very nicely volunteered to go along. His name was Ned Wakeman.

Ned was a pretty tough guy. He was a big man and a black belt in karate. He had been a reserve police officer for several years. It was good of him to volunteer to go along with me, and I later felt sort of bad about what I did to him during the drive down.

Since it was Ian's first day at work, I had never talked with him in any detail about his service in Vietnam, but Police Chief Howard H. Boyd, also a military veteran, had become good friends with him. Chief Boyd had told me when I hired Ian that Ian was the only person he had ever met who had *killed* more people in his lifetime than Boyd had ever *arrested*! This and the fact that Ian had been a lieutenant colonel in the Special Forces were all I knew about Ian's military service at the time. But I felt well armed for what I had in mind.

Ned Wakeman was one of those macho guys who enjoys bragging about the tough situations he has faced. One of his favorite stories, which I had heard more than once, was about the one time in his career as a reserve offi-cer when he had been forced to draw his gun in the line of duty. A big guy with an ax handle was coming toward him. Ned pulled his gun and told him to drop it. The man hesitated, and Ned decided that he would shoot the guy dead if he advanced another step. The decision was made. The guy was going to get shot. After a long and tense standoff, however, the man finally dropped the ax handle and thereby saved his own life.

On the way to the Scott County courthouse, Ned sat in the front seat of my car, and Ian sat in the back. We were not far outside Cape Girardeau when I decided to have a little fun at Ned's expense.

"So tell me, Ned, have you ever had to draw your gun in the line of duty?"

Ned leaped at the opening like a schnauzer after a rabbit and quickly regaled us with his macho story. By golly, as always, he had made that decision that he would indeed shoot the guy to death if he took another step. As always, the guy with the ax handle wised up at the last minute. Ned told it as well as he had ever told it, I'll give him that.

I know that what I did next sounds a bit malicious, but I am really not mean-spirited very often. And, as I said, I do genuinely feel a bit remorseful about my behavior.

"Wow, Ned, that's something," I said. I looked at Ian's reflection in the rearview mirror.

"So, Ian," I asked innocently. "Were you ever in combat in Vietnam?"

"Well, I cleared bunkers."

"What's that mean?"

"It means you throw a grenade into a bunker and then go in and machine-gun anyone who's still moving."

We drove in silence for a couple of miles. To my knowledge, Ned never told his tough-guy story again. Sorry, Ned.

⚖

Ian's organizational skills were amazing. I could dump a ton of cases on him to handle, but his desk would always be spotless. His method was to look at every piece of paper only once, and then make sure it got into the proper file. While my desk was always piled high with clutter and case files, his was always shiny and neat. I still do not completely understand how he did it.

In his fifteen years at my office, Ian tried 123 jury trials, mostly felonies. I was able to go off and try long murder cases without worrying because I always knew Ian could handle anything that came up. After just a year or two, he could have left the job to make far more money in private practice, but he chose to remain a public prosecutor for his entire legal career.

We were both in complete agreement with Justice George Sutherland (no relation to Ian), famous for his remark that the duty of the prosecutor is to strike hard blows, but fair ones. We worked hard at making ourselves the best trial lawyers we could be, while always keeping in mind that our first duty was to achieve justice, not just to win convictions. Ian never lost sight of that principle. Consequently, he was well respected even by the criminals he prosecuted.

I could always get a rise out of Ian by going to the latest war movie and then sauntering into his office the next day and telling him that the movie's portrayal of combat seemed very realistic. I did this the last time with *Saving Private Ryan*. In fact, it occurred to me this might be one instance when Ian would agree that yes, this particular movie had been realistic.

No way. Ian went off about how Tom Hanks's character was unbelievable because he was such a milquetoast. He informed me that once you have reached the position of captain, leading men into battle, you don't sit around struggling with reflective angst, debating the pros and cons of what you are doing. By that point you are a killing machine; it is literally kill or be killed, and you are not philosophizing about it.

⚖

I could also get an entertaining rise out of Ian by mentioning the name Horace Bixby. Bixby's case was our first DNA jury trial in Cape Girardeau County. This was back when forensic DNA was brand-spanking new. Nobody had ever heard of it yet as a crime-solving tool. The Horace Bixby case presented the classic scenario. Bixby was a twenty-four-year-old burglar who had cut himself during a burglary and had left a blood trail as he fled the victim's house. Testing matched his DNA to the blood left at the scene. Voila! He was caught.

He had donated his blood to the crime scene in an interesting way. He shattered the bathroom window of an apartment near the university campus at 3:50 one hot July morning as the victim, a forty-five-year-old woman, slept on the couch in her living room. She awoke to find her yellow blanket pulled over her head and a knife pressed to her throat. A man was telling her to shut up or he would kill her. She struggled with him. She never saw his face, but through the blanket she saw the hand holding the knife. Her three-year-old grandson began crying in the next room. The intruder brought the knife back and whopped her on top of her head with its hilt. When he brought the knife back again, preparing to strike her a second time, he stabbed himself in the face. The woman screamed, her grandson cried, and the burglar howled in pain. He fled the house, leaving his blood on the yellow blanket and on the floor. Patrolman Lawrence Fleming collected the blood at the scene. Detective Tracy Lemonds obtained a sample of Horace Bixby's blood via a search warrant after officers reported seeing Bixby, a known burglar, in the vicinity that night. A fresh cut to his face had helped provide the probable cause for the issuance of the search warrant.

Today, the case would be a slam dunk. Everyone understands that DNA is the genetic material found in all human cells, and that each person's is unique. DNA amounts to a genetic fingerprint. In criminal cases, DNA is left at the scene through the defendant's blood, semen, saliva, and skin or hair follicles. Nowadays, a DNA match is the best possible evidence for a prosecutor. Back then, it was new and confusing to a jury and challenging evidence to present effectively in court.

To make the case even more bizarre, Horace Bixby opted to serve as his own defense lawyer. It really was not a bad idea. With his three prior felony convictions, he had logged more courtroom experience than many of the young lawyers at the public defender's office. In fact, it was an almost brilliant stroke because of those very same convictions.

It is always difficult for the prosecutor when the defendant represents himself. If you object to improper questions or evidence offered by the defendant, you look like a bully, even when your objections are sustained. Thus, you tend to let him get away with things a real lawyer could never get away with.

And then there was the matter of those prior convictions. All of them were for burglary and stealing. The dilemma for Horace Bixby was that if he took the stand to claim that the blood was not his, Ian could cross-examine him about those priors. If Bixby did not take the stand, the prosecution could not tell the jury about the prior convictions, but, in that event, Bixby would never have the opportunity to deny that the blood was his. Despite the jury instruction that a defendant is not obligated to testify, sometimes a jury wants to hear a defendant say he did not do the crime before they will acquit.

So, Horace Bixby had a strategic problem. To testify or not to testify, that was the question. Bixby solved it by representing himself and giving his own closing argument.

Ian did his usual competent and workmanlike job of presenting the state's case. Dr. Allen Gathman, a biology professor from Southeast Missouri State University, explained the genetics of DNA to the jury. Dr. Dwight Adams from the FBI's new DNA analysis unit in Washington, D.C., flew in to tell the jury that the DNA in the blood left at the scene matched the blood drawn from the body of Horace Bixby, and that only one in 645,000 people would be a match. As the expert explained the new DNA technology, Ian thought some of the jurors' eyes seemed to glaze over, but still, the expert made it clear that the statistical probability clearly indicated that blood left at the scene of the crime was a match to Horace Bixby.

When it came time for Horace Bixby to cross-examine the expert, Bixby simply said, "I don't know how to question him. I don't have any questions for him."

After Ian rested the state's case, Horace Bixby offered no evidence. Soon, it was time for closing arguments. Ian summarized the evidence, patiently reminding the jury how DNA testing had proven that the blood on the blanket and the floor belonged to Horace Bixby, so he must have been the burglar.

Then it was Bixby's turn for closing argument. Ethical rules prohibiting prosecutors from lying to the jury did not apply to him; he could tell a few whoppers without worrying about a perjury charge. Bixby was off and running. It was his chance to testify without being cross-examined about his prior convictions. Truth be damned! He soared like an eagle.

"I don't know nothin' about that newfangled DNA stuff," Horace Bixby complained. "All I know is they got the wrong guy. I wasn't there. Don't ask me what went wrong with that DNA testing. I don't know. All I know is I wasn't there. I wasn't there! This ain't right!"

When the jury pronounced Bixby not guilty, the entire office was shocked. Ian was hard to live with for a few days. It is bad enough losing a case, but losing it to a guy who represents himself! Oh, this was painful for Ian and priceless for the rest of us.

Horace Bixby's considerable trial skills did not immediately return him to the streets. He went back to prison, anyway, to finish serving his time for the other burglary convictions since his parole had been revoked.

And, of course, if you now wanted to get a rise out of Ian, you had two options. You could talk about how realistic the latest war movie seemed to be, or you could simply mention the name Horace Bixby.

⚖

Ian kept himself in fantastic physical condition. He swam laps at the municipal swimming pool every morning at some ungodly hour and went parachuting every other weekend when the weather was nice. He often traveled to Fort Bragg to give parachuting tips to new soldiers. When he turned seventy, he looked to be about fifty-five.

It came as a terrible shock to me one Saturday morning when I got a telephone call that Ian had been killed in a parachuting accident in Charleston, Missouri. At age seventy, he had gone on one of his routine weekend parachute jumps. His regular chute failed, and then his backup failed, and he was killed when he hit the ground. I was the person called to the funeral home to identify his body.

Ian's ex-wife, Debbie, and I planned his memorial service. We went through his private photo albums and scrapbooks together, and I gathered material to use in his eulogy.

Remarkably, it was not until his death that I learned that this amazing man had been a hero during his combat service in Vietnam. He had won the Silver Star and five Bronze Stars, which are only awarded for heroism in combat. When he won the Silver Star, it was for risking his own life to save other soldiers who were pinned down by an enemy machine gun nest. Ian charged it, armed with only grenades and a pistol, and wiped out the enemy, allowing the other Americans to escape to safety. Each Bronze Star was for a separate act of combat heroism. He had also won numerous other decorations and awards.

Ian had worked out of the office right next to mine for *fifteen years* and had never once bothered to tell me that he had won a Silver Star, which is just a notch or two below the Congressional Medal of Honor. Had I ever won a Silver Star, I suspect that anyone who ever met me for the rest of my life would find out about it within fifteen minutes of meeting me. Not so with Ian. Just like the fan letter from Colin Powell, Ian kept his medals locked away at home. His life now consisted of his public service as the chief assistant prosecuting attorney of Cape Girardeau County, Missouri. He was not one to upstage his boss.

By the time he died, Ian had caught up with me in the number of jury trials prosecuted. Several exciting trials loomed in his near future. He was writing a sequel to his military history book and had just completed a novel based upon his experiences rescuing prisoners of war in Vietnam. He had a life worth living.

I was devastated when Ian was killed. I really felt like my right arm had been severed. But I took some comfort in knowing that of all the men I have ever known, Ian was one who simply could not have tolerated being an invalid in some old folks' home. He was a vigorous and energetic man's man. He lived his life to its fullest, right up until the moment he died.

Fool for a Client

If there is any truth to the old proverb that
"one who is his own lawyer has a fool for a
client," the Court by its opinion today now
bestows a *constitutional* right on one to make a
fool of himself.

> —Harry A. Blackmun

The very first time I cross-examined a witness,
as a direct and immediate consequence
of my cross-examination of that witness, my
client went to jail. It took me a long while to
realize that there is something with which to
reassure yourself about it. No matter
[how badly you do in your cross-examination],
it is *the client* who goes to jail.

> —Irving Younger

Although Horace Bixby was able to beat Assistant Prosecuting Attorney Ian Sutherland in our county's first trial involving DNA, and renowned defense attorney Clarence Darrow secured an acquittal when he defended himself against charges of attempted jury bribery in 1912, self-representation does not usually end so happily for a criminal defendant. One murderer who undoubtedly regretted his choice of attorneys was Anthony C. McGee.

McGee stabbed Robert Earl Battles to death in broad daylight on Good Hope Street in Cape Girardeau on a scorching August afternoon. With an angry thrust of his knife, McGee ended Battles's life. The blade went clear through the victim's heart. During the violent attack, McGee also stabbed Battles in the neck and the belly.

The stabbing was witnessed by two or three people, so the state's case was pretty strong. I was a bit disappointed when McGee chose to represent himself, since it would likely make the trial cumbersome, tedious, and lengthy. The judge would undoubtedly give the defendant wide latitude in questioning the jury panel during voir dire, delivering his opening statement, cross-examining the state's witnesses, performing the direct examination of the defense witnesses, and presenting his own closing argument. I would have much preferred facing a real lawyer.

Several times in the weeks leading up to the trial, Circuit Judge A. J. Seier questioned McGee on the record, encouraging him to change his mind. He repeatedly warned him about the pitfalls of self-representation. In fact, some of the nicest things the brilliant but cantankerous Judge Seier ever said about me were uttered as he tried to scare Anthony McGee into requesting a lawyer—things like "Mr. Swingle is a skillful prosecutor. He knows the law backward and forward. You aren't likely to be a match for him." Over and over, the judge pointed out to him the disadvantages of representing himself, warning him that he would be forced to comply with the rules of evidence just like a regular lawyer. Of course, I knew the last part was not entirely true. As a practical matter, the judge would not want the case to be reversed, so he was likely to give McGee free rein to say or do practically anything he wanted during the opening statement and closing argument, and to ask witnesses whatever questions popped into his head.

At one point prior to trial, Judge Seier specifically told him, "You know, there's an old saying that a lawyer who represents himself has a fool for a client. There's some truth to that. Are you positive that you don't want me to appoint a lawyer to represent you?"

"I want to do it myself," McGee insisted.

"Very well," the judge replied. "I find that you have the intellectual capacity to do so. It's your choice."

Most of the trial proved to be unremarkable, as far as homicides go. Of course, the killing of another human being is always a tragedy. We had the obligatory gruesome photographs of the dead body, plus the testimony of the medical examiner, along with the testimony of officers Steve Shields and Steve Strong, who had responded to the crime scene. But there really was not any disagreement over the cause of death. Both sides agreed that Battles had been stabbed through the heart.

The courtroom battle was over whether the killing was justified as self-defense. McGee claimed that Robert Earl Battles had confronted him and had initiated the fight in the street. McGee maintained that he had fought to defend himself. If the jury believed McGee, he would be entitled to an acquittal.

I worked night and day to prepare the case for trial. Not only would an acquittal be a terrible miscarriage of justice, since the key witness was adamant that McGee had attacked Battles, but a loss to a defendant representing himself would be especially painful. I was fully aware that getting shellacked by this *pro se* defendant would subject me to the sort of wisecracks Ian faced after the Horace Bixby debacle. Since I had delivered many of those wisecracks myself, I prepared for the McGee trial as if F. Lee Bailey were on the other side.

Anthony McGee looked dapper and lawyerlike in his gray suit, but he did not prove to be an F. Lee Bailey. He did, however, make several appropriate and timely objections and did a reasonably competent job overall. Until, that is, he decided to call a young woman to the stand as a witness for the defense.

"Your Honor," he said, "I call Ms. Maggie Smith."

Smith was a last-minute witness. McGee had not disclosed her as a potential witness until after the trial had begun.

Outside the hearing of the jury earlier that morning, I had objected to his calling her since he had not listed her as a witness prior to trial. I pointed out that in his role as the defense attorney, Anthony McGee had violated basic discovery rules by failing to provide me with the required advance notice. As a result, the judge had the power to either prohibit the defense from calling her or allow the prosecution to interview her prior to her testimony. The judge opted for the latter. He would allow me to have an officer take her statement as long as I provided a copy to the defense.

Detective Steve Strong from the Cape Girardeau Police Department questioned Maggie Smith for me while other witnesses were testifying. She gave him a handwritten statement. In it, she said that on the day before the killing, Anthony McGee told her that he was going "to kill Robert Earl and get the [explicative deleted] out of Cape."

Strong provided me with the statement, and in turn, I immediately handed a photocopy to Anthony McGee. When I read what Maggie Smith had written, I realized that McGee would be a fool to call her as a witness. I was sure he would decide not to use her. Her testimony, that on the day *before* the killing McGee had specifically told her that he was going to kill Robert Earl Battles and get out of town, completely destroyed his self-defense claim. In fact, had I known this important piece of information before filing the charge, I would have charged him with *first-degree* rather than second-degree murder, since it established deliberation and premeditation. It was too late to increase the charge now, though.

When I handed the two-page statement to Anthony McGee, he glanced through it and then casually dropped it onto his counsel table. Much to my surprise, even after getting a copy of her statement, he still chose to call Maggie Smith to the stand.

The young woman glared at him as she made her way to the witness box. She had been the girlfriend of the murder victim. Calling her to the stand was risky business for even an experienced trial lawyer.

She proved to be a feisty adversary for the killer-turned-attorney. She obviously did not appreciate being subpoenaed to testify. She clearly bore a grudge against McGee for killing her lover. Whatever McGee had hoped to accomplish by calling her as a witness failed miserably as she traded jabs with him during his inept questioning. His direct examination turned into a cross-examination, since she disagreed with virtually everything that came out of his mouth. Exasperated, he finally gave up. At that point, I am sure he would have agreed with the observation of the great nineteenth-century trial lawyer Francis L. Wellman that cross-examination is "the most difficult to be acquired of all the accomplishments of the advocate."

When my turn came, I stood up, her statement in my hand.

"Did you know Anthony McGee back in August when this stabbing took place?"

"Yes."

"Did you ever hear him make any threats about Robert Battles?"

"Yes, I did."

"Out of Anthony McGee's mouth?"

"Yes."

"What did you hear him say?"

"He told me on the day before the stabbing that he was going to kill Robert Earl and get the [explicative deleted] out of Cape."

I exchanged knowing glances with several jurors.

"No further questions," I said.

The best cross-examinations are short and to the point. In the words of Irving Younger, an effective cross-examination is a commando raid, not the Normandy invasion.

Anthony McGee knew he had been wounded. He jumped to his feet as if he had been stung by a scorpion. He clutched her written statement in his fist.

"I told you *when*?" he yelled.

"Thursday, the day before the stabbing."

"When did I tell you that? What *time* did I tell you that?"

"I don't know the time, but we were on William Street. It was night."

"Why didn't you tell somebody about this, before?"

"Because nobody asked me about this before. This is my first time being questioned."

"You were the girlfriend, right?"

"At the time I was Robert Earl's girlfriend, right."

"And you state you heard me say I am going to kill this man?"

"Yes."

"*Why* would I call you for a witness if that's what you're going to say?"

She tilted her head back and studied him with dignified disdain.

"I don't know. You tell *me* why you called me for a witness."

The commotion went on for a few more minutes, but the trial was pretty much over from that point on. I cannot in good conscience claim it as an earned Perry Mason moment because Perry Mason had nothing to do with it. The bombshell was delivered by Maggie Smith, but it had been ordered by Anthony McGee. He (and his defense) suffered a self-inflicted wound. I was little more than a spectator.

I have always wondered if McGee actually read Maggie Smith's statement after I handed it to him. It appeared he was reading it. Perhaps he had so looked forward to hearing himself question her that he had not listened to the alarm bells that must have been ringing. Sometimes neophyte lawyers (or people acting as lawyers) are so busy thinking of their next questions that they do not pay attention to what is actually happening in the courtroom. On the other hand, perhaps he just was not as smart as he looked.

The jury found Anthony C. McGee guilty of second-degree murder and armed criminal action. They recommended a life sentence on the murder count and thirty years for armed criminal action. Months later, with a degree of audacity remarkable in its scope, McGee argued on appeal that his conviction should be reversed because his lawyer had been incompetent!

The Missouri Court of Appeals was unsympathetic. Judge Gerald M. Smith wrote for a unanimous three-judge panel:

> The trial court meticulously, patiently, and carefully explained, over forty pages of transcript, the dangers and conditions of self-representation. It further questioned the defendant at length to determine his competence to defend himself. It would be difficult indeed to find a case in which a defendant was more fully advised of the consequences of his decision to represent himself or in which he more adamantly insisted upon self-representation.

Candid Culprit

By trying we can easily learn to endure
adversity—another man's, I mean.

—Mark Twain

One often-overlooked aspect of trying a criminal case is the logistical difficulty of getting all of the witnesses to the right place at the right time. When a case is moved to another county on a change of venue, or when a complicated case involves dozens of witnesses and takes more than a week to try, scheduling and transporting witnesses can be formidable tasks. Since the Sixth Amendment gives a criminal defendant the constitutional right to confront his witnesses, the prosecutor must make sure they show up. This involves not only getting them served with subpoenas, but cutting down on their wasted time by staggering the days they are required to appear. Sometimes the prosecutor's office must provide transportation for them because they have no other way to get to court. Things like vacation schedules, sickness, and general uncooperativeness can also make life difficult for the prosecutor trying to coordinate the arrival times of all of the witnesses. In a big case, the prosecutor dreads a call from a witness claiming a scheduling problem, because no matter when the trial gets rescheduled, it inevitably will cause a calendar conflict for someone else. More than once, I have had to ruin someone's vacation or work schedule.

One of the better excuses for not coming to court came from a Southeast Missouri Drug Task Force officer named Darren Bullard. The undercover officer called me a couple of weeks before a preliminary hearing to tell me that the court date for a defendant named Robert Funt had landed smack in the middle of his honeymoon. He was scheduled to be in Jamaica on the date of the hearing. He asked if it would be possible to get the hearing rescheduled. I put him on hold and tracked down the file.

Robert Funt, age nineteen, was charged with one count of sale of crack cocaine. He had made the sale directly to Bullard one summer afternoon on Hanover Street in Cape Girardeau. Bullard, along with Bill Bohnert and Dan Seger from the Cape Girardeau Police Department, had equipped a ratty-looking van with state-of-the-art video cameras. Funt was one of the many street-level drug dealers Bullard had nabbed by cruising through drug-infested parts of town, driving slowly, acting disheveled and stupid, and giving his best imitation of a desperate "crackhead" trying to buy another rock of crack cocaine. Bullard, a bright officer, always did an outstanding job of looking stupid. Drug dealers flocked to his van like catfish to stink bait. He sometimes had to fend off the more aggressive ones to give other dealers a chance to earn their fair share of indictments.

The videotaping equipment was the best I had seen in my career as a prosecutor. A camera on the outside of the van got a good shot of the dealer as he approached the van to talk to Bullard. When the young entrepreneur reached the driver's window, Bullard would press a hidden button and switch cameras. The second camera was positioned to provide a full-color, sharp-image videotape of the drug dealer's face and of his hand as he passed the crack cocaine into the van and received the cash from Bullard. A concealed microphone also captured the entire conversation on tape, perfect for playing later in court. These cases tended to be ironclad. Winning them did not usually require anything close to a Perry Mason moment.

Robert Funt had been caught on videotape selling one rock of crack cocaine to Darren Bullard for twenty dollars. I read through Bullard's police report as he and I discussed what we were going to do about his honeymoon plans.

Even though a preliminary hearing only tests for "probable cause," the rules of evidence still apply. Thus, since Bullard had been alone in the van when he bought the crack cocaine from Funt, it looked like I would need Bullard for court. Then I noticed something. Funt was representing himself. He had waived his right to a lawyer.

"Go ahead and have a happy honeymoon," I boldly told Bullard. "I don't even need to postpone the case. I can get by without you."

Darren Bullard, a veteran officer, was skeptical.

"How can you possibly prove the case without me?" he asked. "I'm the one who made the drug buy. No one else was with me in the van. Bohnert and Seger were waiting back at the starting point."

"I see that," I said. "But you've got a videotape of the entire buy. The defendant won't know the law of evidence well enough to make a hearsay objection. I imagine I'll get the tape admitted into evidence whether you show up or not."

Although he did not completely share my confidence in the outcome of the preliminary hearing, Bullard happily left for his honeymoon. Meanwhile, I made sure that Bill Bohnert had been subpoenaed for the hearing.

I was not being as reckless as it might seem. Double jeopardy does not apply to a preliminary hearing. Even if things fell apart for me at the hearing, I could always dismiss the case and refile it later.

On the day of Robert Funt's preliminary hearing before Associate Circuit Judge Gary A. Kamp, the courtroom was packed. Not because this was a big case, but because Judge Kamp had a huge docket. The judge had scheduled lots of preliminary hearings that afternoon. The entire first row of the spectator section of the courtroom was filled with defendants. Each wore an orange, jail-issue jumpsuit. They watched one another's preliminary hearings as the judge plowed through his busy afternoon. They were packed shoulder-to-shoulder in a row behind the counsel table, where Robert Funt sat drumming his fingers on the tabletop, perhaps debating the wisdom of self-representation. The judge had called his case, though, and it was time to get started.

"Call your first witness," the judge told me.

"The state calls Bill Bohnert."

Bohnert, an experienced narcotics officer, dutifully described how he and Darren Bullard had checked the video cameras prior to the Funt drug sale to make sure they were properly working. He told how he had put a new tape into the recorder, turned the recorder on, handed Bullard the cash to use to buy the drugs, and sent him off on his way.

"Did you go with him to make the buy?" I asked.

"No. I waited at our prearranged location."

"What happened next?" I asked.

"Bullard was gone for about five minutes. When he came back to where I was waiting he handed me some crack cocaine. I packaged it and later took it to the crime lab."

"Did he say where he got it?" I asked casually, trying not to make eye contact with the judge as I blatantly offered a question calling for hearsay. This was the point at which an objection would have shut us down. Funt not only failed to object, he seemed interested in hearing the answer.

"He told me he had just bought it with the twenty dollars I had given him," Bohnert testified.

"Did he say *where* he'd bought it?"

"In the three hundred block of Hanover Street."

"Did you and he check to see if the video camera worked?"

"Yes. We watched the tape together."

"Did Bullard confirm that the tape was a fair and accurate portrayal of the drug buy he had just made?"

"He did."

"Your honor, I offer into evidence State's Exhibit 1, the videotape of the drug buy."

The judge paused, giving Robert Funt time to object. He did not. Once again, a hearsay objection would have prevented the videotape from being admitted into evidence and would have ended the hearing.

"The tape is admitted," the judge finally said.

We were home free! I requested permission to play the tape. Since it had been admitted into evidence without objection, the judge let me play it.

As Bohnert got the tape going, the prisoners sitting behind Robert Funt jostled for a clear view of the television screen. The trip to the courtroom sometimes proved to be the highlight of an otherwise boring day in jail. They were not disappointed. When Robert Funt's face filled the twenty-four-inch screen, bigger than life and sharply focused, several of the kibitzers groaned in sympathy. When Funt could be seen actually handing the crack cocaine into the van, right into Bullard's outstretched hand, one of the orange-clad observers made the ungrammatical but accurate assessment, "You in a *lot* of trouble!" The other prisoners snickered.

Robert Funt did not look happy. Perhaps he had harbored hopes of beating the charge. Maybe he was counting on the tape being fuzzy or his face unrecognizable. If so, the tape clearly dashed any dreams of an acquittal.

Don't misunderstand me. I am not claiming a Perry Mason moment for sliding a bit of hearsay past a *pro se* defendant. Practically any lawyer could have done it. I stake my claim for the memorable moment on what happened next, something I did not see coming.

When the tape was over, I closed my direct examination of Bill Bohnert by asking, "Detective Bohnert, do you see in the courtroom today the man we just saw on the tape, *selling* the crack cocaine to Darren Bullard?"

Bohnert pointed to Robert Funt.

"He's right there. . . ."

I heard more laughter in the courtroom. Once more, the orange-clad prisoners were being highly entertained. I glanced at the defendant, who had dutifully raised his hand.

The prisoners behind him were guffawing. They recognized a Perry Mason moment when they saw one.

Bohnert continued, "He's the one with his hand raised in the air."

Although it borders on the shameful to pad one's stats with victories acquired against criminals unrepresented by counsel, I am not above nominating this tiny bit of courtroom drama as a Perry Mason moment. I do so with full recognition that my only role in the comedy was to provide Robert Funt with the opportunity to make his candid and dramatic courtroom confession.

Millionaire Murderer

Whenever I prosecuted a murder case, I always
at least aspired to a masterpiece. Whether I
achieved it or not is another story.

—Vincent Bugliosi

An ideal client [for a criminal defense lawyer]
is a very rich man, thoroughly scared.

—Frank J. Hogan

Jefferson County Prosecuting Attorney William L. Johnson buttered me up to get me to serve as the special prosecutor in the William Nick Pagano case.

"I saw you give that presentation at the prosecutor's association last fall," he told me over the telephone. "You were terrific. Really, really outstanding. Hey, by the way, I've got this case here in my county where I need a special prosecutor, and I was hoping you'd be willing to do it."

"What's it about?" I asked.

"One guy shot another guy in a garage. It's probably self-defense. It's politically sensitive, though, because the shooter is the ex-police chief of Festus. I can't handle it because he offered me a campaign contribution in cash recently, and I don't think it would look right for me to keep the case."

Probably self-defense. I calculated the amount of time I would likely spend on this case if I took it. I would need to drive to Hillsboro, meet with the investigating officers, read the entire police and autopsy reports, and issue some sort of official statement explaining why I was declining to file the charge based upon the law of self-defense. I surmised it would take about two full days of work.

"I'll do it," I said. "What's the suspect's name again?"

"Pagano. William Nick Pagano."

Little did I realize that I had just signed onto a case that would end in one of longest state court criminal jury trials in modern Missouri history.

Of such things are good stories born.

⚖

The next day I drove to Hillsboro to meet with Buck Buerger, the sheriff of Jefferson County, and his chief of detectives, Wally Gansmann. I knew going into the meeting that Buerger considered the shooting a matter of justifiable self-defense because I had seen his quote in the *St. Louis Post-Dispatch:* "If it were up to me, I would not issue charges. I think the shooting was justifiable." I went to the meeting fully expecting it to be the only meeting I would need to attend in regard to the Pagano investigation.

Buck Buerger was sixty-three years old. He had been the sheriff of Jefferson County, Missouri, for twenty-five years. Gansmann also had two decades of experience in law enforcement. We all sat at a table as Gansmann told me the background of the shooter and his victim. "Bill Pagano was the police chief of Festus for many years. He started a private security business on the side. It grew bigger and bigger to the point where it provides security for several big businesses in the St. Louis area, plus the local hospital and Lambert Airport. He employs more than 200 people. He eventually resigned as police chief because his private business had grown so big. He's now a self-made millionaire."

"So who did he shoot?" I asked.

"Tim Todd, the right-hand man in his security business. Todd was a young police officer when Pagano was the chief of police. Pagano lured him away from the department to be his second-in-command at the security company. They were extremely close. Pagano shot him to death in Pagano's garage last Monday morning. He says it was self-defense. Todd was a big guy, 6' 6" and 253 pounds. He was 33 years old and a bodybuilder. Pagano was 5' 11", 42 years old, and a bit fat. He said he had to shoot him to protect himself."

"What kind of gun did he use?"

"A 12-gauge shotgun, loaded with double-aught buck."

Double-aught buckshot consists of pellets the size of large peas. A blast may include a dozen pellets, which spread out and make a mess of whatever they hit.

"Where did he hit him," I asked, "the heart or the head?"

Every legitimate self-defense case I had seen involved a shooter who had been backing away from an aggressor, who kept coming at him, until the shooter finally had to pull the trigger, and the one shot hit the aggressor in either the heart or the head, killing him.

"Well," Gansmann said uncomfortably, "he shot him twice: once in the face, and once in the back of the head."

I sat in stunned silence. The face *and* the back of the head! The case no longer sounded like self-defense. It began to dawn upon me that this undertaking was going to consume far more than two days of my time.

I soon learned that fully half of the deputies at the Jefferson County Sheriff's Department were or had been on Pagano's payroll, working part-time for his security company even though they were full-time employees of Jefferson County. The sheriff's wife, too, had worked for Pagano, and Pagano had made big contributions to Buerger's election campaigns. In fact, Pagano had promised Buerger a job when he wanted it, once he retired from the sheriff's department. After a few days, I requested that the Missouri Highway Patrol help with the investigation, since I had no idea whom I could trust at the Jefferson County Sheriff's Department. Most were dedicated law enforcement professionals. Some were good buddies of Bill Pagano. You could not tell allegiances by appearances.

It turned out that Tim Todd, a married man, had been having an affair with one of Pagano's daughters for eighteen months. The affair had started when the girl was in her late teens. It was unclear whether the affair was still going on at the time of the killing or the two had broken up. What was clear was that Todd was already seeing yet another young woman, Katie Leary. In fact, he was to meet Katie later in the afternoon on the day he was killed. Yet he was still living at home with his wife and children. He had just come from their house when summoned to Pagano's garage. Romantically, he led an extraordinarily complicated life.

Pagano had also taken out a 1.5 million-dollar life insurance policy on the life of Tim Todd. It was payable to Pagano's company. Pagano explained that it was a "key man" policy, meaning that Todd was so indispensable to the company that his life was insured so Pagano's company could collect the money to survive the hardship it would suffer should anything happen to Todd.

On the day before the killing, two twelve-year-old girls, unconnected to either Todd or Pagano, noticed them arguing on a parking lot outside a fitness center. Pagano had poked Todd in the chest angrily, yelling, "It has got to stop!" Todd had shrugged in response, saying, "She's a grown woman."

The deeper I delved into the investigation, the less it sounded like self-defense. Pagano had at least three possible motives for the killing. Either

Pagano was mad because Todd was committing adultery with his daughter, or Pagano was mad because Todd had hurt his daughter by two-timing her, or Pagano had decided to cash in on the 1.5 million-dollar insurance policy. Fortunately, the prosecutor in a homicide case is not required to prove motive. Motive is relevant and interesting but not an element of the crime. The prosecutor need only prove that the defendant did the killing and that it was not self-defense.

Pagano presented a lengthy explanation as to why the shooting was justified. He claimed that Tim Todd had been planning to kill his wife, Patricia, to whom Todd had been married for almost sixteen years. Pagano claimed that Todd had asked him to find a hit man. Pagano had secretly tape-recorded some of the conversations, and the tapes did include conversations between Todd and Pagano about killing Patricia Todd. Pagano tipped off his good friend, Sheriff Buck Buerger, informing him that Todd seemed mentally unstable and was making comments about killing his wife. Pagano claimed that Buerger told him to arrest Todd and bring him in for an involuntary mental health commitment.

Under Missouri law, papers can be filed with a judge to temporarily commit to a mental health facility any person who presents a danger to himself or others due to mental illness. But Pagano had taken no steps to prepare any paperwork for the signature of a judge. Nor had any arrest warrant been issued for Tim Todd for conspiracy to commit murder. Instead, Pagano claimed he decided to play along with Todd about finding the hit man, all the while planning to use his shotgun to arrest Todd at an opportune time. Sheriff Buerger confirmed that Pagano had relayed Todd's comments about killing his wife, and Buerger had approved of the idea of arresting him and forcing him to be evaluated at a mental health facility, but the sheriff was adamant that he had never intended for Pagano to try to make the arrest by himself.

On the morning of the shooting, Pagano paged Todd to come to his home in a subdivision called Seclusion Woods. Pagano claimed that when Todd arrived, he brought with him a photograph of Patricia for Pagano to provide to the hit man and some typed information about Patricia's schedule so the hit man would be able to decide on the best time and place to make the hit. Pagano, who had secretly and successfully recorded many other conversations with Tim Todd, chose not to record the tragic developments on this eventful day.

Pagano explained that he pulled the gun on Tim Todd in the garage, telling him that he was under arrest for conspiracy to murder his wife. Both Pagano and Todd had been issued reserve deputy badges, so Pagano did have the power of arrest.

Only one car was in the two-car garage. The men faced each other across the vacant space where a second car would have been. Pagano stood near the entrance to the house at the front end of the car. Todd was standing near the rear of the car about sixteen feet away. The garage door was down.

Explaining why it was necessary to shoot Todd in both the face *and* the back of the head was the tricky part. Pagano claimed that Todd was carrying a revolver in his waistband. He added that Todd was a user of anabolic steroids. Pagano had heard how steroid users could go into rages and lash out in violent attacks. According to Pagano, when he pulled the shotgun on Todd, the big man raised his hands above his head, let out a "demonic" scream, and made a move as if to go for his gun. Pagano fired. Todd seemed to be moving toward the trunk of the car, as if trying to get around behind it to fire at Pagano from cover. Pagano fired again. After the two shots, Todd lay sprawled on his back on the concrete floor of the garage, his feet toward Pagano and his bloody head touching the garage door.

The Jefferson County deputies who first interviewed Pagano were former employees of his. They were obviously nervous about interviewing their former boss. They let him get away with being vague as to which shot had come first and whether he had actually seen a gun in Todd's hand.

In a phone call to Buerger immediately after the shooting, in which he told the surprised sheriff that he had just tried to arrest Todd single-handedly, Pagano exclaimed, "He came up with a gun! I had to shoot his ass!"

Before deciding whether or not to file charges, I wanted Pagano to be reinterviewed. The second interview was conducted by Karen Buchheit and Joe Swearengen. Buchheit was the investigator for my office. Swearengen was a criminal investigator with the Missouri Highway Patrol. This time, Pagano was forced to be specific about details. The first shot had been the one to the back of the head, he said, and the second shot had been to the face. The shot to the back of the head was necessary, he asserted, because Todd was in the process of spinning to try to get behind the car, and Pagano knew that if Todd made it to the back of the car, he would probably turn and shoot Pagano to death. The second shot was necessary, he said, because he was not sure he had hit him with the first shot. Todd was spinning, and he wanted to make sure he got him. He admitted never seeing a gun in Todd's hand.

Another twist was that Tim Todd had another loaded gun tucked between the front seats of his car, which was parked in Pagano's driveway. The loaded stainless steel Smith and Wesson revolver found next to Todd's body was owned by Pagano's security company. Each of the company's handguns bore a numerical stamp. This one was stamped with the number one. It seemed possible that the gun next to Tim Todd had been planted by Pagano. The theory made sense; gun number one of Pagano's company would logically be issued to the number-one man in the company—William Nick Pagano. Yet Pagano provided a business record showing that the gun had purportedly been issued to Todd.

A person is allowed to use deadly force in self-defense to stop someone from killing him. The question was whether Pagano had reasonably believed Todd was trying to kill him or had simply killed Todd and was now trying to make it look like self-defense.

Another cause for concern was the way Sheriff Buerger had handled the matter. After the shooting, the sheriff responded to the scene to console his friend, Bill Pagano. The sheriff immediately announced that the shooting was clearly self-defense and told the deputies to remove the body and hose the blood from the garage. Wally Gansmann, in a move that was heroic in hindsight and must have taken courage at the time, told the sheriff that they should handle the shooting just like any other homicide investigation. They should photograph the scene and collect the evidence and not move the body until the routine crime-scene work was completed. Buerger eventually agreed.

Dr. Gordon L. Johnson, the medical examiner for Jefferson County, also responded to Pagano's home. Rather than spending much time in the garage examining the body, Johnson joined the sheriff in Pagano's home, and the three shared a few mixed drinks as the deputies worked in the garage. At one point Johnson called his partner at the hospital to let him know that the autopsy room should be prepared for use.

Again, Wally Gansmann spoke up. He pointed out that since Pagano had been the person who got Dr. Johnson his job at the hospital (Pagano was head of security at the hospital and had been influential with the county commissioners who hired Johnson) perhaps the autopsy should be conducted by a doctor with no ties to Pagano. It was finally agreed that the autopsy would be done by the St. Louis Medical Examiner's Office.

Dr. Mary Case was the physician who performed the autopsy. The justice system got a big break when the case went to her. She is one of the premier medical examiners in the United States. At the time, she was one of only four in the country to be board certified in forensic pathology, anatomical pathology, and neuropathology. She had performed more than four thousand autopsies and had authored numerous articles and chapters of books in her field. She had testified in a few of my homicide cases in the past and was the best expert witness I had ever seen. Brilliant and articulate, she also had a knack for teaching and could explain complicated things to a jury in a way that every single person could understand. She was an interesting person, too. When I met with her at her office, I noticed some rather unusual photographs upon her wall. One was a picture of a headstone. The other showed Dr. Case and her husband in their swimsuits next to a swimming pool.

Brilliant people tend to be characters, and Dr. Case was no exception. I came to find out that you never knew what sort of outfit and hairstyle she would be sporting when she testified in court. Always petite and trim, she often changed other aspects of her appearance drastically between trials. Most times, she showed up with stylish, short blonde hair. At one trial she surprised me by coming to court with jet black hair, spiked. On that occasion she wore lots of silver-and-jade jewelry, including a belt buckle the width of a softball. No matter what she wore, once she started speaking, her garb did not matter. She knew her field better than any person I ever met.

So I was glad the body went to her for the autopsy. Her insights proved invaluable. She was able to point out that the shot to the face clearly came *after* Tim Todd was lying on his back on the floor; otherwise gravity would have made the blood streak down his shirt. Instead, the front of the shirt was clean; the blood had flowed *down* the sides of Tim Todd's face. The idea that he had been in the process of spinning when he was shot in the face was, in a phrase, blown away. Tim Todd, already shot in the back of the head, had been shot again in the face as he lay helpless upon the concrete.

It was an execution.

I charged William Nick Pagano with first-degree murder and armed criminal action. Bond was set at a quarter of a million dollars. He bonded out of jail within two hours.

⚖️

It has always been extremely important to me to treat every defendant the same, no matter what that defendant's wealth, race, or social status. In that sense, it was almost providential that I happened to be the prosecutor who ended up with the Pagano case. I have always felt a kinship to the fictional Eliot Ness in the movie *The Untouchables*. (The real Eliot Ness had alcohol problems and did not live up to the image presented in the TV show and the movie.) But like the fictional character, I *am* untouchable. I have flaws, of course. I make mistakes. I have lost cases I should have won. I have been too self-confident in filing cases where the evidence was circumstantial. I have based decisions on my heart rather than my brain. But my mistakes are honest mistakes, not sellouts. I would rather lose my job and everything I own than sell out the result of a particular case for money or power or anything else. I have low tolerance for people who do not think the same way.

Back when I was a fledgling prosecutor who had only been in office for three months, I got a telephone call from one of the county commissioners. The three commissioners oversee the budgets of all county offices. They have nothing to do with the day-to-day operations of the prosecutor's office, though, other than budgetary matters. It was unusual to get a call from one of them.

"I'm calling about a speeding ticket a state representative got in our county the other day," he said.

"Well, if he doesn't want to come to court, he can pay it by mail," I said.

"No, I want it to go away."

"Excuse me?"

"I want the ticket to just go away."

"That's not the way I do things," I said.

The county commissioner growled. "Sometimes you have to scratch somebody's back, so they'll scratch yours later on."

"That's not the way I do things," I repeated. "I'll treat him like anybody else. If he's not guilty he can set it for a bench trial. If he's guilty he can either appear in court or pay it by mail."

The commissioner unleashed a tirade of profanity at me, but I held my ground. Eventually I said, "I'm sorry you feel that way" and hung up on him.

I never had a good relationship with that county commissioner from that point forward. He always did his best to try to embarrass me at budget hearings. There was no way, though, that I was going to run my office in his "Good Old Boy" mold. No other county commissioner has ever asked me to do anything improper.

Bill Pagano, on the other hand, raised the "Good Old Boy" way of doing things to an art form in Jefferson County. Extremely wealthy, he had made huge contributions to almost every politician in the county. He had recently donated over thirty thousand dollars to a Democratic congressman, and thirty-four thousand to the incumbent Republican attorney general of Missouri. His good word could get someone a job at the hospital or at a government office. He had just offered the local prosecuting attorney a cash contribution for the prosecutor's reelection campaign but had withdrawn the offer when the prosecutor responded that he would be required to report the contribution on mandatory reporting forms. Much like the character played by Sorrell Booke in the television show *The Dukes of Hazzard,* Pagano was the "Boss Hogg" of Jefferson County.

William Nick Pagano and I were cut from very different cloth.

The Pagano investigation continued well after the charges were filed. I learned from the FBI that Pagano had been investigated fifteen years earlier while he was still the chief of police in Festus. An informant working with Festus police officers to buy drugs had, instead, told the local drug dealers the true identities of the undercover drug officers. In a rage, Pagano threw a knife at the informant. It stuck in the wall by the man's head. Pagano then pulled the knife out of the wall and told three officers to come out into the hallway with him. He said, "We've got to get rid of him. Take him on a one-way ride." When the officers asked what that meant, he explained that he wanted them to take the informant for a drive, push him out of the car, and shoot him with a shotgun, claiming he was trying to escape. An officer protested that no one would believe the shooting had been necessary. Pagano took the knife and cut the officer's sleeve, nicking his skin in the process. "There," he said, "the guy attacked you with the knife. You had to shoot him." The Festus police officers refused to do their boss's bidding. All three later gave the same account to the FBI after Pagano fired them.

The investigation of Pagano for violating the informant's civil rights landed on the desk of a bright young federal prosecutor, an assistant United States attorney who later became a federal judge. She read the statements of the three officers but balanced them against Pagano's version. Pagano denied the entire incident. He claimed the officers were fired for other reasons and were just making up the story to get even with him. An elderly officer at the department corroborated Pagano's account by claiming he had heard the three officers talking about ways to get even with Pagano for firing them. The young prosecutor, perhaps applying her own "Where's the Beef?" test, declined to file the charge against Pagano.

Fifteen years later he killed Tim Todd.

The incident brings to mind Justice Robert H. Jackson's observation about the prosecutor having more control over a person's life, liberty, and reputation than any other person in America. I often wonder whether Pagano would have been in a position to kill Tim Todd had he been prosecuted for the civil rights violation years earlier. I'm not saying that the prosecutor necessarily made the wrong decision, nor that most prosecutors would not have made exactly the same decision. It is one of those questions that can never be answered. It simply shows how decisions made by a prosecutor can have ramifications even years later.

The issue of potential influence upon a prosecutor also comes into play when considering whether the prosecutor should be elected or appointed. In Missouri, as in most states, the prosecutor is elected by the citizens of his jurisdiction. He is accountable only to them. This allows the prosecutor, when a county commissioner calls to try to tell him what to do with his friend's case, to say no and keep his job. On the other hand, federal prosecutors, or U.S. attorneys, are appointed by the president. The advantage is that they do not have to run for election every four years. The bad thing is that when that call comes from the White House or the Justice Department, they have to listen. Although running for office is my least-favorite part of the job, I much prefer being independent. Being elected allows me to march to my own drummer as prosecutor. I am at the mercy of no politician. Rather, I am answerable to no one but the public and my own conscience.

⚖

When the Pagano case went to trial, I was hoping it might be tried in one week. I grossly underestimated the long-windedness of the defense lawyers, who stretched the jury-selection process into a four-day affair, and kept our first witness, Detective Jan Vessel, the crime-scene officer, on the witness stand for five hours of cross-examination. When we reached the end of the first week, I had only called one witness, with nineteen still left to take the stand. I telephoned my wife from a motel room and told her that it would be a long time before I would be home.

The case was tried in Waynesville, Missouri, on a change of venue, before Circuit Judge Douglas E. Long, Jr. He was an impressive man. A former FBI agent, he had been a judge for seventeen years. He knew criminal law and the rules of evidence inside and out. Good-natured but capable of running a courtroom with a firm hand, he was the perfect judge for the case.

Pagano was represented by a pair of lawyers whose styles differed greatly. Timothy M. Finnical was a former prosecutor. During almost seven years at the Missouri Attorney General's Office, he had traveled throughout the state serving as a special prosecutor when small-town prosecutors needed help trying complicated homicide cases. He had acquired the nickname "Doctor Death" because he put more defendants on death row than any other prosecutor in the state. Tall, auburn-haired, and a bit wild-eyed, he took pride in his flamboyant style and merciless cross-examinations. James E. Bowles, on the other hand, a former Sunday school teacher, was clean-cut and fastidiously groomed. He was a highly intelligent and careful attorney, thoroughly prepared and extremely articulate. They made an effective team.

During the pretrial conference, Finnical, who had taught voir dire for prosecutors at a seminar I had attended in the past, grinned at me and said, "If you get *lucky* and win this case, it will be extremely inconvenient for me because I'm planning to be out of the country in October, when I'd have to be working on the motion for new trial." It was clear he did not expect to lose.

The Pagano trial was one of the rare times in my career when the prosecutor was truly the underdog. Going into it, Pagano certainly expected to win. In fact, he mugged for cameras outside the courthouse, telling reporters, "I feel terrific, very confident." His attorneys undoubtedly expected to win. The public, too, whose speculation was fueled by information about Pagano's connections, expected him to be acquitted. After all, as *St. Louis Sun* columnist Kevin Horrigan had written: "The sheriff, good ol' Buck Buerger, was so impressed with the story [of self-defense] that his old pal Pagano told him that he decided the shooting was justifiable almost before the body hit the ground." How could a conviction be expected?

I endured life in a Waynesville motel during the four-week-long trial. Actually, I wasn't in the motel room very much. Evenings and weekends were spent in the courtroom or in a borrowed room at the local prosecutor's office preparing for the next day's action. My workdays were fifteen to twenty hours long. I often ran laps at the Waynesville High School track to relieve stress and keep in shape. Joe Swearengen sometimes ran with me. I lost about ten pounds during the course of the trial.

For the first time in my life, I felt the need to have someone watch my back during a trial. Pagano and his lawyers had tried desperately for a postponement, even going so far as to request a writ of prohibition from the Missouri Supreme Court to overrule Judge Long's order denying their last-minute request for a continuance. One time when I was in Jefferson County preparing the case, I came outside to find the gas tank cover of my car standing wide open, as if it had been tampered with. Later, word reached me that Pagano was trying to tamper with witnesses. Pagano's security company employed more than two hundred employees, all investigator types. Police officer friends of mine suggested that the easiest way to make sure the case did not go to trial was to cause something unpleasant to happen to the prosecutor before or during the trial.

When I mentioned my concerns to some detectives at the Cape Girardeau Police Department, a group of them took comp time to alternate serving as my bodyguard during the trial. One by one they made the trip to Waynesville to watch my back so I could do my job without looking over my shoulder. Detectives Keith May, John Volkerding, Tracy Lemonds, Zeb Williams, Kenton Martin, and John Brown will forever have my appreciation for the time they spent watching out for me during the month-long ordeal of a trial.

A prosecutor should try to come up with a graphic exhibit that will effectively drive home the key point he wants to make to the jury. In this case, that exhibit was a drawing Dr. Mary Case made as a part of her autopsy report. It was a standard form, containing both a front and back view of a human head. She used it when she prepared her report to show the extensive damage the shotgun pellets had done to Tim Todd's head. The face view showed the ten separate entry wounds, each the diameter of a pencil. The diagram of the back of the head showed the cluster of entry wounds blasting their way into the back of his skull. The diagram demonstrated the point that this man had been shot both from the front *and* the back, a key fact to keep in mind when the claim is self-defense. I enlarged the diagram into a huge poster, four feet in diameter. No juror would go into the jury room to deliberate with even a trace of confusion about where the shots had hit Tim Todd.

It was really the testimony of Annie Moffett, however, that was the turning point in the trial. She was twelve years old. She was one of the girls who had watched Pagano cursing and poking Todd in the chest on the day before the killing. Annie made a terrific witness. She recalled how Pagano had yelled at Todd, "This has got to stop!" and Todd had responded, "She's a grown woman." It was clear that she was telling the truth. The defense tried to shake her testimony with a vigorous cross-examination, but she held her ground.

During the evenings, I fine-tuned my closing argument. As was my custom, I had written a rough draft before making the trip to Waynesville, but each night I tweaked it to better conform to that day's testimony. I practiced it in the hotel room, over and over, working toward that point where I would be able to deliver it with little or no use of my notes. I knew that the closing arguments would be tremendously important in this case.

Among the defense witnesses was a professor from Harvard Medical School, Dr. Harrison Pope, a world-renowned expert on anabolic steroids.

The autopsy had revealed anabolic steroids in the body of Tim Todd. The defense jumped on this fact and called Pope to suggest how *reasonable* it was for Pagano to fear that someone on steroids might go into a violent rage. The testimony was relevant on the issue of self-defense.

Pope proved to be one of the most self-satisfied witnesses I have ever seen on the witness stand. Minutes after being asked the first question, he turned to the jury and sniffed, "You may have seen me on *60 Minutes* last week." That coolness may play well in some circles, but I have found that Missouri juries prefer a bit of humility, even from expert witnesses. There were no surprises during Pope's direct examination, but I had carefully prepared his cross-examination.

A cross-examination of an expert witness, such as a doctor, is the most challenging part of being a trial lawyer. The expert is always going to know far more than you do about his or her field of expertise. There is no way you can match him or her when it comes to background knowledge of the subject matter. Yet, you can score points against the expert on cross-examination if you do your homework.

If possible, you should read everything that expert witness has ever published, especially if it relates to the topic for which he is being called. You should also track down transcripts of prior testimony the expert has given in other cases. If the witness is a "hired gun" who goes around the country making his living testifying as an expert, you should take his deposition to find out exactly how much money he makes as a witness-for-hire and what percentage of his income comes from testifying.

As to Dr. Harrison Pope, I knew I could not attack his credentials. Teaching at Harvard Medical School is the gold standard for respectability in the field of medicine. An honest expert witness, though, will agree with truthful things you present to him, even if the answer is harmful to the side that called him. I decided to approach him from that angle, knowing full well what use of his answers I planned to make later.

In my closing argument, I intended to ridicule the idea that it was okay to shoot the victim in the back of the head just because he was on steroids. In medical journals, I found articles about the number of people in the United States, especially football players, who were using anabolic steroids. When Pope was on the stand, I first got him to agree that most steroid abusers did not exhibit notably more aggressive behavior. He then conceded that the medical journal figures concerning percentages of football players using steroids seemed accurate to him. I stopped my questioning right there. I had what I needed for closing argument. Later, during my summation, I made my point:

> I want to talk about steroids. You know, they put on a lot of testimony about steroids. The two doctors testified to you about the dangers of steroids. But the bottom line is that just because a person is on steroids does not give you the right to shoot him in the back and then shoot him in the face when he is down.
>
> Dr. Pope testified that there are about one million steroid users in the United States; that 20 percent of college athletes are on steroids; 96 percent of pro football players have been on steroids; and 6.6 percent of high school males have been on steroids. Does that mean it is open season on these people? That it is all right to shoot them down because they are on steroids? Obviously not.
>
> It doesn't matter if Tim Todd was on steroids; it is still not all right to shoot him in the back of the head.
>
> And, another thing: Here is this guy who is supposed to be so crazed and so dangerous and on steroids, and Pagano is the one who is letting him carry a gun and work for his company. Pagano is the one who treats him like a son. This guy who was supposed to be so violent and dangerous is the guy Pagano has as his right-hand man. If he is that violent and dangerous, why in the world does he have him come to his garage to be alone with him, if he is that violent and crazed and dangerous?

Using cross-examination to pull facts from an expert witness for later use during closing argument is a useful technique for a trial lawyer. The key thing for budding prosecutors to keep in mind is that I came up with my argument and cross-examination *after* reading everything I could find about anabolic steroids. Success in court is 99 percent perspiration and 1 percent inspiration. A good trial lawyer will identify with a comment made by former Chief Justice Charles Evans Hughes that "the Lord created Sunday so there would be one day in the week when a man could work with relatively little interruption from telephone calls."

I spent countless hours preparing my closing argument in the Pagano case. Sometimes a Perry Mason moment is strictly the result of painstaking preparation. The hours spent editing and practicing it in the hotel room paid off. I reached the point where I could deliver it without looking at my notes. Eye contact with the jury is tremendously important for closing argument. My argument lasted more than an hour. I began the speech with words I hoped would be memorable:

Ladies and gentlemen. On March 26th, 1990, William Nick Pagano shot and killed Mark Tim Todd by shooting him twice with a shotgun. He deliberately killed him.

You heard the testimony. The first shot was to the back of the head, and the next shot was to the face, as he was lying on the ground. He admitted to Corporal Joe Swearengen that the man was on the ground when he shot him that second time.

And recall the testimony of Dr. Mary Case, that that first shot to the back of the head would have caused an explosion of blood at the time that first shot hit. He knew when he shot him that second time that he had already hit him that first time. You know he knew he did.

And, ladies and gentlemen, there were two people in that garage, and one of them lived to tell the officers his version of why it was necessary to shoot a man in the back. But by that second shot, he was making sure Tim Todd was dead. He was making sure that Tim Todd's lips were sealed, that he would never have the chance to give his version of what really happened between them.

You have heard all of the evidence in the case. It has been now over three weeks of your life given in service to your community. But when this trial is over at least you can leave with the satisfaction of knowing that by serving as a juror in a case as important as this one, you have performed one of the biggest functions you can do for your community, because this is an important case.

Murder and armed criminal action are two of the most important crimes. And ladies and gentlemen, by your verdict, you will send a message to William Nick Pagano, in particular, and also to other people out there who might shoot somebody in the back and then shoot them in the face when they are down, and claim that it was self-defense, that the people of Pulaski County don't buy that kind of story on an execution killing like this.

You are not just twelve individuals. As a group you are representatives. And the message needs to be sent that no matter who you are, no matter how much money you have, no matter who you know, you can't get away with murder. And it is murder to shoot somebody in the back and then shoot them again in the face, when they are down on the ground.

You know, William Nick Pagano is an example of what is wrong with law enforcement in some parts of the country, and, in particular, in Jefferson County, Missouri. This notion that whether you are going to be arrested, whether you are going to be prosecuted, whether you are going to be convicted of a crime, depends on who you are, who you know, how much money you have.

You heard some testimony in this case I would like to remind you about. Remember the Herculaneum police officer who had been chasing Tim Todd when Tim Todd was speeding 85 miles an hour when his daughter was in the emergency room. Did Tim Todd end up getting prosecuted for that offense? No. And the officer said, "It wasn't because I necessarily checked to see if the daughter was in the hospital. Once I found out he was a deputy, I tore up the ticket."

Tim Todd slapped a woman at a Little League game, and it is right in front of police officers where it happens. Was Tim Todd prosecuted? No. The police officers talked the woman into not having the case prosecuted.

Tim Todd, when he is a police officer working for William Nick Pagano, files a false police report saying he had been shot, when he really hadn't been. Does he get prosecuted for the crime of filing a false police report? You heard the conversation between the two of them on the tape. Bill Pagano took care of that, so that he did not get charged with that crime.

Tim Todd plots to kill his wife, and according to Pagano, he had paid Pagano $5,000 to get the hit man, clearly enough evidence for Tim Todd, if that's true, to be prosecuted for conspiracy under Missouri law. William Nick Pagano, a deputy sheriff, who has a deputy's commission by his own testimony, does he have any intention whatsoever that Tim Todd is going to be prosecuted? Not for one second.

And, interestingly, do you remember when the sheriff was testifying, that Mr. Finnical asked him a question, "Now, it would be up to the prosecutor whether or not Tim Todd would be prosecuted [for conspiracy to murder his wife], wouldn't it?"

The sheriff actually said something that was very, very true, and that was: "It would be up to the prosecutor *and Mr. Pagano.*" Why should it be up to Mr. Pagano whether Tim Todd gets prosecuted for conspiracy to murder his wife?

And the fifth thing I wanted to point to your attention on that issue was, Bill Pagano shoots a man in the back of the head. He shoots him a second time when he is lying on the ground. Is he going to be prosecuted and convicted for murder? Not if his friend, the lord high sheriff, has anything to say about it.

Bill Pagano, I submit to you, has been a big frog in a small pond of Jefferson County, making big contributions to all the politicians, getting his way on everything. And I submit to you that he thinks money and connections of who you know and who you are, can buy you anything, including murder, including the death of a man that had been working for him.

You have heard the old saying that a good defense is the best offense. Well, they have tried that in this case. They have tried to prosecute the Jefferson County Sheriff's Department. They have tried to go on the offensive and say, "Well, the Sheriff's Department made up all this evidence. They fabricated evidence to frame this poor, innocent man, Bill Pagano."

Well, I submit to you that the fact of the matter is, there was never for one second, never one iota of a chance that an innocent man was going to get framed for this. The real danger in this case, the real and true danger, was that there was going to be a cover-up, and that because of *who* he knew, because he was a friend of the sheriff, because he was a friend of the medical examiner, because of *who* he was, there would be a cover-up and he wouldn't get prosecuted at all. That was the real danger in this case, *not* that the Sheriff's Department was going to make up any evidence. Fortunately for the system of justice, his friends were not willing to go as far as that for him.

After going over the evidence and the jury instructions, I lauded the real hero in the case, Wally Gansmann.

In everyday life, every now and then, somebody gets to meet a real hero. You got to hear a real hero testify in this trial, and that real hero was Wally Gansmann, the Chief of Detectives for the Jefferson County Sheriff's Department. Because look at the situation he was in at 3:06 in the afternoon on March 26, 1990, when he went to the garage of William Nick Pagano. He gets there and the sheriff is consoling Bill Pagano. The sheriff doesn't even realize at that point that there is a shot to the back of the head of the man who is dead.

Wally Gansmann knows the sheriff is a good friend of Pagano's. He knows the medical examiner is a good friend. And it was Wally Gansmann who suggested we should have somebody else outside Jefferson County do the autopsy in this case. And it was Wally Gansmann who worked this case as thoroughly as he has worked the other 75 homicide cases he has been involved in, and saw that an honest investigation was done and that this did not turn into a cover-up of the sheriff's friend, William Nick Pagano.

You know, while the sheriff was consoling his friend, Bill Pagano, while the medical examiner was making drinks for himself and Bill Pagano, it was Wally Gansmann and his detectives who worked four days straight, around the clock, to interview witnesses and gather the evidence in this case, to be sure that this wasn't going to be a cover-up, to be sure that an honest investigation was done.

It would have been easier for Wally Gansmann just to look the other way and say, "Oh, yes, let's just have Jan Vessel take a few photographs and we will call this self-defense." It would have been easier to go through it like that, but he saw that it was worked as an honest investigation, that all of these leads were pursued.

P. J. Mertens, the sergeant of the Highway Patrol, testified to you that when he got involved in this case on April 2, 1990, by that time in the investigation there were no holes in the investigation. Every lead he could see basically had been pursued. He did some follow-up leads, had some witnesses reinterviewed, but, basically, the Jefferson County Sheriff's Department, led by Wally Gansmann, had thoroughly investigated this case before he even got involved.

Wally Gansmann was a hero, and, for the sake of justice, Jefferson County was lucky that he was there in the garage of Bill Pagano on March 26th of 1990.

After six hours of deliberation, the jury found William Nick Pagano guilty of the lesser-included offense of second-degree murder and of armed criminal action. They recommended a sentence of twenty years on the murder charge and three years on the armed criminal action charge. Judge Long ordered that the sentences run consecutively.

When I made it back to my office after the trial, I found a thoughtful note of congratulations from Ian Sutherland, my chief assistant prosecutor. It was short, concise, and pure Ian: "Boss Man—You took no prisoners and left nothing but hair, teeth and eyeballs. Good show."

Much to my surprise, Pagano remained free on bond during his appeal. Under the law at the time, even a person convicted of murder could remain free while he was appealing his case, as long as he was rich enough to make the big bond. As a direct result of the Pagano case, the Missouri legislature later changed the law. Now when a person is convicted of first- or second-degree murder, he must remain in prison during his appeal.

The media and the public were pleasantly surprised by the conviction. It sent a strong message that no one was above the law, not even "Boss Hogg" Bill Pagano. My favorite reaction came from Bill McClellan, a columnist with the *St. Louis Post-Dispatch*. He wrote: "Prosecutor Morley Swingle is young and handsome, and in this trial, he came across as the Lone Ranger, the law-man who rode into Jefferson County to fight for Right and Justice." For some-one who grew up watching *The Lone Ranger* on television, at the feet of his father, a Missouri State Highway Patrolman, this was high praise indeed. Whether intended or not, he absolutely captured my view of the role of the prosecutor. It's always nice to be called young and handsome, but I found his comment somewhat less flattering when I learned that his favored breed of dog is the pug, and he has called them handsome, too. So much for my looks.

Later that year the FBI nominated me to attend their weeklong training session for prosecutors at the FBI Academy at Quantico, Virginia. They pick one prosecutor from each state to attend the training. I knew the hard work I had put in on the Pagano case had earned me the trip. The audience at the training seminar proved to be as interesting as the presenters. On one side of me sat Michael McCann, the district attorney from Milwaukee who had pros-ecuted serial killer Jeffrey Dahmer. On the other side of the room sat Greg Garrison of Indianapolis, who had prosecuted boxer Mike Tyson for rape.

In one last surprising twist, Bill Pagano avoided serving even one day of prison. On the day his conviction was affirmed, officers went to pick him up to take him to the department of corrections. He met them at the door and asked if he could take a moment to change clothes. They allowed him to leave the front door, unrestrained. Instead of donning his going-to-prison clothes, Pagano grabbed a gun and killed himself right in front of them.

To the very end, William Nick Pagano had been treated differently by vir-tually everyone in Jefferson County except chief of detectives Wally Gans-mann. Had any other person whose murder conviction had just been affirmed greeted officers at his front door, the handcuffs would have appeared immedi-ately. Because of *who* he was, Pagano was allowed to go into the other room with his hands free. The officers were just lucky he did not decide to take them with him into the next world.

Thug-Tossed Crack

[A] trial lawyer has to be confident in front
of the jury. If he's not, then he has to be a
good actor and at least appear to be confident.
It's one of the most important ingredients of a
successful trial lawyer. If he's not confident,
the jury will pick it up just like that—in the
way he walks, the expression on his face, the
inflection in his voice.

—Vincent Bugliosi

Circuit Judge William L. Syler, Jr., worked as an assistant prosecutor in Kansas City before moving to Cape Girardeau. He tells a good story about the resourcefulness of a particular Kansas City criminal defense attorney.

As prosecutor, Syler had two separate rape cases pending against clients of this wily old lawyer. They happened to be set for jury trials just weeks apart.

When the first case went to trial, the rape victim wanted to watch the closing arguments. Syler felt she not only had the right to do so, but he considered it such a good idea that he put her in the front row of the spectator seats. During the defense attorney's closing argument, the veteran litigator, after arguing that the woman was trying to railroad his innocent client, pointed to her and exclaimed, "Just look at her! She's sitting there like a vulture, just waiting for you to do her dirty work for her!"

A few weeks later, when the second rape case went to trial, Syler cautioned the second rape victim that with *this* lawyer on the other side, it might be a good idea if she did not sit in the courtroom during the closing arguments. Minutes later, when the defense attorney was wrapping up his summation, he pointed dramatically to the empty spectator seats and proclaimed: "That woman who claimed my client did such a terrible thing to her? Why, she didn't even care enough about what you'll do to him to stay around to see what happens!"

There's a lesson in that story somewhere.

Judge Syler presided over a drug case I prosecuted shortly after the O. J. Simpson murder trial. In case you lived in a cave in 1994, Simpson was a legendary NFL running back, Heisman Trophy winner, and movie star who stood trial in California for stabbing to death his ex-wife, Nicole Brown Simpson, and her friend, Ronald Goldman. A highlight of the trial occurred when one of the gaggle of prosecutors, Christopher Darden, asked Simpson to try on bloody gloves. The left-hand glove had been found at the murder scene; its right-hand mate had been found on the grounds of Simpson's estate. The latter bore traces of the blood of both Nicole Brown Simpson and Ronald Goldman. O. J. Simpson, a professional actor, made it appear that the gloves were too small. "They don't fit," he muttered loudly enough for the jury to hear as he seemingly struggled in an effort to put them on. *Newsweek* magazine called his performance either the greatest acting job ever by an actor of limited skills or one of the biggest bungles ever committed by a prosecutor or both. I share their assessment.

Darden had spectacularly violated a cardinal principle of cross-examination: never ask a question of a witness unless you either already know or do not care what the answer will be. He should have known that the chances were nil that Simpson would slip on the glove and proclaim, "Shucks! It fits! I guess I'm guilty!" Showy defense attorney Johnnie Cochran alertly capitalized upon the mistake by adding to his closing argument a reminder of the botched courtroom demonstration, concluding with the catchy rhyme: "If it doesn't fit, you must acquit!" It was not exactly courtroom eloquence of the caliber of Daniel Webster or Clarence Darrow, but it worked. Simpson was acquitted. Two of the jurors, when talking with the media after the long trial, repeated the phrase verbatim, sounding like parrots.

My post–O. J. Simpson trial in front of Judge Syler was a bit more mundane.

Two young men were in a white Mercury Sable station wagon on Good Hope Street in Cape Girardeau at 12:57 A.M. when Patrolman Dan Seger spotted them. Seger recognized the driver, Artemus Ward, and knew his driver's license had been revoked. He began following the car. Dan Dequille, a known drug dealer, was the other man in the car. He was riding in the front passenger seat. Seger pulled close behind them and illuminated the interior of their car with his spotlight at the same time he activated his red lights and siren, indicating that Ward should pull over.

Seger watched closely as Dequille stuck his arm outside the window and tossed something. Seger pulled them over. Once backup officers arrived, he walked back to the place where the item had struck the ground and found a sandwich-sized baggie containing one gram of methamphetamine. Methamphetamine, for those law-abiding, non-news-watching readers who may be unfamiliar with the substance, is a highly addictive drug made by cooking the ephedrine contained in routine cold medication with such appetizing edibles as Liquid Drano, anhydrous ammonia, and lithium batteries.

The reports were waiting for me when I stopped by the police station the next morning. I was already familiar with Dan Dequille. I had been helping him build his criminal record for years. He already had a felony conviction for trafficking in drugs. Also, he had testified as a witness for the defense when I prosecuted his younger brother for murder. In this new case, I charged him with possession of a controlled substance (for having the methamphetamine in the first place) and with attempted tampering with evidence (for tossing it out the window).

At trial, the defense tried to suggest that the driver, Artemus Ward, had been the one who threw the drugs out the passenger window. This was an absurd claim, since Seger had specifically seen Dequille's hand and arm extending outside the window as he threw the item, but a prosecutor can never be overconfident. You never know what a jury will do. Did I mention O. J. Simpson?

Obviously, the outcome of the trial would depend upon the jury understanding and believing that Dequille was definitely the one who threw the bag. Once a trial lawyer has identified the key issue in the case, and the specific evidence that supports his side of that issue, everything he does during the trial should be geared toward driving that point home.

When Seger testified, I spent a lot of time asking questions aimed at proving that he had a good view of the interior of the car, that he could tell the driver was driving, and that the passenger was definitely the person whose arm stuck out the window as the meth was being tossed. During the direct examination, the prosecutor wants to focus the jurors on the witness. One way of accomplishing this is to stand near the far end of the jury box so the witness is looking toward the jury as he is answering the questions.

In my closing argument, I referred to an old song lyric, the one chanting a litany of body parts, including the line: "The ankle bone's connected to the *shin bone,* the shin bone's connected to the *knee bone.*" It goes on ad nauseam until one runs out of body parts. I reminded the jury that the hand bone was connected to the arm bone, the arm bone was connected to the shoulder bone, the shoulder bone was connected to the neck bone, the neck bone was connected to the head bone, and the bonehead was Dan Dequille. Well, I didn't really say "bonehead." But my little analogy did drive home the point that if the drugs came out of Dequille's hand, the jury should find him guilty.

I thought it was pretty clever, but that was not the full extent of my cleverness in this particular case. Oh, no. I also had my own little courtroom demonstration planned. Aware of Christopher Darden's spectacular catastrophe with the gloves, I had thought this through carefully. At least I thought I had.

When the defendant took the stand, I grilled him for a while about his prior criminal convictions. This is always safe ground for the prosecutor. I then decided it was time to spring my courtroom demonstration. I handed him the small plastic bag of methamphetamine and asked him to show the jury how far he could throw it.

"How far do you *want* me to throw it?"

"As far as you can."

I felt pretty smug. Since the baggie was so light, I was sure it would not go far. This would play right into my anticipated closing argument, where I'd be pointing out that this demonstration was one more bit of proof showing that the *driver* could not have thrown it. Why, it would have barely made it out of the car, much less to the spot where Seger found it.

In hindsight, what I failed to take into account was that the evidence unit had repackaged the light sandwich baggie inside a heavier plastic evidence bag. When turned sideways, it was transformed by the laws of physics into a drug-juiced *Frisbee.* I had never been very good at physics.

I managed to keep a poker face as this spinning bag of speed flew like a jet-propelled flying saucer over the full length of the courtroom, forty-three feet, six inches, finally banging off the wall underneath the clock. Another cardinal principle for a trial lawyer is that you never, *ever* show the jury that you are surprised or upset by something horrible that has just happened to your case right in front of them.

"Thank you, Mr. Dequille," I said confidently, as I hiked to the back of the courtroom and retrieved the exhibit. Fortunately, I had saved some other decent cross-examination questions for just such an emergency, and I moved right into them, pretending that my backside was not full of arrows.

The jurors probably spent the rest of the trial wondering what in the world I had been trying to prove. "What was up with that meth toss?" I imagined them saying once they got back into the jury room to deliberate. Undoubtedly, the jury, with that collective wisdom it possessed, would figure out exactly what I had been trying to prove and would realize that I had screwed up royally.

Undaunted by the speed bump on the road to conviction, I persevered with my trial plan. I had one last bit of cleverness in store for the jury.

At various points in the trial, the state's witnesses had testified to the different street nicknames for methamphetamine, including such things as "meth," "crank," "speed," and "shit." It had not been accidental when I asked the questions calling for that testimony. I was building the record to support my Johnnie-Cochranesque spectacular and memorable closing-argument grand finale.

During closing argument, the prosecutor goes first, summarizing the evidence and asserting that the facts and the law support a guilty verdict. The defense lawyer then delivers a closing argument, offering grounds for reasonable doubt. Finally, the prosecutor gets the last crack in rebuttal, addressing anything the defense raised in its argument.

Everything in the Dequille closing arguments went as expected. During my rebuttal I was soaring to the heights of eloquence when I reached the final two sentences of my carefully prepared closing argument: "Finally, ladies and gentlemen, to paraphrase a flamboyant defense attorney from a well-known trial in another part of the country, this case boils down to whether or not Dan Dequille threw that bag of methamphetamine, and the bottom line is this: *If he threw the shit, you must not acquit!*"

On that triumphant note, I sat down, feeling extremely clever.

The bailiff handed the jury their written instructions, and the members filed out of the courtroom into the adjacent deliberation room. The door had barely closed before Judge Syler was scolding me.

"Mr. Swingle, don't ever use that kind of language in my courtroom again!"

My bubble burst. I thought the little ditty distilled the case to its most important point, and in a very memorable way. Every word I had said, even *that* word, had been testified to in open court and was part of the evidence in the case. Commenting upon the evidence is appropriate in closing argument. Nevertheless, I got the judge's point. What had seemed clever to me might have seemed a tad unprofessional to others. It was the judge's courtroom. Everyone in it had to play by his rules.

"Yes, sir," I said humbly.

Fortunately, whether or not the jury considered my words poetic or vulgar, they quickly returned guilty verdicts on both counts. As a prior drug offender, Dequille was sentenced to twelve years in prison.

So, what worked for Johnnie Cochran in sunny California had worked for Morley Swingle on the banks of the muddy Mississippi. Not that I will ever again allow myself to soar to such heights of vulgar eloquence in Judge Syler's courtroom.

Forgetful Drunk

No one can seriously dispute the magnitude
of the drunken driving problem or the States'
interest in eradicating it. Media reports of
alcohol-related death and mutilation on the
Nation's roads are legion. The anecdotal is
confirmed by the statistical. "Drunk drivers
cause an annual death toll of over 25,000 and
in the same time span cause nearly one million
personal injuries and more than five billion
dollars in property damage." For decades, this
Court has "repeatedly lamented the tragedy.
The increasing slaughter on our highways now
reaches the astounding figures only heard of
on the battlefield."

—William H. Rehnquist

The year was 1907. Teddy Roosevelt was president. Babe Ruth was twelve years old. Missouri had been a state fewer than one hundred years. In that year, the Missouri legislature enacted an important new law, one that would still be around for prosecutors to enforce many generations later—the state's first drunk-driving statute.

The remarkable thing was how quickly the legislature learned that a new law was needed to protect the public from people who drink and drive. The first gasoline-powered automobile was invented by a man named Frank Duryea in 1893. Henry Ford had just started Ford Motor Company in 1903, but was yet to make his first Model T. Even in the infancy of automobile travel, Missouri found it necessary to pass a law prohibiting and punishing drinking and driving. Quite simply, huge, fast cars and liquored-up drivers had immediately proved to be a deadly combination.

The dangers of drunk driving continue to this day. "The Case of the Forgetful Drunk" is the story of a DWI prosecution, but it also involves the St. Louis Cardinals baseball team. But before I delve into the drunk-driving incident, I want to tell you about the time I almost became a crime victim at a Cardinals game.

⚖️

I have been an avid Cardinals fan since childhood, when Bob Gibson forged his sparkling earned-run average of 1.12 in 1968. After dreaming about attending spring training for years, I finally got the chance when my oldest daughter was thirteen. Years of grooming her as a baseball fan finally paid off when she did the heavy lifting of convincing her mother that this was a vacation the family should take. Bless her heart!

The Cardinals played their spring training games at the Roger Dean Stadium in Jupiter, Florida. The stadium seated only seven thousand people, so no matter where we sat, the view was better than what we were accustomed to from the seats in the ozone levels of the fifty-thousand-seat Busch Stadium in St. Louis. A special area was roped off for children where the players would sign autographs for the kids before, after, and sometimes even during the game. My youngest daughter, Veronica, at age six, was our cleanup hitter in the autograph department, snagging thirty-three autographs on baseballs during the week, plus a broken bat from John Mabry, who immediately became her favorite player.

We had so much fun attending the Cardinals' home games at Roger Dean Stadium, in fact, that the two most avid fans in the family, thirteen-year-old Olivia and I, decided to make a road trip to Fort Lauderdale, to watch the Cardinals play the Baltimore Orioles. I called to see if any tickets remained.

"Do you want the best seats available?" the ticket-seller asked.

"Yes."

"They'll be waiting at the window."

Much to our shock and delight, the seats proved to be in the fourth row, right behind the Orioles' dugout. Since this was Hall-of-Famer Cal Ripkin's last year with the Orioles, we were especially pleased to be sitting so close; however, I soon discovered that there are certain risks to sitting right next to the action.

Midway through the game, a Cardinals batter hit a high pop-up. The Baltimore first baseman, a minor-leaguer named Calvin Pickering, lumbered toward the Orioles' dugout to make the catch. Pickering had been playing on the Orioles' farm team, the Rochester Red Wings. He was trying out for the Show.

Lumbered is exactly the correct verb, because Pickering was huge: 6' 6", and 278 pounds. He zeroed in on that ball like a bear trying to catch a falling honey-filled beehive.

Did I mention that we were sitting just four rows behind the dugout? They were great seats. We could see the beads of perspiration on Pickering's face as he strained to make the catch. The ball hit the center of Pickering's glove and bounced right out. Instinctively, I yelled the sort of insult frequently uttered from the safety of the nosebleed section at Busch Stadium.

"Hey, there must be a hole in that glove!"

As an experienced prosecutor, I think fast. Clever phrases come naturally to me, whereas the average fan might require days to think up a comment so witty, pithy and situationally appropriate.

Pickering spun and unleashed an angry tirade at me, including his own situationally appropriate insults and a stream of profanity impressive from someone born outside the United States, who might have learned English as a second language. He advanced toward the stands. It seemed likely he would come over the wall and that I soon would be making a visit to a Florida emergency room, if not the morgue. I handed my camera to Olivia, determined to depart the world like a true attorney.

"Get a good picture if he assaults me."

As he moved closer, a fan a few seats to my left yelled an even better zinger: "*Rochester* is a great place to spend the summer!"

Rochester, of course, was the home of the minor league team for the Orioles. Players not good enough to make the Orioles would end up at Rochester. This fan was pretty good with the insults, himself. He must have been a brain surgeon or a professional comedian.

Pickering turned and fired a verbal barrage at his latest critic. His teammates ultimately dragged him back to first base, and the game continued.

I have followed Calvin Pickering's career with a certain amount of interest since that exciting day. His fielding percentage has improved each year. He finally made the majors after spending ten years or so in the minor leagues. So far, however, his major league batting average is a somewhat meager .232.

With such dismal hitting, he has either developed a thicker skin or has left many dismembered fans in ballparks across the country.

Back to "The Case of the Forgetful Drunk."

⚖

Isaiah Sellers, thirty-three, was a successful Cape Girardeau businessman. It was the beginning of October, a fine time for true baseball aficionados. The St. Louis Cardinals were in the playoffs. Sellers had scored some tickets to a playoff game, and they were terrific seats. What better way to spend the day than to travel the one hundred miles from Cape Girardeau to St. Louis to attend a major league playoff game?

Sellers drove himself, his wife, and another couple to St. Louis for the big event. He parked his blue minivan in a parking garage across from the stadium, and the four Cape Girardeau residents, dutifully wearing the red of "Cardinal Nation," joined the throng at the packed stadium to take in the big game.

Despite the exorbitant prices of ballpark hotdogs and beer, Sellers kept the supply coming. By the third inning, he was drunk. By the fifth inning he was looped. By the seventh inning he was soused. Babe Ruth himself was probably never quite so drunk in a ballpark.

Inconveniently, the stadium beer vendors quit selling their product after the seventh inning, pursuant to an admirable policy aimed at cutting down the number of drunk drivers exiting the gates and taking to the roadways at the close of each game. Sellers, highly disappointed that his beer supply had been cut off, excused himself during the eighth inning, after promising to come right back, and headed to the parking garage, where a cooler with several cans of iced Miller Lite awaited him.

The Cardinals were locked in a pivotal game with the Atlanta Braves, but Isaiah Sellers was well past the point of caring who won.

⚖

Sergeant Blaine Adams of the Missouri Highway Patrol has won awards for his aggressive efforts to rid southeast Missouri highways of drunk drivers. He currently ranks second in the state for career DWI arrests by an active officer, and in various years he has held single-season records in DWI arrests and convictions both in his troop and in the state. His accomplishments have been recognized by Mothers Against Drunk Driving, as well as by the patrol itself. And his feats have been achieved without the use of anabolic steroids.

A graduate of Southeast Missouri State University, and a former probation officer with the Missouri Board of Probation and Parole, Adams is a very intelligent man. Unlike some police officers, who are content to wait for drunk drivers to come to them, Adams stalks the intoxicated motorist like a lion after a wildebeest. Where is the lion likely to find the wildebeest? At the watering hole, of course. One of Adams's most effective techniques is to regularly cruise past local bars and taverns. When he spots a car weaving all over the road as it leaves the parking lot, he pulls it over. Not only has he thereby added another statistic to his hall-of-fame-caliber DWI numbers, but he has quite possibly saved the life of some innocent motorist who otherwise would have met the drunk driver in a head-on collision later in the night.

Defense lawyers have vociferously criticized Adams for lurking around bars while on patrol, particularly the successful and flamboyant Albert C. Lowes, who is quite fond of such watering holes himself. "It's unfair!" he and other attorneys thunder to juries. Adams is just out to "pad his stats!" Better he should stick to patrolling rural roadways, hoping he might stumble across a drunk driver weaving along next to some cornfield, than proactively seek them out at the places they are likely to be. Why, it's practically *entrapment* to nab a drunk driver right after he's left the parking lot of the bar! Doesn't he have something better to do with his time? Isn't there a murderer, rapist, or robber he could be catching?

"Don't worry," Adams assures them. "If I get a call about a murder, rape or robbery, I'll be there in seconds. In the meantime, I'm going to take another drunk driver off the streets."

Not long ago, a candidate for sheriff in neighboring Perry County, Missouri, also in Blaine Adams's territory, placed a paid advertisement in the newspaper proclaiming that he did not believe in arresting people for driving while intoxicated, and promising that he would fire a deputy for lurking outside a bar to arrest a drunk driver. He received 112 votes. Did 112 people agree with his position on DWI enforcement, or did he have that many drinking buddies in the county? Either thought was a bit scary.

In Cape Girardeau County, we consider it important to catch drunk drivers. Many law enforcement tactics are used.

One weekend night the Missouri Highway Patrol and the Cape Girardeau Police Department set up a sobriety checkpoint right after midnight at the foot of the long, narrow bridge spanning the wide Mississippi River. They stopped every car that crossed from Illinois to Missouri and asked to see each driver's license. If the driver seemed sober, the car was allowed to go on its way within thirty seconds or so. If the driver appeared to be impaired or smelled of alcohol, he was asked to submit to field sobriety tests, such as reciting the alphabet, touching his finger to his nose, or walking a straight line. Those drivers who proved to be intoxicated were arrested.

Sobering fact: Of the 500 people pulled over that night, 102 drivers had been drinking, and 23 were intoxicated to the point that they were arrested and later convicted. In other words, if you were crossing over to Illinois that dark night and saw a set of headlights coming right at you on the narrow bridge, there was a 20 percent chance the person behind the wheel had been drinking and nearly a 5 percent chance that the car hurtling toward you was being operated by a drunk driver.

As a veteran prosecutor, I now grip the steering wheel with white knuckles when I am driving on a two-lane highway at night and see a set of headlights coming toward me. Sometimes I wish I were still oblivious to the danger, like everyone else in the world who has not yet seen a drunk driver take the life of someone they love.

I have personally prosecuted 10 cases where a drunk driver killed someone. The dead include Cathy A. Wilson, 21; Russell Scott McLain, 20; James Beussink, 38; Lydia Beussink, 37; Stanley Nenninger, 45; Martin L. Haupt, 85; William Householder, 25; Patricia Young, 46; John M. Endrizzi, 44; Carl Scott Ford, 41; Tracie Diane Ford, 29; Rebecca Larkin, 36; Terry J. Webb, 21; Bonnie Carol Wolf, 27; Jane E. Mallonee, 36; and Jason Mallonee, 10. Every one of these human beings would be alive today had it not been for their killers choosing to get behind the wheel of a car while intoxicated. These are tragedies that could have been prevented. Heroic officers like Blaine Adams, who not only do their duty, but do it aggressively and tirelessly, are truly making the world a safer place.

Blaine Adams happened to be the officer patrolling the interstate highway between St. Louis and Cape Girardeau on the night the Cardinals were playing the Braves. He was working the four-to-midnight shift. He was thirty-six years old and had been with the patrol for almost ten years. Rather than listening to the big game, he was out looking for drunk drivers.

⚖

Absalom Grimes was an accountant. He was driving south on I-55 from St. Louis at 11:40 P.M. when he saw the blue minivan in his rearview mirror. It was weaving all over the roadway. At one point it drove between two other cars, both traveling south, one in the regular lane and one in the passing lane.

The cars moved apart to give him room to careen between them. Grimes cringed as he watched the near-wreck and breathed a sigh of relief when Isaiah Sellers pulled ahead of him.

Using his cell phone, he dialed 9-1-1 and reported the weaving driver. The dispatcher asked his whereabouts. He spotted a mile-marker sign and relayed the information. He also provided a detailed description of the minivan, complete with its license number.

⚖

After hearing the dispatch about the van, Blaine Adams set up at a position where he thought he might rendezvous with it. As he lay in wait, he spotted an unusual sight, something he had never before seen during his many years of patrolling the roads and highways of southeast Missouri. A St. Louis cab, the station-wagon type often seen at the airport, was cruising down the highway near Cape Girardeau, its fare light on. He wondered what a St. Louis cabbie was doing over one hundred miles from St. Louis. But he could not think about that right now. He had a drunk driver to catch. After waiting a while in the same place, Adams finally doubled back toward St. Louis.

A few minutes later, he spotted the blue minivan pulled over on the shoulder just north of the Jackson exit. Sellers was behind the wheel, but the motor was shut off.

Isaiah Sellers was incredibly drunk. His sharp mind, the same one that had allowed him to build a highly successful business and accumulate great wealth, was suddenly having difficulty coming up with the letters of the alphabet. In fact, when asked to recite them, like many drunks, he experienced an almost uncontrollable urge to sing the letters. Surely the officer would find that amusing! He must have thought, *That'll show him I'm a funny guy!*

Adams did not find Sellers particularly amusing. It was October 14. This was his fifty-second DWI arrest for the year. He read Sellers the *Miranda* warnings and asked him a few questions.

"Have you been drinking?"

"Yes."

"What were you drinking?"

"Beer."

"How many?"

Sellers was uncontrollably and inexplicably compelled by the DWI laws of nature to give the answer uttered by perhaps 98 percent of the nation's drunk drivers.

"Two."

The ground beneath him was rolling like ocean waves. He scrunched up his eyes and peered closely at Adams. *Had he fooled him? Did the trooper believe it? Darn! Didn't look like it. He was getting out the handcuffs.*

"Where've you been tonight?" Adams asked genially as he applied the steel cuffs.

Sellers dimly recalled being at a sporting event. That might make for good conversation. Unfortunately, he was so intoxicated he could not even remember which sport he had been watching.

"I'm coming from the Rams football game," he announced with slurred speech, his eyes watery and glassy. "We had some good seats!"

"We?" Adams asked, glancing into the minivan. "Who were you with?"

Sellers stared dumbly into the empty van. *Where the hell were the others?*

⚖

At the station, Sellers registered a .255 on the breathalyzer machine, more than three times the reading of .08, which indicates intoxication. A 175-pound man who drank two beers in one hour would still be under a level of .04. A reading of .255 would be the result of drinking approximately seventeen beers over a three-hour time frame.

From the police station, Blaine Adams called Sellers's home. He had a hunch about that St. Louis taxi. Sure enough, Sellers's wife and the other couple had been its occupants. They had waited and waited for Sellers to return to the stadium. Eventually, they had checked the parking garage and found, to their shock and dismay, that the minivan was gone. Finally, in exasperation, his wife had flagged down a St. Louis cabbie and hired him to make the two-hundred-mile roundtrip from the ballpark to her home. It was an incredibly expensive fare.

"Your husband is in jail for drunk driving," Adams told her.

"Is he hurt?"

"No."

"Thank goodness!"

Her voice became a tad cold.

"The [blankety-blank]!" she hissed.

Isaiah Sellers pled guilty to drunk driving before Associate Circuit Judge Scott Thomsen, thereby depriving the world of the opportunity to hear the colorful testimony about his eventful night at the ballgame. To my knowledge, his marriage is still intact. It would have been enlightening, however, to have been in a position to hear the conversation when his wife bailed him out of jail.

Isaiah Sellers was not the only person who got plastered on that particular October night. The Cardinals were blown out by the Atlanta Braves 14–0, starting a downward spiral that cost them the National League Championship Series four games to three.

Girl in the Shower

Not even the abuses, the mishandlings, and the
puerilities which are so often associated with
cross-examination have availed to nullify its
value. It may be that in more than one sense
it takes the place in our system which torture
occupied in the medieval system of the civil-
ians. Nevertheless, it is beyond any doubt the
greatest engine ever invented for the discovery
of truth.

—John Henry Wigmore

The issue of a cause rarely depends upon a
speech and is but seldom even affected by it.
But there is never a cause contested, the
result of which is not mainly dependent upon
the skill with which the advocate conducts
his cross-examination.

—Francis L. Wellman

I am often asked: "What case was your most painful loss?" This
assumes, of course, that I have lost a case.
Unfortunately, I have. Several.
Any prosecutor worth his salt has lost some cases over the course of his
career. Show me a prosecutor who brags that he has never lost a case, and I
will show you a prosecutor who has not been aggressive enough in taking difficult cases to trial, or who has not handled many sex crimes or domestic
assaults. Sometimes, a tough case needs to be filed, and its outcome will

depend mostly upon the credibility and believability of one key witness. Many cases of rape, child molestation, or domestic violence rest almost completely upon the testimony of one particular victim, often a family member of the defendant. Many DWI cases rest solely upon the testimony of one traffic cop who can testify that the suspect was drunk. In all of these cases, if the prosecutor truly believes that one witness, and thinks he has a reasonably good shot at convincing all twelve jurors that the witness is telling the truth, the prosecutor has an ethical duty to file the case, as long as it clears the "Where's the Beef?" threshold. Too many criminals would get away with their crimes without the public even having a shot at justice if a prosecutor put too much pride in his or her win/loss record.

So, yes, I've lost some cases.

As of this writing, I have tried 116 jury trials, one civil and the rest criminal. I won convictions in 89 of the criminal trials. Of course, that means I suffered through 26 acquittals. But let's not dwell on those painful memories. I'm sure each loss was someone else's fault! A bit better statistic is that of the 66 people I have prosecuted for homicide, all but one were convicted. Of the 23 murderers who chose to take their cases to jury trial, 22 were found guilty. The rest pled guilty. The one homicide I lost had peculiar facts. The defendant had punched a man in a street fight, and the man fell and hit his head on the curb. He died a day later. Our pathologist thought the death was a result of the blow to the head. Dr. Scott Gibbs, a respected local brain surgeon, testified for the defense that it was possible the death could have been the result of a prior aneurysm in the victim's brain. The jury felt Dr. Gibbs's testimony provided sufficient reasonable doubt to acquit the defendant of the murder charge. To my surprise, they even acquitted him of the assault for punching the victim. They bought the defendant's claim of self-defense. But the homicide loss was not my most painful one. That dubious honor goes to "The Case of the Girl in the Shower."

⚖

Carlo Ranaldi was married to the girl's mother. The girl—Ashton—was fourteen. She was a well-developed fourteen, with long, dark hair, an adorable face, and a slender body already developing the curves of young womanhood. Carlo Ranaldi, her stepfather, had noticed.

He was captivated by the budding sexuality of this lovely girl living under his roof, a girl to whom he was not related by blood. He and Ashton's mother had their own three-year-old daughter, but Ashton was not his biological child. He was becoming obsessed with her.

Carlo Ranaldi was not a model citizen, either. He had served time in prison for selling cocaine. He had met Ashton's mother, Priscilla, when he got out of prison.

As his secret obsession with his stepdaughter grew, he developed an extraordinarily despicable plan. He rigged a video camera to film Ashton as she showered. Not just once, but many, many times.

The shower was a stand-alone unit in the basement of the home. It had a shower curtain, which at first presented an obstacle for Carlo Ranaldi's film-making career. He solved it by complaining that the curtain was getting in his way when he showered. He took it down. Neither his wife nor Ashton became suspicious.

Next, he placed a brown paper grocery bag on a shelf on the basement's opposite wall, amid some clutter. The bag blended right in with the other junk on the shelves. The silver-dollar-sized hole—just the right size for the unblinking eye of the camera—went undetected.

He spent an entire summer videotaping Ashton's showers. He kept the videocassette locked in his toolbox in the closet of the carport.

Priscilla began noticing her husband's secretive behavior as the weeks passed. Something did not seem right. When she noted that he had begun keeping his toolbox locked, she became convinced that he was up to something. He had never locked it before.

One Saturday morning, while Carlo Ranaldi slept late, his wife removed his keys from his pants and went out to the carport closet, where she quietly opened the toolbox. It was empty. Convinced Ranaldi was hiding something from her, she searched the cardboard boxes in the vicinity. Eventually, she found something that changed her life forever.

First, she was baffled by the solitary, unmarked videocassette wrapped in a cloth towel. Why in the world would a man keep a videotape wrapped in a towel inside a box? Extremely curious, Priscilla took the tape to the living room and popped it into the videocassette player. Within seconds, she found herself watching images of her naked daughter taking a shower. Aghast, she froze in front of the television, her eyes riveted to the screen, absorbing the awful truth. She felt herself becoming physically sick.

Priscilla grabbed the tape and hurried to Ashton's bedroom and woke her. She then plucked her three-year-old from bed and fled with her two daughters to her mother's home on the other side of town. In the safety of her mother's house, she watched the entire videotape, beginning to end. It proved to be a collection of six shower scenes totaling fifty-two minutes covering a period of many weeks. Ashton was depicted from the knees up, taking shower after shower. Sometimes she danced in the shower. Sometimes she practiced cheers. Sometimes she softly caressed herself as she soaped her body. It was obvious from her changing tan lines that the secret filming had gone on most of the summer.

The tape was an appalling violation of privacy. Priscilla called the police as soon as she finished watching it. Patrolman Jack Wimp responded quickly. Wimp is an excellent police officer; with his name, he has to be. He watched enough of the tape to get the picture. He and other officers returned with her to her home, where Carlo Ranaldi was still sleeping. They found the grocery bag with its telltale hole. They collected the toolbox. They arrested Carlo Ranaldi. Ranaldi denied knowing anything about the tape.

I watched the videotape while assessing the strength of the evidence before deciding how the case should be charged. I felt embarrassed as I watched it, even though I was alone in the conference room at the prosecutor's office. I felt humiliated for this innocent and pretty young girl, completely unaware that she was being filmed. I was acutely aware that I was seeing something I was not meant to see—that no one was meant to see. This poor girl's privacy was violated anew every time someone else in law enforcement watched the tape, including me.

I felt guilty as I watched it. Afterward, I made sure it was kept in the evidence unit under lock and key, to be viewed only by those who had a legitimate reason to watch it.

At Jack Wimp's request, Karen Buchheit, the investigator for my office, questioned Ashton. She revealed for the first time that Ranaldi had recently molested her by touching her in inappropriate ways and by having her touch him. She had never told her mother because he had threatened to hurt her and to take her little sister away from her mother if she told anybody.

I charged Carlo Ranaldi with child abuse under a statute that makes it a felony to film a naked child for sexual purposes, with sodomy, and with sexual abuse. The case looked open and shut to me. Even though the medical examination of the girl could neither confirm nor deny the sexual molestation, the things she had alleged were not acts that would leave visible damage to her body. We had the tape. We had the grocery bag. We had the mother and daughter as very sympathetic witnesses. Carlo Ranaldi, convicted drug dealer, was going back to prison, if I had anything to say about it.

As the trial date drew near, I met with Ashton and her mother to prepare them for court. Testifying is never easy, and here was a fourteen-year-old girl who was going to be required to testify about being filmed as she showered and about being touched in inappropriate ways. As she looked at the jury, she would know that every juror in the box—man or woman—had either already viewed or soon would view the tape in which she was completely naked. Criminal trials are public events. The judge cannot close the courtroom. Thus, not only the jurors, but the judge, the court reporter, the defense lawyer, the defendant, and any courtroom spectators would have the opportunity of watching her taking shower after shower as the tape was played in open court. Priscilla, too, was in a stressful position. Here was a mother who would be required to testify publicly about the betrayal of trust by her husband—a betrayal almost breathtaking in its scope.

I was impressed by Ashton when I met her. She was bright and articulate. I was confident she would do just fine when the time came to take the witness stand. I was worried about Priscilla, though. She now felt such obvious hatred for the man who had violated her daughter's privacy that it might play poorly with the jury. People who hate passionately will sometimes stretch the truth. Yet, what mother in her position would not have felt white-hot hatred toward Carlo Ranaldi?

The case went before a jury one autumn in front of Circuit Judge William L. Syler, Jr. The state's case went smoothly. The defense attorney, Malcolm Montgomery, was aggressive in his questioning of Ashton and Priscilla, but I did not feel he made much of a dent in their testimony.

When it came time for the defense to present its case, Ranaldi's claim seemed absurd and pathetic. The defense was actually arguing that the mother and daughter had created the tape themselves and were framing Carlo Ranaldi so the mother could get a bigger share of the marital property in the divorce. I practically laughed at the lameness of the defense. Being the father of two daughters and having spent years watching their mother's love for them, I knew that no mother in the world would videotape her own daughter naked to be shown in an open courtroom. The whole idea was pure bunkum.

The big surprise in the case came when Montgomery, an experienced defense attorney, called Carlo Ranaldi to testify in his own defense. Normally, a defendant with a criminal record will not take the stand. Under Missouri law, if the defendant does not take the stand, the prosecutor may not tell the jury about his criminal history. If he does testify, however, his credibility becomes an issue in the case, and his criminal record becomes relevant to his credibility and fair game for cross-examination.

When preparing for trial, I always write questions for a possible cross-examination of every defense witness, even those I do not expect will testify. When Malcolm Montgomery called out Carlo Ranaldi's name, I reached for my prepared cross-examination questions for Ranaldi.

Bring it on!

I probably rolled my eyes as I listened to Carlo Ranaldi giving his direct testimony under the patient questioning of Malcolm Montgomery. He claimed to know nothing about the existence of the tape. He had certainly not made it himself. He had absolutely never touched his stepdaughter in an inappropriate manner. His wife and he had been contemplating a divorce for some time. She was out to get him. Blah, blah, blah. I was itching for my shot at him.

When it came, I bludgeoned him with my first question: "Isn't it true, sir, that you have a felony conviction for selling cocaine?"

"Yes, I do."

"Isn't it true that you received a sentence of four years in prison for that offense?"

"Yes, sir."

"So, you're a convicted felon?

"Yes, sir."

I was definitely off to a good start.

Different lawyers have different styles of cross-examination. Some charge in like playground bullies, administering a merciless verbal beating, pummeling witnesses with difficult, embarrassing, and downright rude questions. Others take a quiet approach, buttering up witnesses, almost schmoozing them, to draw out admissions. The best trial lawyers vary their approaches, depending upon the witnesses and the facts of each case. You can be a lot tougher on a swarthy convicted felon than you can be on a defendant's little old mother.

I felt I could be very aggressive with Carlo Ranaldi. The jury was not likely to feel sorry for him if I attacked him hard. He was, after all, a convicted felon, an admitted drug dealer, and an alleged pervert.

I took off the gloves.

"The tape was found in *your* toolbox, wasn't it?" I thundered.

"That's what Priscilla claimed. I didn't put it there. I never saw it before in my life."

"You were the *only* one with the key to the toolbox, right?"

"Well, Priscilla and I lived in the same house. She had access to my keys."

I got louder.

"You hid that camera in that paper bag, didn't you?"

"No."

"You videotaped Ashton taking those showers, didn't you?

"No."

"You fondled her, didn't you?"

"No!"

I ridiculed him and grilled him, but he would not admit a thing. Nevertheless, it seemed to me that his denials rang false. I had scored some points. What a lying weasel! I sat down, feeling pretty satisfied with myself.

The closing arguments went even better. I emphasized once again the magnitude of the invasion of Ashton's privacy. I masterfully (I thought) countered Malcolm Montgomery's closing argument by pointing out that if this mother and daughter had wanted to frame this convicted drug dealer for a crime, all they had to do was plant a baggie of marijuana in his car and tip off the police. Such an easy plan wouldn't involve the needless and distressing embarrassment of filming your daughter naked and subjecting her to a rather invasive medical examination. Also, Ashton's changing tan lines showed that the videotape had been made over a long period of time. It wasn't something that mother and daughter had just cooked up on the spur of the moment. They would have to be impressively diabolical to carry out this devious plan throughout an entire summer!

When the jury disappeared into the jury room to begin its deliberations, I was feeling pretty good. I always feel a tremendous rush of adrenaline during my closing argument. It is my favorite part of the trial. The adrenaline glow lasts for several minutes after I sit down.

Even Malcolm Montgomery was impressed with the pearls of wisdom scattered throughout my closing argument. Privately, he agreed with me that Ranaldi was going to be found guilty. The only real question was what sentence the judge would wind up giving him. Always the advocate for his client, Malcolm began working on me to try to get me to agree that Ranaldi could remain free on bond while awaiting his sentencing. I, however, was not so sure I was willing to be magnanimous. I had developed a good solid loathing for Ranaldi. I was planning to request an increase in his bond once the jury nailed him.

I grew a bit nervous as the hours passed. The jury moved into its eighth hour of deliberations, and the voices in the jury room were becoming quite loud. Normally, you cannot hear a thing from the jury room. During this deliberation, the shouting grew so loud that even from our seats in the court-room we could hear some of the loudest comments. I grew especially uneasy when I heard one male voice yell, "The prosecutor really went after him hard on cross-examination, but he held up well!"

I cringed. A cardinal principle of cross-examination is to never waste time trying to get the witness to admit something he will *never* be willing to admit. His refusal to admit wrongdoing in response to your vigorous cross will be more memorable than his protestations of innocence during his direct exam-ination. Ranaldi's vehement denials during my cross-examination had become the most memorable moments of the trial. I had violated the rule precisely because I thought Carlo Ranaldi was so despicable that his denials would be obvious lies. I had never really expected him to crumble under my aggressive cross-examination and admit he made the tape or fondled the girl. In hindsight, I realized that I had outsmarted myself.

Eventually, the jury knocked. They had their verdict.

I watched as they filed back into the courtroom. No matter how strong or weak the case, this is always the most suspenseful moment of the trial. You never know what a jury will do. Sometimes you can guess the verdict as jurors come into the courtroom by looking at their faces. If they are glaring at the defendant, it is a guilty verdict for sure. If they won't make eye contact with him, they probably found him guilty. I have actually had jurors wink at me, signaling a guilty verdict. On the other hand, if they smile at the defen-dant, they are sending him home a free man.

With the Ranaldi jury, I simply could not tell. They were not smiling, but no one was winking, either.

The words *not guilty* came like a kick to my gut. Behind me, I heard Priscilla and Ashton sob. Malcolm Montgomery, quickly overcoming his sur-prise, proudly shook his client's hand. He had certainly earned his fee. I hoped it was huge. I gathered up my file and left the courtroom.

The moments following a not guilty verdict are some of the loneliest of a prosecutor's life. It is a deflating feeling to realize you were unsuccessful in per-suading the jury to decide the case your way. Seeing the victims crying never helps, either, especially when you know they put their faith in you to get jus-tice for them. Try as you might to deflect blame, there is really no one else to hold responsible. You either did not accurately assess the strength of the case in the first place, or you failed in your job of proving a winnable case.

It turned out that some of the jurors believed the claptrap that Ashton and her mother were trying to frame Ranaldi. They'd seen the hatred Priscilla felt for him. They'd seen—Aghhh!!—how well Ranaldi had stood up under my withering cross-examination. The burden of proof, after all, had been on the prosecution. It was mother and daughter's word against Ranaldi's. Under the law, Ranaldi was entitled to win any ties. The jury simply did not believe the testimony of the mother and daughter reached the level necessary to prove guilt beyond a reasonable doubt. Those voting for his guilt eventually caved in to those who felt the evidence was not sufficient to support a conviction.

Needless to say, Ashton and her mother were crushed. It was hard to explain to them that although juries almost always reach the correct result, this particular jury had not felt we proved the case beyond a reasonable doubt. Ashton and Priscilla knew Ranaldi's defense had been a pack of lies. It astounded them to hear that at least some of the jurors had bought it. I apologized to Ashton and Priscilla for losing the case and urged them not to take the verdict personally. To this day, I believe I would have won the trial had I done a more effective job of cross-examining the defendant. I should have gone after him with a scalpel instead of a sledgehammer. I completely agree with an observation made by one of my heroes, famed prosecutor Vincent Bugliosi: "Cross-examination is a lost art, and I doubt you could find more than a handful of superb cross-examiners in the entire country." A skillful cross-examination would have exposed Ranaldi for the louse he was. I had struck out.

A few weeks later Karen Buchheit destroyed the videotape of Ashton. At least no one else would ever see it. The continuing invasion of her privacy begun by Carlo Ranaldi had officially come to an end.

Almost.

I have seen Ashton around town a few times since the trial took place years ago. For a while, she worked in the drive-through window at *Taco Bell*. Every time I came to her window I remembered the videotape. She undoubtedly recalled it, too. I felt ashamed every time I saw her, not just for losing the trial, but for having watched that videotape, and thus becoming one more person who had violated her privacy.

The case concluded with something of a silver lining in its clouded ending. Allegations surfaced of other unsavory activity on the part of Carlo Ranaldi, and instead of maintaining a prolonged fight with Priscilla over the custody of their three-year-old daughter, he instead agreed to the termination of his parental rights. Priscilla did not need to worry about letting her baby go to Ranaldi for unsupervised visitation. Ranaldi was out of her life, forever, I hoped.

Cross-examination is the hardest part of a trial to master. It takes preparation, skill, study, practice, and an instinct for detecting and emphasizing a provable lie. I have read and reread the classic book *The Art of Cross-Examination* by Francis L. Wellman. I have read everything Vincent Bugliosi has ever written. I have studied the training videotapes of Irving Younger. I have pored over trial transcripts of effective cross-examinations. I have read countless treatises and articles. I have attended numerous seminars on trial techniques. Like other trial lawyers, I am still perfecting my craft.

That's why they call it *practicing* law.

Stone-Dead Blood Stone Villain

Plea bargaining is "a fish market that ought to be hosed down" and "a concession to the burned-out DA."

—Ralph Adam Fine

Plea bargaining is an essential component of the administration of justice. Properly administered, it is to be encouraged. It leads to prompt and largely final disposition of most criminal cases.

—Warren E. Burger

One of the most severely criticized aspects of the criminal justice system is the prevalence of plea bargaining. It has reached the point where, like racism or communism, it is automatically perceived as a negative thing by the general public. Plea bargaining is a favorite whipping boy of the media, but, in truth, it has received something of a bad rap.

Plea bargaining *can* be bad. But before we discuss its pros and cons, let's make it clear what we are talking about. Plea bargaining occurs when the prosecutor says to the defense, if your client will plead guilty, I will reward him with some sort of a break in exchange for his giving up his constitutional right to take his case to trial. Sometimes the prosecutor is reducing the charge to a lesser offense. Sometimes he is dismissing some counts in return for a plea to others. At times he is agreeing to a shorter sentence than the maximum for a particular crime. Often he is agreeing that the defendant will get probation and various types of counseling instead of jail time. Plea bargaining is an agreement between the prosecution and the defense giving the defendant some incentive to plead guilty.

Is this a bad thing? It completely depends upon what the prosecutor has offered. It can be very, very bad. But at other times it can be the best solution.

Plea bargaining is bad when the prosecutor has sold out the criminal justice system. When that happens, you step back and study the big picture, and the plea bargain makes your nose wrinkle. "That stinks!" you say. "It would have been better to lose the case than agree to *that*!"

Consider a homicide case where the prosecutor realizes the case may very well be lost completely should it go to trial. Let's say two men were in a bar and one man killed the other with a knife. The defendant claims it was self-defense. Two friends of the victim claim the defendant stabbed the victim with absolutely no provocation. Two other spectators, friends of the defendant, back his version that the victim was attacking him. This sort of case is a nightmare for a prosecutor, but unless a coroner's inquest or a grand jury rules the killing justifiable self-defense, any prosecutor is going to file the charge because an intentional killing occurred and the only issue is a questionable claim of self-defense. Questionable issues in a murder case are for a jury to decide.

A lazy prosecutor, or one who does not keep his eye on the big picture of justice, or one who is too covetous of a perfect win/loss record, might go too far in making a plea offer. After charging the defendant with second-degree murder, which carries a range of punishment from ten years to life, the prosecutor might reasonably offer voluntary manslaughter under those facts.

Whether such an offer is made will depend upon the strength of the case, the wishes of the victim's family, the prosecutor's desire to make an example of the defendant (in an effort to discourage the use of knives in bar fights), any bad conduct on the part of the victim suggesting that he deserved what happened, or any other fact indicating that justice would still be served even after a reduction of the charge. The lesser voluntary manslaughter charge carries a range of punishment of five to fifteen years in prison. Often it might be better to convict the defendant of a lower level of homicide than to let him get off completely. In rare cases, the prosecutor might even consider reducing the charge to involuntary manslaughter, which carries up to seven years in prison. A person commits involuntary manslaughter when he recklessly kills another person, even though he did not intentionally kill him. The defense might convince the prosecutor that involuntary manslaughter is appropriate because even though the defendant believed he was justified by self-defense, he recklessly used too much force and accidentally killed his assailant. At some point, however, based upon the facts of the case, the prosecutor should stop slinging plea offers. In general, my practice in homicide cases is to file the highest charge supported by the evidence and stick with it all the way to trial or guilty plea. I have made exceptions when cases have weakened after I filed them.

Theoretically, the prosecutor *could* keep improving the plea offer until he came up with one so irresistible that even an innocent person would plead guilty to it rather than take the case to trial. In our hypothetical, the prosecutor, his knees trembling violently at the prospect of taking the case to a jury, might finally offer the misdemeanor of peace disturbance for fighting in public, and further agree that the defendant would merely get a fifty-dollar fine. Any defendant charged with murder would be a fool to turn down such a slap on the wrist, even if he had not even been at the bar when the stabbing took place!

This shows the double whammy of sleaziness one has to guard against in plea bargaining. First, you don't want to make an offer that simply is not the right thing to do in the overall scheme of things. If a man stabbed a person to death at a bar, he is either guilty of murder or manslaughter or is not guilty of anything. Better to lose the case than agree to let him plead to peace disturbance. Also, the integrity of the system is compromised when a plea bargain is so lenient that it actually coerces an innocent person into pleading guilty. Our goal is to convict the guilty, not to pressure the innocent into pleading guilty. On the other hand, plea bargaining has its advantages.

Offering a plea bargain can be the most effective use of time and resources. There are only 365 days in a year, a certain number of them Sundays. There are only a finite number of courtrooms and judges available to hear jury trials. My office files twenty-five hundred criminal cases per year. It is not feasible that every one of them could go to jury trial. When a first offender is caught with marijuana, and would most likely receive probation if he pled guilty, where is the harm in making a plea offer guaranteeing he will get probation and drug counseling if he pleads guilty? You are giving him the certainty that he will not be going to jail in return for his giving up his right to go to trial, but you are not compromising the criminal justice system. He is simply getting the *same* sentence he probably would have received from the judge, anyway. Effective plea bargaining streamlines the court system and moves the cases that *ought* to be pled faster and more economically than if no plea offers were made in those cases.

Plea bargaining also helps develop informants in order to nab criminals higher up on the food chain. For example, a college kid caught with a small amount of marijuana might be able to lead you to the community's biggest drug dealer. You might want to make a deal with the kid to wear a tape recorder and go make controlled buys from his supplier. Becoming a snitch is not something most people are going to do out of the goodness of their hearts. They expect something in return, like guaranteed probation or an agreement not to file the misdemeanor marijuana possession charge.

The prosecutor and the judge have the duty and the power to make sure plea bargaining is done properly. Most of this responsibility rests squarely upon the shoulders of the prosecutor.

The prosecutor should put considerable thought into that big picture I talked about. He should develop policies governing plea bargaining by his office. He should spell out what offer should be made to a DWI first offender, or to a major drug dealer, or to a shoplifter, or to a bad-check writer. He should make sure all assistant prosecutors are aware of the parameters and stay within them. The office should strive for fairness and consistency.

Finally, the trial judge *always* has the right to reject a plea bargain as to a specific sentence. When a judge rejects a plea bargain, the defendant is entitled to withdraw his guilty plea and take his case to trial. The admissions he made during his aborted guilty plea cannot be used against him. The judge sits as the final arbiter to make sure that a plea bargain is not so lenient that it would have been better to have no plea bargain at all.

One case vividly illustrating plea bargaining in the real world is "The Case of the Stone-Dead Blood Stone Villain."

⚖

Cameron Allyn Childs, twenty, aka Al Shaw, aka "Short Dog," aka "Dolow," was a drug dealer from Los Angeles who set up business in Cape Girardeau. He was a member of a well-known street gang called the Blood Stone Villains, commonly referred to as the "Bloods." As the months went by, he developed a feud with a local rival named Michael O. Smith. Smith, twenty-one, had grown up in Cape Girardeau. As the bad blood between the two of them grew badder and badder, Smith finally decided it had reached the point of "kill or be killed."

Michael O. Smith knew where Childs lived. At 8:30 one April evening, he went to Childs's home on Bloomfield Road, armed with a Taurus .357 Magnum revolver. He was accompanied by his brother, Johnny E. "Pousie" Smith.

He walked up a set of wooden steps to the door of the apartment, knocked, and asked Childs to come outside to talk. He then descended the steps and waited.

Childs was at home with his roommate, twenty-two-year-old Artemus Ward. The two of them were entertaining their girlfriends, Hannah Fuller, twenty, and Abby Wharton, twenty-one. The four young people had been watching television and eating pizza. After Smith invited Childs outside, Childs and Ward slipped out the door. The two girls remained in the apartment.

Childs and Ward walked down the seven wooden steps to the yard. They faced the Smiths.

"How come you shot at me the other day?" Michael O. Smith asked.

"I didn't shoot at you," Childs protested. "I don't even know what you're talking about."

Without further discussion, Michael O. Smith pulled his gun and began firing. His first shot struck Childs in the gut near his navel. The second hit him in the chest, passing through the left lung and severing his aorta. Childs turned and tried to run up the steps. Smith kept firing, hitting him twice more in the shoulder and arm. Childs collapsed at the top of the steps, blood pouring from his mouth.

Michael O. Smith then turned the gun on Artemus Ward, who stood staring at him in shock. Smith knew Ward. They were cousins. They had grown up together. They had been friends before Ward started hanging out with Cameron Childs. As he looked down the gun barrel at Ward, Smith considered killing him, but finally concluded Ward would not tell on him. After all, they were friends. Michael O. Smith and his brother turned and ran off.

Smith had underestimated Artemus Ward. Sure, they had been friends, but so had Ward and Cameron Childs. Ward's sense of right and wrong told him that he owed it to his dead buddy to tell the police what had happened. When they arrived, he did so.

Once the investigation was complete, I charged Michael O. Smith with second-degree murder and armed criminal action, for committing a homicide with a firearm. Eleven months later, the FBI found him hiding in Springfield, Illinois, and arrested him. He was brought back to Cape Girardeau to face the charges.

I knew going into it that this trial would be a professional challenge. Artemus Ward was my star witness. I could not make the case without him. I could not win the case unless the jury found him believable, and I knew he would be lugging plenty of baggage with him to the witness stand.

At the preliminary hearing, Smith was represented by a veteran public defender named Renee Murphy from Farmington, Missouri. Her cross-examination was skillful. First, she got Artemus Ward to deny that he was a member of the Blood Stone Villains or that he had ever had anything to do with the Blood Stone Villains. Next, she showed Ward the autopsy photo of the arm of Cameron Childs and got Ward to admit that the tattoo of the letters *BSV* on Childs's arm stood for Blood Stone Villains. Finally, she asked him to raise his own shirt sleeve.

Lo and behold, he had the tattoo BSV on his own arm.

I had not known that little fact going into the hearing. It was an unpleasant discovery, one I would have preferred to make *before* I was sitting in the courtroom.

"So, you have a Blood Stone Villain tattoo on your own arm, don't you?" she said.

"No," Ward answered.

All of us in the courtroom were awed by the audacity of his answer. We had just seen the tattoo ourselves. It was like the Richard Pryor joke about the man caught in the very act of cheating on his wife who says to her, "Who are you going to believe, me or your lying eyes!"

"That's *not* a Blood Stone Villain tattoo on your arm?" Renee Murphy pressed.

"No, it stands for Thirteen Series Virus. You see, the first thing is not the letter *B*, but a 13. There's a space between the one and the three. It looks like a B. I can see where you'd think it was a B, but it's really a 13. Thirteen Series Virus."

Murphy stared at him. Sometimes silence can be an effective cross-examination technique.

"Okay," she said. "I'll bite. What does Thirteen Series Virus mean?"

"Nothing."

"Nothing? It must mean something, for it to be tattooed on your arm?"

"No, it's just something I did myself when I was fourteen. I was just goofing around."

This murder prosecution was imploding right in front of my eyes.

"No further questions," Renee Murphy announced.

I found out that day that a Perry Mason moment is not all it is cracked up to be when it is the lawyer on the other side who is experiencing it.

Since the burden of proof on the prosecutor at a preliminary hearing is met by merely showing probable cause, I did not lose the case at that point. Even though his credibility had been badly damaged, Ward's testimony that he had seen Michael O. Smith shoot Cameron Childs was sufficient evidence to get the case bound over to the circuit court level for trial. But just as Renee Murphy intended, I knew my case was in trouble. At trial, my burden of proof would be much heavier. I would need to prove the case beyond a reasonable doubt. The jury would be required to agree unanimously that Artemus Ward was believable. If even one juror had a reasonable doubt that Artemus Ward was telling the truth about seeing Michael O. Smith shoot Cameron Childs, Smith would get off scot-free.

This is where plea bargaining has its place in the criminal justice system. As she had hoped I would, I offered Renee Murphy a deal for her client. If Smith would plead guilty to voluntary manslaughter and armed criminal action, I would agree to a twenty-year sentence. It was a good thing for the people of my community because Smith would not get away with killing another human being, but would instead get a significant prison sentence. It was a good thing for him, though, because a murder conviction would have rendered him ineligible for parole until he had served 85 percent of his sentence. Had he rolled the dice and taken the case to trial and been hit with a murder conviction, he would have served at least twenty-seven years behind bars had the jury recommended a life sentence. As it was, he might get out of prison after serving eight years or so.

Michael O. Smith took the deal. I was spared the spectacle of watching Renee Murphy rip Artemus Ward to shreds in front of a jury. In the big picture, twenty years seemed adequate under the circumstances for the death of a drug-dealing gangster from Los Angeles.

Artemus Ward turned out to be a good guy. Since being a witness for the prosecution, he has held down regular jobs and was so proud of his first child that he even brought the baby by my office for me to admire. I have no doubt that Artemus was telling the truth about the shooting. As for the tattoo? Well, who knows?

But I have a bit of advice for prosecutors. Find out about the tattoos of a witness before putting that witness on the stand. It is much better for your blood pressure to discover bad news like that in the privacy of your own office rather than in open court in front of the whole world.

Luckless Lawyer

> If there were no bad people there would be no good lawyers.
>
> —Charles Dickens

Every time the brilliant and flamboyant trial lawyer Melvin Belli won a big case, he would proudly hoist a flag bearing a skull and crossbones above his law office. He won lots of cases, so the Jolly Roger flew often. You've got to admire that kind of spunk. Most lawyers lack not only Belli's trial skill, but also his sense of humor. Not surprisingly, they try to distance themselves from direct comparisons to pirates, sharks, or other unsavory predators.

By far the vast majority of lawyers I have met during my years practicing law are honorable people, both intelligent and high-minded. Most consider the practice of law a calling and a chance to serve other people. They are valued members of their communities, not only because of the work they do as attorneys, but also because of the time they spend on a wide assortment of efforts to improve the lot of mankind.

Of course, there are exceptions. The most egregious exceptions end up facing disbarment and jail time.

I have prosecuted many lawyers during my career, including several for driving while intoxicated, two for domestic assault, one for possession of a firearm while intoxicated, two for possession of marijuana, one for passing bad checks, one for shoplifting, one for forging a court file, one for statutory rape, and one for practicing law after his law license was suspended. There are a few others I fully expect to prosecute some day, depending upon how long I remain a prosecutor and how careless they become.

One especially memorable attorney-on-the-wrong-side-of-the-law case was the prosecution of W. Epaminondas Adrastus Blab. (This is not the lawyer's real name, by the way. Rather, it is an early pseudonym used by Samuel Clemens before he settled upon Mark Twain. Since he cast it aside, I am happy to use it here.) Before I graduated from law school, "Eppie" Blab was already a fixture in the legal community of Cape Girardeau, Missouri. Smart, suave, and charming, he acquired the nicknames "Fast Eppie" and "Fix" because he could allegedly fix anything for anybody. I guess those are good nicknames for a lawyer. Unsavory, yet highly marketable. On the whole they are not ones I would choose.

By the time I was working at the prosecutor's office, Blab was an older man, but still very successful. He handled many criminal cases in state, municipal, and federal courts. His nicknames bothered me tremendously, and I was always extremely careful not to make any attractive plea offers to his clients. I was determined he would never be able to justify his nicknames in any of *my* cases. In fact, the nickname "Fix" probably hurt him more than it helped him in cases against my office.

Blab's downfall came from a combination of drunk driving and organized crime. He had nothing to do with organized crime until the very end of his career. As you will see, his one brush with it was brief but explosive.

At 8:05 on a dark December night, two deputy United States marshals were transporting a federally protected witness to Cape Girardeau from St. Louis to be housed in secret as a part of the federal witness protection program. The witness was key to an investigation into one of the most dangerous organized crime gangs in St. Louis, the Moorish Science Temple. Members of the temple had been behind numerous murders in the metropolitan area. Several members were being prosecuted under federal racketeering statutes. The tension surrounding the cases was incredible.

Deputy marshals Kenny Schaefer and Skip Rutkowski were two of the "hot dogs" with the marshal's service. They were often given dangerous assignments. They were alert to every possible danger as they rode with their protected witness in a dark blue Chevrolet Impala down I-55 to Cape Girardeau. They had no intention of letting any harm come to the witness. They knew the most likely time for an assassination attempt was during the transportation of the witness from hideout to hideout or to and from the courthouse. Nothing was going to happen to him on their watch.

The federal agents were armed to the teeth and wired for trouble. They carried their standard-issue .357 Magnum handguns, plus a Whippet gun, which was a cut-down Remington 870 shotgun with a handgrip. Just in case, they also carried AR-15 Colt .223-caliber rifles. They would not lose their witness without putting up a tough fight. Anyone who messed with them was risking his life.

Deputy Marshal Schaefer was behind the wheel. He eased the big car onto the exit ramp at Cape Girardeau and cruised toward the stoplight at the intersection with Route K. Deputy Marshal Skip Rutkowski rode shotgun. The protected witness was in the backseat.

They stopped at the red light, many feet behind the car in front of them, allowing them room to maneuver if needed. Schaefer glanced in his rearview mirror. He spotted headlights bearing down upon them from behind. As he watched, it eventually became clear to him that the car driving straight toward them was not slowing down.

"Look out, he's going to hit us!" he yelled.

A second later, a huge crash enveloped their car. The back windshield shattered. The Impala was knocked forward thirty feet into the rear of the car in front of them. The violent jerk slammed Rutkowski's head into the dashboard even though he was wearing his seatbelt. The shotgun next to him bounced against his leg. Schaefer had braced himself to keep from eating the steering wheel.

In the backseat, the protected witness lay in the seat as the trunk of the car was crushed right up to the backseat. With growing terror, he realized that the killers from the Moorish Science Temple had caught up with him in spite of his federal protection.

Rutkowski's head spun. He felt as if he were taking "an eight count" in a boxing match. His ears were ringing. He did his best to shake off the cobwebs and leaped out of the car, gun in hand. He had a witness to protect.

Their government-issued sedan had just been rear-ended by a big, blue Cadillac Deville. The Cadillac had been going between fifty-five and seventy miles per hour when it crashed into them. Its driver had never even applied his brakes. It was a good way to disorientate the federal marshals before gunning them down.

The Cadillac was now rolling backward down the ramp. It veered off the roadway and stopped in the grass. Its driver leaped out, his face covered with blood. He glanced at Rutkowski and instead of shooting at him ran away across the grass toward I-55. Perhaps this was not an assassination attempt, after all. Rutkowski reluctantly abandoned his plan to put multiple bullets into the driver.

Rutkowski checked on the protected witness. He was okay, except for some glass in his eyes. Seeing that Schaefer was taking control of the witness, Rutkowski chased the man who had slammed into them.

"Stop!" he yelled.

The man picked up speed. Rutkowski chugged after him. The man was not fast. Rutkowski eventually caught him and threw him to the ground.

"You're not getting away," Rutkowski said.

"I thought I was still on the highway," the man babbled, trying to pull away from the marshal.

Rutkowski yanked him to his feet and walked him back toward the Impala. The man again tried to pull away. This time he kicked Rutkowski. The federal marshal then slammed him to the ground and handcuffed him. Disheveled and distraught, the man finally quit struggling.

The man turned out to be sixty-seven-year-old attorney W. Epaminondas Adrastus Blab.

He was in a fix.

It turned out that Blab had been driving with a blood-alcohol level of .13. He, too, had been driving down to Cape Girardeau from St. Louis. Despite his impaired condition, he had taken the correct exit. Unfortunately for him, he had been unprepared to stop for the red light. He had not been trying to kill a protected witness in an organized crime case. Far from it. He had simply been driving drunk.

The case came to my office. I assigned it to Assistant Prosecuting Attorney Kenny C. Hulshof. Blab ultimately pled guilty to drunk driving, careless and imprudent driving, and failure to wear a seatbelt. But that was not the last we heard of "Fast Eppie."

Blab practiced law for a few more years. Eventually federal authorities ran into him again. This time they caught him committing scoundrel-like behavior pertaining to the distribution of cocaine. The drug case was prosecuted in federal court, so it was not one of mine. Blab was ultimately sent to prison and disbarred. I have always wondered if Rutkowski and Schaefer drew the assignment of chauffeuring him to the federal penitentiary.

"Fast Eppie" had been a talented lawyer, but a combination of drugs, alcohol, and greed brought a sad ending to a long career. In the end, he had not been able to fix the most important thing of all—himself.

Embarrassing Defense

> Why is there always a secret singing
> When a lawyer cashes in?
> Why does the hearse horse snicker
> Hauling a lawyer away?
>
> —Carl Sandburg

The case of W. Epaminondas Adrastus Blab was not the weirdest attorney-as-defendant case ever pursued by my office. That honor goes to "The Case of the Embarrassing Defense." The lawyer involved was Thomas Jefferson Snodgrass. (Once again, this is not the lawyer's real name, but another early pseudonym discarded by Mark Twain.) This particular case involved the crime of indecent exposure; it is more commonly known in the sometimes coarse world of law enforcment as a "weenie-waver" case. Whatever you call the crime, it is a sad morality tale.

Snodgrass was a sixty-three-year-old lawyer embroiled in a nasty divorce. He and his wife handled their split-up the All-American way: each hired a private investigator. Hers, however, trumped his.

Her investigator learned that since the breakup, Thomas Jefferson Snodgrass had been directing some rather strange behavior toward an attractive twenty-three-year-old waitress who lived across the alley from him. At night, Snodgrass would position himself in front of a second-story window directly across from a window of her apartment. Whenever he could catch the young lady's attention, he would expose himself to her. This is said to be somewhat akin to the mating ritual of the red-butt monkeys of Argentina. I am assuming the monkeys have better success with their romantic endeavors, however, because the response of the young waitress was to notify the police that she was being stalked by a "Peeping Tom" across the street. It was certainly not the response Snodgrass had sought.

Indecent exposure cases demonstrate a fundamental difference between men and women. A woman is not thrilled by having a strange man display his genitals to her without an express invitation to do so. By contrast, virtually no man would call 9-1-1 if a woman across the street raised her shirt or skirt for him. Most men would scramble to find their cameras or rush across the street while being victimized in such a way. In fact, in all of my years as a prosecutor—and over one hundred cases of indecent exposure—I have never once seen a police report where a man complained about being flashed by a woman. All the defendants have been male. Had the tables been turned, Thomas Jefferson Snodgrass would certainly not have been complaining had his neighbor been giving him a peep show.

Detective Judy Gentry from the Cape Girardeau Police Department worked the Snodgrass case. Eventually, both she and the private investigator captured Snodgrass on videotape, exposing his well-aged genitalia to this girl young enough to be his granddaughter. One tape showed Snodgrass in a bathrobe, holding up a bottle of beer, toasting the girl with his beverage while he waved at her, in a manner of speaking. It left nothing to the imagination.

The case fell to Ian Sutherland to prosecute. Ian charged Snodgrass in the alternative with the misdemeanors of stalking and indecent exposure. Charging in the alternative meant that the jury could find the lawyer guilty of either offense, but not both. Since we had the videotapes of the incidents, this looked like a case that would never go to trial. All aspects of the case had been revealed.

We were wrong.

Much to our surprise, Snodgrass vigorously fought the charges. He pled not guilty and filed a motion for a change of venue. The case landed in Jefferson County, Missouri, where it went all the way to a jury trial in front of Associate Circuit Judge Carol Bader in Hillsboro. I sent Ian Sutherland to try the case. I had seen all of Snodgrass I cared to see.

The prosecution's case went smoothly. The girl testified about the man in the window. She described the whole incident as disgusting and frightening. The videotapes were played for the jury. The state rested.

Snodgrass's defense was creative. Snodgrass called Steve Robertson, a widely respected professional photographer, as an expert witness. Robertson testified that the video camera used by the police to catch Snodgrass in the act was equipped with a zoom lens. He pointed out that the particular part of the male anatomy shown in all its glory on the videotape had been so clearly visible on the television screen only because of the zoom lens. The zoom lens made it appear seven to ten times larger than real life. He maintained that the girl could not have seen the anatomical part from the place where she stood in the window of her own home without the aid of a zoom lens. Thus, there would have been no exposure, indecent nor otherwise. In short, the body part was too small to be seen from across the alley.

Prior to trial, Snodgrass endorsed the photographer as his expert witness. Going into the trial, Ian and I knew what was coming. We discussed this novel defense at length. We both came to the conclusion that had we been charged with indecent exposure, and had our only defense been that this particular part of our anatomy was too small to be seen, we would have thrown in the towel and pled guilty. You have to keep a proper perspective on things. These crimes were only misdemeanors, carrying merely county jail time or fines. A man has his reputation to maintain, after all.

Snodgrass, however, chose to unveil the embarrassing defense for the jury. Unfortunately for him, it did not stand up in court.

The judge did not let the photographer state all of his opinions for the jury. She ruled some irrelevant. After hearing the admissible evidence, the jury found Snodgrass guilty of stalking. He received a fine of one thousand dollars, the maximum fine possible for the offense.

When a lawyer in Missouri is convicted of a felony or of a misdemeanor involving moral turpitude, he will usually lose his license to practice law. So it went in this case. Snodgrass lost his law license as a result of the conviction. To this day, however, Thomas Jefferson Snodgrass insists he was wrongly convicted. He still claims he was set up by the private investigator, the young waitress, and his ex-wife. The jury, obviously, believed otherwise.

⚖

I recently told Buchanan County Circuit Judge Patrick Robb about "The Case of the Embarrassing Defense." He, in turn, told me about an indecent-exposure case he had handled during his years as a prosecutor. It seems every prosecutor has his favorite such case. Diabolical flashers must be running amok across the Show-Me State.

In Robb's case, an older man developed a fixation upon his twelve-year-old papergirl. He began lurking just inside his front door, waiting for the tantalizing plop of the daily paper hitting the step. When it sounded, he would rush outside, stark naked, grab his newspaper, leer at the girl, and dash back inside. Unappreciative of his idea of a tip, she told her parents, who called the police. Prosecutor Robb slapped him with an indecent-exposure charge.

The defense lawyer made a full-scale assault upon Robb's sense of mercy. It turned out the man was afflicted with cancer and was not expected to live long.

"He's going to die soon, anyway," the lawyer argued. "Be a good sport and dismiss this case. What's the use of prosecuting him, anyway?"

Eventually, Robb agreed and dismissed it. He would let the man go to his grave with a clean criminal record.

The old man resumed his scandalous behavior a month later. The police were called, and they set up surveillance and caught the whole mad dash-and-flash on videotape. Robb charged him again. Once more, the glib lawyer came to Robb's office to plead his client's case.

"Come on," he urged. "My client's dying. What does the State gain by prosecuting him?"

"I believe I've heard that one before," Robb said. "Look, your client violated our plea agreement. He was supposed to *die*. Doesn't a binding plea agreement mean anything to him? No, the girl and her parents are upset. I'm not dismissing it this time."

A couple of weeks later, the attorney returned to Robb's office and dropped his client's obituary onto Robb's desk.

"There," he said. "Satisfied?"

Robb dismissed the case.

Which brings to mind the great line in Clarence Darrow's autobiography, *The Story of My Life*: "All men have the emotion to kill; when they strongly dislike someone they involuntarily wish he was dead. I have never killed anyone, but I have read some obituary notices with great satisfaction."

Green-Speckled Coffee

Perjury is a tough rap to prove.
                        —Richard M. Nixon

Perjury in a civil case is rarely prosecuted.
                        —Monica Lewinsky

I felt a bit provoked by Monica Lewinsky and various apologists for President Bill Clinton when they publicly claimed that perjury cases are never prosecuted. People who did not know better made this assertion while arguing that the investigation of the president for lying under oath during a deposition was politically motivated. They said Special Prosecutor Ken Starr never would have pursued the matter had the suspect not been the president of the United States. Now, I agree that Starr's investigation reeked of politics. A professional prosecutor never discusses an unfiled criminal case in the media, and his office leaked information like old-school politicians doing a hatchet job on an opponent. But the suspect was the most prominent politician in the country. Of course the case had political overtones. Nevertheless, the claim that perjury cases are never prosecuted was simply not true. At the time the impeachment brouhaha was enveloping Bill Clinton, I had personally prosecuted over twenty perjury cases in my medium-sized Missouri county.

Perjury, of course, is lying under oath in an official proceeding about a material fact in the case. It is a very serious crime. Our legal system could not work if perjury were allowed to run rampant. The entire system is based upon the premise that each side in a dispute will come to court and present its side of the case. The judge and jury will decide the facts and apply the law. The side that should win will prevail. The entire system falls apart if either

139

side can get away with presenting perjured testimony, thereby causing the verdict to be based upon a foundation of lies.

When I was first elected prosecuting attorney, I sent a letter to every judge and lawyer in the county. I encouraged them to let me know when they encountered a case of perjury in a matter they were handling. I urged them to report directly to me so I could make sure any complaint was thoroughly investigated and vigorously prosecuted.

One of the lawyers who took me up on my pledge was Richard G. Steele, a prominent civil trial lawyer. He referred to my office the most interesting perjury case I ever prosecuted: "The Case of the Green-Speckled Coffee."

⚖

Now, the *green-speckled* coffee was not the most disgusting coffee I ever heard about during my career as a prosecutor. That distinction goes to the thick brown sludge belonging to Patrolman Rick Fehr of the Cape Girardeau Police Department.

Fehr arrested a drunk one night and placed him in the front seat of his patrol car to take him to the station. As they cruised down the road, the drunk spotted Fehr's Styrofoam coffee cup on the dashboard and grabbed it. Before Fehr could protest, the drunk took a big gulp. What the man did not know was that Fehr, a tobacco-chewer, had been using the coffee cup as a spittoon throughout the evening. The syrupy liquid in the cup was brown and wet, but, well, it was not 100 percent pure Colombian coffee.

"Agggghhh!" the drunk exclaimed. "That's the *worst* coffee I ever tasted!"

Fehr said nothing. He did not want the truth to unsettle the stomach of his passenger. He was the one who would be forced to clean up the squad car if the drunk could not take the truth.

No, the green-speckled coffee was not the most revolting coffee I had ever heard of. It was, however, the most lethal.

⚖

The case began as a civil matter between Isabella Hooker, fifty-four, and her estranged husband, John Hooker. They had been divorced over a year. John was now living alone in his ranch-style duplex on a scenic roadway called Cape Rock Drive.

As the weeks went by, John Hooker, a healthy man when he and his wife split, began to feel unwell. He developed stomach problems and numbness in certain parts of his body. He suffered headaches and nausea. His doctors were perplexed. As time went by, his symptoms worsened.

John Hooker wore glasses. He normally did not wear them in the mornings, however, when he went through the ritual of fixing his morning coffee.

One morning he *did* put on his glasses, though, and what he saw in his jar of Folgers Classic Decaf alarmed him. Green speckles nestled among the rich brown crystals. Puzzled, he took them to his divorce lawyer, Richard G. Steele, who provided them to a chemist for analysis. The green speckles proved to be rat poison.

John Hooker was aghast. He had been dosing himself with rat poison every morning when he made his coffee. Needless to say, he immediately suspected his ex-wife as the culprit, but he had no solid proof. Nevertheless, he obtained a court order to keep her away from him and out of his house. He also changed his locks and installed a surveillance video camera triggered by a motion detector. Shortly thereafter, he eased his troubled mind with a trip to Cancun with his new girlfriend.

While John Hooker was out of town, an intruder entered his house. She was caught on videotape making her excursion through the home. When she reached the kitchen, she looked into his refrigerator and leafed through the mail lying on his kitchen table. She walked through the kitchen and disappeared off camera through a door to the garage, returning a few minutes later. (The car was not damaged on this occasion, but in a previous incident, an unknown intruder had entered the garage and scratched John Hooker's car with a nail or key.) The trespasser caught on tape this time was none other than Isabella Hooker. It was impossible to view the tape and fail to recognize her.

When John Hooker returned from vacation he watched the videotape of his estranged wife traipsing through his home. Outraged, he took it to Richard G. Steele. The timing could not have been better for Steele because a court hearing had just been scheduled for the purpose of determining whether the temporary order barring Isabella Hooker from entering John Hooker's home should be extended into a permanent order. Isabella Hooker and her lawyer were claiming the order should not be extended because she had never trespassed upon John Hooker's property nor harassed him in any way. Their position was that the temporary order should never have been issued in the first place because the allegations were, in the words of her lawyer, "unfounded."

Steele knew the tape would be invaluable at the hearing. And it would be a surprise because he was not required to disclose it to the other side prior to the hearing, since the discovery process had not yet kicked in.

Richard G. Steele is a lawyer's lawyer. He is intelligent, eloquent, and always thoroughly prepared. It was almost overkill to have a lawyer of his skill handling the hearing over the order of protection. Armed with that videotape, the worst lawyer in the county could have enjoyed a Perry Mason moment.

The hearing took place in front of Associate Circuit Judge Peter L. Statler. Steele startled everyone in the courtroom by calling Isabella Hooker as his first witness. It is always a shock to be called as a witness for the other side. Isabella Hooker must have been extremely surprised.

Steele asked her if she had ever "molested, maligned, annoyed or troubled" his client since their separation. She admitted letting the air out of his tires on one occasion and putting nails under his tires on another.

He asked if she had ever gone into John Hooker's home without John's permission. She admitted coming to his house when she thought he was not home, opening the door, and stepping inside. She claimed that when she heard a television playing, she changed her mind about going inside and left immediately. Under Steele's questioning she was adamant that she had merely stepped *one foot* into the house. Unaware she had been caught on tape, and of the ease with which Steele would prove she was lying, she boldly and confidently committed perjury. No, she insisted, she only took *one step* inside the house, but immediately turned and left. She denied going further inside. She denied opening the refrigerator. She denied going into the garage.

After she testified, Steele presented testimony from John Hooker and the technician who had installed the video camera. The tape was played. Not surprisingly, Judge Statler decided to extend the order of protection.

When Steele referred the perjury case to my office I was delighted to get it. Ian Sutherland and I did some legal research and considered charging Isabella Hooker with attempted murder, but we decided we simply could not prove beyond a reasonable doubt that she was the scoundrel who had put the rat poison in the coffee jar. Other people had access to the home. She vehemently denied doing it. It was one of those instances where you felt the suspect *probably* committed the crime, but the proof was insufficient.

The perjury offense, however, was another matter. We were certain we could prove she had lied on the witness stand when she claimed she had only stepped one foot into his house on the day she was videotaped going through his house, opening his refrigerator, and looking through his mail. Not only did we have the tape, we had also located a locksmith with damning information. Isabella Hooker had contacted him after John Hooker had changed his locks. She had claimed she still lived with her husband and was locked out of the house. The bamboozled locksmith let her in and made her a key.

I was surprised when Isabella Hooker and her lawyer decided to take her perjury case to trial. It looked like an open-and-shut case to me. Ian and I tried it together.

The jury heard the testimony, watched the tape, and rather quickly found Isabella Hooker guilty of perjury. The defense waived jury sentencing, meaning that the issue of punishment would be completely up to the judge.

The proper punishment was a difficult decision for Circuit Judge John W. Grimm. On the one hand, Isabella Hooker deserved to go to prison for lying under oath in court. Shipping her to the penitentiary would send a strong message to other would-be perjurers. On the other hand, she had come across as a pathetic creature. Her lawyer portrayed her as a woman who had never done anything wrong in her life but became so distraught when her marriage ended that she went off the deep end. She came across as a somewhat frumpy middle-aged woman whose husband had dumped her for a younger woman. This pitiful image elicited the sympathy of both the judge and the prosecutors. Judge Grimm followed my recommendation and sentenced her to five years in prison, but suspended the execution of the sentence and placed her on supervised probation for five years. He also imposed a five-thousand-dollar fine, which she was forced to pay out of her own pocket.

I had hoped the case would send a strong message to the public that if you commit perjury you will pay a price. Maybe it did. Maybe not. To my mind, the clearer message is that you should wear your glasses when you fix your instant coffee in the morning, and that you should never, under any circumstances, drink green-speckled coffee. It calls to mind something Jean Rostand once said: "Never feel remorse for what you have thought about your wife; she has thought much worse things about you."

Homicidal Energizer Bunny

A prosecutor hopes and expects to be a judge,
and after that he will aspire to be governor,
then senator, and President, in their regular
turn. To accomplish this noble ambition he
must in each position give the people what
they want, and more; and there are no rungs
in the ladder of fame upon which lawyers can
plant their feet like the dead bodies of
their victims.

—Clarence Darrow

I've always considered final summation the most
important part of the trial for the lawyer.
It's the climax of the case, where the lawyer
has his last and best opportunity to convince
the jury of the rightness of his cause. . . .
In fact, before the first witness at a trial
has even been called, I've usually prepared my
summation to the jury. As soon as I learn the
strengths and weaknesses of my case I begin to
work on how I'm going to argue these strengths
and what I'm going to say in response to the
opposition's attacks on the weaknesses.

—Vincent Bugliosi

One of the unavoidable consequences of being a prosecutor is that you come face to face with a truly evil person every now and then. Fortunately, they are few and far between. While prosecuting the criminals of your community, often multiple generations of the same families, you quickly realize that the vast majority of them come nowhere close to deserving the epithet *evil*. Most committed their crimes because they were stupid, drunk, drugged-out, mentally unbalanced, or temporarily overwhelmed by passion, lust, or greed. By the time they appear in court, almost all of them accept that they made a mistake and are willing to face the consequences. Most really believe they are going to change their lives for the better. Many actually do.

Every now and then, though, you run across a sociopath, someone genuinely evil, who takes pleasure in hurting other people. Typically, a sociopath has enjoyed causing pain to others since childhood, and his pattern of selfish and cold-blooded behavior has existed for years. One local murderer prosecuted by one of my predecessors liked to play with cats as a child. His idea of a good time with a kitty, though, was to bury the cat up to its neck and then run over its head with a lawnmower. He graduated to human beings and began stalking an elderly woman who lived in the neighborhood. For several nights, he tapped on her windows and made noises to scare her. When this no longer sufficiently excited him, he broke into her home, terrorized her, and stabbed her to death.

As a prosecutor, when you recognize that someone is a true menace to society, you feel the weight on your shoulders of life-and-death litigation. You know that if you fail to put this monster away, he will almost certainly hurt or kill another human being in the future. You feel a responsibility to that unknown future victim to keep the killer from showing up at his or her door. The sense that an innocent life is at stake motivates the prosecutor to know the law of evidence better than anyone in the courtroom, to agonize over just the right words for the opening statement and closing argument, to spend hours working up cross-examination questions likely to be effective in discrediting the defendant, and to literally abandon family and friends during the time it takes to adequately prepare for trial.

Over the years, my family has learned the hard truth that when I am in what my daughters call my "trial mode" in the days leading up to a trial and throughout the trial itself, they are probably better off avoiding me. A prosecutor who is the last thing standing between a sociopath and the streets is not in a proper mood to shop for Barbie dolls or listen attentively to piano practice.

The pressure of getting justice is focused squarely on him until the verdict is read and the word *guilty* lifts that weight from his shoulders.

A prosecutor who is not willing to set aside everything else in his life when trying a case against someone who is truly evil has no business being a prosecutor, at least not in a violent-crime unit. The stakes are simply too high.

As the prosecutor for a medium-sized midwestern community, I prosecute five or six sociopaths every year, usually for homicides, rapes, or assaults. When I think about those cold-blooded predators, one who sticks out in my mind is the villain in "The Case of the Homicidal Energizer Bunny."

⚖

Russell Earl Bucklew may be the most evil person I have ever prosecuted. He gunned down Michael H. Sanders, age twenty-seven, a virtual stranger, in Sanders's own home in front of his two sons, ages six and four. As with many murders, it was over a woman.

Her name was Stephanie Lovitt. She was an exotic dancer but had taken a break from topless dancing to work at a ceramics factory. She was twenty-one years old, blonde and shapely. She had been the girlfriend of Russell Earl Bucklew, also twenty-seven. He had lived with her in her mother's home for almost a year, but then he and Stephanie moved into a mobile home with Stephanie's two daughters by a previous marriage. Within a few months, Stephanie decided to break up. Sometimes, as the song says, breaking up is hard to do.

When she told him her plans, Bucklew refused to accept the fact that she no longer wanted to see him. After hours of arguing, she finally drove him to his parents' home in Troy, Missouri, a bit west of St. Louis. She dumped him off, telling him in no uncertain terms that it was over. She drove back to Cape Girardeau, thinking she was rid of him.

Russell Earl Bucklew had never been violent with her before. She had no idea what lay in store.

A week after the breakup, Stephanie came home from the grocery store about 6:45 P.M. When she and her two girls entered the mobile home, Bucklew was waiting for her. He grabbed her and dragged her to the bedroom. He threw her onto the bed, leaped on top of her, and held a knife to her face, nicking her chin. Over and over he insisted that she take him back. She told him to get lost and fought to get him off. Finally, he punched her one last time and stormed out of her home. Stephanie gathered up her children and hurried to her car. She immediately reported the assault to the police. Afraid to go back home, she ended up staying the night with a friend from the ceramics factory, Michael H. Sanders.

Sanders, a nice guy, let Stephanie and her girls stay with him and his two sons. At first, they were not romantically involved. He was just a friend from work, giving her a safe place to stay, a place where Russell Earl Bucklew would never think to look for her.

The next day, at work, Stephanie got a phone call from Bucklew. He vowed to kill her two children in front of her, to cut them up while making her watch, and to kill her afterward. Later that day, Stephanie got an order of protection from a judge, requiring Bucklew to stay away from her. Of course, an order of protection is just a piece of paper to a man contemplating murder.

For her own safety, Stephanie kept staying at the home of Michael Sanders. Michael, who knew little about guns, borrowed a shotgun. He kept it in the bedroom closet. One day he took it outside to try to unload it, but then accidentally discharged it in front of Stephanie. Sheepishly, he put it back into the closet with the empty shell still in its chamber.

A week later, Bucklew struck again. This time Stephanie had returned to her mobile home to get some of her things. She left her two daughters waiting in the car while she ran inside. While she was packing, Bucklew burst into the mobile home and grabbed her from behind in a choke hold. He throttled her into unconsciousness. When she awoke, she was tied to the bed by black plastic cables and metal dog chains. He had cut off her shirt with a knife. Over the course of several hours, he alternately threatened her and begged her to take him back. He tried to force her to have sex with him, but she refused, claiming she would rather die. At one point she slipped out of the chains and dashed out of the trailer, but he caught her, punched her, and then banged her head against the concrete steps until she again lost consciousness. When she awoke, she was once again tied up. Bucklew had moved her daughters from the car into the mobile home.

She was eventually able to persuade Bucklew that in spite of everything, she still might consider being his girlfriend if he would just let her go. She claimed that one of her girls was sick and needed medicine. Eventually, he untied her and drove them to a pharmacy. She convinced him that if he would just leave, she would drop the charges she had pressed against him, and they could start all over again. She promised to meet him a week later at a gas station near St. Louis.

After he left, she immediately reported this latest assault to the police. I typed up a warrant for his arrest. The judge set the bond at $100,000. But no one knew where Bucklew had gone. He had disappeared.

By this point, Stephanie was afraid for her life. She was still staying with Michael Sanders. She did not know where Bucklew was hiding, but Bucklew did not know where *she* was, either.

During the time Michael Sanders gave her sanctuary, Stephanie and Michael fell in love. Things suddenly seemed to be going better for her.

Meanwhile, she still went to work at the ceramics factory every day. That was how Russell Earl Bucklew found her the last time.

He had been living with relatives near Troy, Missouri. On the day he killed Michael Sanders he armed himself with two guns, two knives, two sets of handcuffs, duct tape, rubber gloves, and extra ammunition, and drove his nephew's car, a gray Honda, to the place where he knew Stephanie would be picking up her paycheck at a particular time. He then followed Stephanie to Michael Sanders's home.

When Stephanie arrived, Michael Sanders met her at the door. The two of them went inside with the four children, ages six, four, two, and two. They locked the door.

Minutes later, Bucklew was at the front door. Sanders peered from the kitchen window and saw him. He hurried to the bedroom to get the shotgun.

Meanwhile, the six-year-old boy, trying to be helpful, and assuming that the man at the door was a friend of his daddy's, unlocked the door. I do not know how long you have to be a prosecutor before you lose the special sadness that comes from seeing anyone's kindness and trust, especially a child's, turned against him. I have not reached that point. My heart still goes out to that boy every time I think about what happened next.

Bucklew barged in, a gun in each hand. As soon as he spotted Michael Sanders coming down the hallway from the bedroom, shotgun in hand, Bucklew opened fire. He shot Michael Sanders four times. Michael fell to the floor. The shotgun discharged harmlessly as he fell, blowing a hole in the wall.

Bucklew had been advancing up the hallway as he kept shooting Michael Sanders. Michael was still conscious when Bucklew arrived next to him and pointed the gun at Michael's head.

Michael said, "I'm down, man, I'm cool. I'm down."

Stephanie pushed herself between Bucklew and Sanders. She begged Bucklew not to shoot him again. Bucklew grabbed her and dragged her to the kitchen. He pistol-whipped and handcuffed her. He then dragged her to his

car and drove away with her. A neighbor got a good look at the Honda and
called 9-1-1.

As they sped away, he boasted that Michael Sanders would bleed to death
before any ambulance could arrive. He drove her around the rural part of the
county for two to three hours, stopping once to rape her in the backseat of
the car. Eventually, he headed north on I-55, toward St. Louis.

Missouri State Trooper James Hedrick, a young officer, heard a broadcast
to be on the lookout for the Honda. He spotted it at 10:30 P.M. in Jefferson
County, Missouri, heading north on I-55. He began following it, radioing for
backup.

More and more patrol cars joined the pursuit. They chased Bucklew at
speeds up to eighty miles per hour. Some troopers drove in front of Bucklew,
lights flashing, warning motorists ahead of them to get out of the way.

Inside the car, Bucklew began telling Stephanie about one of his favorite
Bon Jovi songs. The lyrics spoke of going down in a "blaze of glory" in a gunfight. He told her he planned to shoot it out with the cops, taking as many of
them with him as possible.

Eventually, the police stopped him on the ramp leading from Highway 270
onto Highway 40 in St. Louis. Hedrick's patrol car blocked the road in front
of Bucklew. Other cars on the sides and rear hemmed him in. He was
trapped. He tried to ram Hedrick's car, but his Honda was too small to budge
the big squad car.

Bucklew sat behind the steering wheel of the Honda, brandishing a gun in
each hand. He put one gun to Stephanie's head and pointed the other at
Hedrick.

Hedrick positioned himself near the back of his patrol car, pointing his
handgun at Bucklew. From a distance of twelve feet, he saw Bucklew aiming
at him. They exchanged fire. Hedrick fired three shots in his first burst,
moved to the right, and fired four more shots, keeping them low and to the
driver's side to avoid hitting the hostage.

Bucklew's left-handed return fire missed Hedrick, but with the gun in his
right hand, he shot Stephanie Lovitt through the left thigh.

While Hedrick and Bucklew were shooting, another trooper, James Gau,
used the butt of his shotgun to smash out the Honda's front passenger window. Gau reached in and dragged Stephanie through the window to safety.

Two of Hedrick's shots hit Russell Earl Bucklew. Despite being shot in the
head and chest, Bucklew survived. The glass windshield had slowed the veloc-
ity of the head shot to the point where the bullet did not penetrate his skull.

He lived to face the death penalty.

Over my lifetime, I have vacillated about the death penalty. In my high school years I was in favor of it but had not really given the issue much thought. During my undergraduate college years, I decided I was against it on the simple notion that it was wrong to kill, and two wrongs did not make a right. During my law school years, however, as I immersed myself in the history and reasoning of the law, I swung around again to believe in the usefulness of the death penalty, this time for a good reason: the death penalty can save lives.

I have read the tracts against the death penalty, including the well-written *Dead Man Walking* by Sister Helen Prejean. In fact, I read her book during the evenings while I was preparing for a death-penalty trial. But Prejean and those of like mind do not put enough weight on the deterrent effect of the death penalty.

The death penalty saves lives.

Sure, it will not stop a crazed killer like Charles Manson or Richard Speck or Ted Bundy. But the threat of the death penalty can save a victim's life in the right type of crime with the right type of criminal.

If murder, rape, kidnapping, and robbery were all punishable by the same sentence, life in prison, the criminal would have no reason to spare the life of his victim once he accomplished his underlying crime. The kidnapper who snatches the millionaire's child for ransom will have no incentive to keep the child alive if he knows he will get life in prison whether he kills the child or not. The robber who holds up the bank president or convenience store clerk at gunpoint will have no reason not to pull the trigger if he figures he will get life in prison either way. The rapist who enters his victim's home in the middle of the night knows there is less risk of being caught if he kills his victim. If he leaves her alive, she may identify him later, particularly if she has glimpsed his face. Yet, when a state has the death penalty for murder, some killers who plan out their crimes in advance come up with plans that leave the victims alive, precisely to avoid the risk of being executed.

No, the death penalty does not deter *all* killers. But if it deters one—if *one* innocent kidnapping victim's life is saved—it is worth having. You simply need to make sure that safeguards are in place to ensure that only a truly guilty person is executed and also that the execution takes place swiftly enough that it serves as a forceful deterrent to others. If a person thinks he will hang around on death row for ten or twenty years, the deterrent effect of the death penalty is lost.

It did not take me long to decide that I was going to seek the death penalty for Russell Earl Bucklew. Committing a murder during the course of a kidnapping and rape is a death-penalty offense, and the evidence of his guilt was overwhelming.

What I did not know then was that Russell Earl Bucklew was not through committing crimes. Three months after being confined in the Cape Girardeau County jail, he got access to a telephone in the jail and called Stephanie's mother. He asked where Stephanie was hiding and railed on and on about how she should not have cheated on him.

Stephanie's mother said, "You don't *kill* for any reason."

Bucklew answered, "I do. I did. And I will."

"I'm going to watch you fry," Stephanie's mother sobbed.

"No, I'm going to watch *you* die!" Bucklew vowed.

Shortly after making the phone call, Bucklew became the first person in fifteen years to escape from the Cape Girardeau County jail. He hid in a trash bag and was carried out to the dumpster by a trustee. Since then, the jail has purchased a trash compactor.

On the day Bucklew escaped, Stephanie and her mother went into hiding. The mother moved to a motel, afraid to stay in her own home. Whenever she needed clothing, she would call the police. They would meet her at her home and walk through it before she entered, making sure Bucklew was not there.

Officers assured her that Bucklew, facing murder charges, would be long gone. She knew better. He had told her he would watch her die. She had no doubt he meant to keep his promise.

Two days after his escape, she returned briefly to her home with her fiancé, a male nurse who had recently suffered a stroke. She needed to pick up a few things to take back to the motel. As usual, a police officer checked the house before she entered, then left.

He had not checked the house quite thoroughly enough.

When Stephanie's mother walked past the pantry, the door flew open, and Bucklew emerged. He hit her on the head with a hammer. She screamed. Her boyfriend came running and faced Bucklew, who held the hammer in one hand and a knife in the other. Bucklew hit him four times on the head with the hammer. While they struggled, the injured woman escaped out the back door. Her bleeding fiancé followed her moments later.

Bucklew then ran to a stolen truck and took off.

Thirty minutes later Deputy Richard Walker of the Cape Girardeau County Sheriff's Department spotted Bucklew and pulled him over. Bucklew jumped from the truck. As Bucklew started to flee, Walker pumped his shotgun, pointed it at him, and in true Clint Eastwood fashion warned him that unless he put his hands up and lay down on the ground, he would shoot him. Perhaps the sound of the shotgun being pumped contributed to his decision, but Bucklew apparently changed his mind about going down in a "blaze of glory." He surrendered without further incident.

Professor Irving Younger, who was not only an accomplished trial lawyer, but also a judge and law professor, often said that someone who wants to be an outstanding trial lawyer should read the classics in literature. A trial lawyer needs to be a good storyteller. He needs to be able to keep the attention of the jury as he tells them the facts of the case in opening statement, and as he urges them to see the facts *his way* during closing argument. The opening statement should be structured in a format that is both informative and suspenseful. The closing argument must be persuasive and memorable. By studying Dostoyevesky, Tolstoy, Twain, Dickens, and other great writers, one can perfect the art of storytelling. Reading transcripts of effective closing arguments by other prosecutors and lawyers is also great preparation. While stealing someone else's words constitutes plagiarism in publishing, it is good lawyering in the courtroom.

I spent a great deal of time working on my closing argument in the Bucklew case. It is a sobering thing to ask twelve jurors to take the life of another human being. When the time came to deliver my final summation, the jury had already found him guilty of murder, kidnapping, rape, burglary, and armed criminal action. Now the jurors were deciding punishment. I looked into their eyes as I spoke to them:

> It's a cardinal principle of law, a cardinal principle of justice, that the punishment should fit the crime. This crime was the ultimate crime: the first degree murder of Michael Sanders. It would be hard to image a more premeditated murder. This man equipped himself with two guns, at least thirty-four bullets, two knives, two sets of handcuffs, duct tape, rubber gloves, drove an hour and a half to the scene of the crime, waited another thirty minutes putting the final touches to the plan, and then went in and executed a man in his own home in front of his own children in front of the woman he loved, and then kidnapped and raped the woman. This is the ultimate crime and it deserves the ultimate punishment. The punishment should fit the crime. I'm asking you by your verdict today to send a message to jilted ex-boyfriends who are contemplating stalking and killing their ex-girlfriend and the girlfriend's new boyfriend that if you carry out a plan like that, you *will* get the death penalty.

A few minutes later, I came to my Energizer Bunny analogy. It was based upon a television advertisement where a stuffed bunny rabbit powered by Energizer batteries just keeps going, no matter what happens to it. I had debated long and hard whether I should use the analogy. *Calling a murderer an Energizer Bunny?* Perhaps I would sound a bit too clever for my own good. I certainly didn't want to trivialize the seriousness of the moment. Neverthe-less, when writing my closing argument during the weeks leading up to the trial, I finally decided that the facts of the case fit the analogy so well that it made my point more vividly than anything else I could say.

Looking at the jurors, I decided that they would indeed hear the Energizer Bunny portion of my carefully prepared closing argument.

> As long as this man breathes a breath of air he is a danger to other human beings. He's already shown a willingness and capability to track down and terrorize and traumatize and hurt whomever he happens to be mad at at that particular time. He has shown that like some homici-dal and bloodthirsty Energizer Bunny he just keeps on coming. You can shoot him, you can jail him, you can lock him up, but he'll just keep on coming with any weapon at his disposal, whether it's a gun, a knife or a hammer. He just keeps on coming, wanting to cause hurt to whomever he's mad at at the time.

I then turned to the "blaze of glory" lyrics. Knowing I would refer to them during the closing argument, I had made sure they were discussed during Stephanie's testimony.

> There's a song that goes, "I'm a six-gun lover. I'm a candle in the wind. Yeah, I'm a wanted man." The song ends, "I'm going down in a blaze of glory." And that's what this man saw himself as, a six-gun lover going down in a blaze of glory, a wanted man going down in a blaze of glory. That's how he saw himself. He didn't see himself as a father to his son. And he didn't see himself as a responsible person who cared about or thought about anybody other than his selfish miserable self.

I then directed the attention of the jury to the victim, making a contrast between the two men.

> Michael Sanders has been dead now for over a year. In the last moments of his life he was trying to protect the young woman he had fallen in love with. He was trying to protect his home. He was trying to

protect his children. He had shooed and shushed those children to a bedroom behind him trying to get them to an area where they would be safe. He was thinking of his children in the last moments of his life. Michael Sanders was trying to give sanctuary to a friend from work with whom he had fallen in love and with whom he was looking forward to a life together. He was trying to help someone in the last moments of his life. He was in the sanctity of his own home with the children he loved and with the woman he had fallen in love with. And the last moments of his life, because of this man, ended up being looking at this man over the end of a gun barrel as this man was shooting him again and again and again and again. The last moments of the life of Michael Sanders were intense pain as he felt a shot hitting him in the chest and in the right leg, as he felt a shot hitting his elbow and arm. He had to be feeling intense pain. The last moments of his life were falling to the ground and losing his dignity by begging for his own life when Russell Bucklew stood over him pointing a gun down at him. The last moments of his life were hearing her screams and hearing the screams of her little children as the blood was flowing out of his body. And you saw from the bloodstains that the last moments of his life would have been crawling, trying to go out of that room while the blood was pouring from his body.

I paused before concluding:

What Russell Bucklew wanted was to go out in a blaze of glory. All Michael Sanders wanted to do was create a happy home for his children and Stephanie and her children. It's ironic that Michael Sanders ended up being the one going out in a blaze of glory—unwanted glory for him.

The jury returned a death verdict against Russell Earl Bucklew. His conviction was affirmed on appeal, and he awaits execution by lethal injection.

⚖

Our local newspaper carried a front-page color photograph of the prosecutor delivering his closing argument to the jury. When the photo was snapped, I was holding up the shotgun Michael Sanders had ineffectually used in his attempt to protect his home. In the photo, the trial judge, Frank Conley, can be seen behind me. He happened to be blinking when the photo was taken. One of my friends, a prankster with a notorious sense of humor, used a computer program to alter the front page, changing the headline

"Bucklew Guilty of All Charges" to his new and improved version: "Trial Judge Snoozes As Bucklew Loses."

Contrary to Clarence Darrow's cynical comment about prosecutors seeking the death penalty to advance their own political careers, I can honestly say that I never felt even an inkling of political pressure to seek a death sentence in the Bucklew case nor in any other. I have only sought it when I believed that the facts and the law justified it. Sometimes the judge and jury have agreed with me. Sometimes they have not.

Bucklew is one of four men against whom I have gotten a death sentence. So far, only one has been executed: Gary Lee Roll. Roll murdered a mother and her two sons in a robbery at their home at 31 North Henderson one dark November night. Roll had planned to rob one of the sons, a seventeen-year-old drug dealer. The plan was to steal his marijuana and cash. When the boy recognized Roll, however, Roll, a military veteran, slaughtered the young drug dealer, plus his forty-four-year-old mother and his twenty-two-year old mentally handicapped brother.

At the time Gary Lee Roll was put to death, Missouri's practice was to administer the lethal injection at one minute past midnight. As the prosecutor, I was invited to attend the execution.

Would you want to go?

I decided against it.

For one thing, I was not sure that the vision of him dying was something I wanted to add to my memory bank. He was a cold-blooded killer and deserved the death penalty. But I did not particularly want to watch it happen.

Also, as strange as it may seem, I bore kind thoughts toward the family members of Gary Lee Roll. His mother was a good person. So was his brother. I had met them during the course of the prosecution. I had cross-examined them when they were called as defense witnesses. I felt my attendance at the execution might be a slap in the face, as if I were gloating in some way. I was not gloating. Far from it. I had done my job. I had followed the law. I was pleased and proud to have gotten the death penalty when it was so well deserved. I had been an instrument of justice. But I was not gloating.

I went to bed about 11:00 that night, knowing that Gary Lee Roll had but one hour to live. As I lay in bed it occurred to me that it was much like I had fired a gun six years earlier. The bullet had been tearing through space all this time, like a comet, heading for Gary Lee Roll in his bunk on death row. My bullet was about to strike its victim in just one hour. A killing I had started by making the decision to seek the death penalty was about to come full cycle with the death of a human being.

Talk about premeditation. I had deliberated many hours over whether I should seek the death penalty.

I lay silently in the bed. My wife was next to me, sleeping. I lay awake the entire hour. Midnight came. Somewhere many miles away Gary Lee Roll was being stuck with the needle. I watched the glowing orange numerals of the bedside clock change from one minute to the next. Soon, I knew Gary Lee Roll had to be dead. I felt no different. I felt no remorse. He had made the choice to take the lives of three innocent people. The legal system had held him accountable under the laws of the State of Missouri. I had done what I had to do. Shortly after midnight I fell asleep.

I woke up refreshed and recharged the next day, ready to face another crop of scoundrels. I have never once regretted my role in the death of this triple-murderer. Likewise, I look forward to hearing that Russell Earl Bucklew has breathed his last breath on the day of his execution. The world will be a safer place once he departs it.

Prancing Mare

> I thought I would work in the district attorney's office for about a year and a half, and at the end of that time I would go into private practice and become a great trial lawyer. So I worked sixteen hours a day for the first five years, and ended up by remaining eighteen years, often working until midnight at least five nights a week.
>
> —Earl Warren

I was working in my office late one afternoon when I got a phone call from Deputy John Rich. He was calling from a crime scene, seeking advice from the prosecutor about whether or not he should collect a particular bit of evidence.

"I'm hoping you'll say I don't have to collect it," he confided.

Calls like this are commonplace. A conscientious officer wants to make sure he is gathering all of the evidence the prosecutor will need to successfully prosecute the case. Since the officers work both day and night shifts, the calls can come at any hour, at home or at the office. This one came while I was still at work.

"What have you got?" I asked.

"I'm out at the Locke farm. Mr. Locke spotted a guy coming out of a horse's stall in his barn. The guy was trespassing. He ran off when Locke spotted him. Locke recognized him, though. It's his neighbor. He says the guy is pretty weird."

"What's your question?"

"Well, after the guy ran off, Locke checked out the barn to see if anything was missing. When he got to his mare's stall, he realized what happened."

"And what was that?"

"Well, when this mare gets bred, she always prances around the stall with her tail straight up in the air. You know what I'm saying?"

I had no response.

"When Mr. Locke went into the barn just now, the mare was prancing around the stall. Her tail was straight up in the air, and a wooden box had been dragged to the center of the stall. There were shoeprints all around the box. Plus, there's some white stuff leaking out of the horse's, um, vagina. I think it might be semen. Do I have to collect it? We might have a case of bestiality here."

"You are asking me if you need to do a rape kit on a horse?"

"That's about the size of it."

Fortunately, this was an answer I knew off the top of my head. When Professor Ed Hunvald and a blue-ribbon panel of criminal law experts wrote Missouri's first comprehensive criminal code in 1979, they decided to follow the modern trend and do away with the crime of bestiality.

"I've got some good news for you. Technically, it hasn't been a crime to have sex with a horse since 1979. Your horse-lover committed the crime of trespass. Since Mr. Locke saw him coming out of the barn, we can make the trespassing case with just the eyewitness testimony. You don't need to collect the evidence. It would just be overkill."

"Thank God!"

A few days later, after receiving Rich's paperwork, I charged the neighbor, a thirty-one-year-old white male, with misdemeanor trespass. When I filed the charge, I sort of hoped he would fight it. The case promised to be absurdly entertaining should it go to trial.

Much to my disappointment, the defendant, eager to put the sordid matter behind him, pled guilty during his first appearance in court without any sort of plea agreement whatsoever. For some reason, he was not keen on taking the case to trial and having his avid interest in animal husbandry come out in a public courtroom. He received thirty days in the county jail and a fine of three hundred dollars, but all of the jail time and most of the fine were suspended, and he was placed on probation for one year. It seemed a reasonable punishment for the crime of trespassing in a barn.

In the year 2004, the Missouri legislature, in its infinite wisdom, amended the criminal code to once again make bestiality a crime. It is unclear to me whether this change in the law came about because of any sort of documented crime wave throughout the corrals and stalls of the state, or whether the legislature simply had nothing better to do with its time and resources than pass this law. Whatever the case, in this enlightened age, mares are once again protected from lustful humans. As a result, my advice to a deputy sheriff calling me with the same evidentiary question would now be completely different. I would tell him to collect the evidence, to get some good photographs of the victim and the crime scene, and to send the evidence off for DNA testing. A conclusive DNA test could identify with certainty the culprit who rode the horse.

Considerate Leaper

Barristers' speeches vanish quicker than Chinese dinners, and even the greatest victory in court rarely survives longer than the next Sunday's papers.

—Horace Rumpole

As a prosecutor whose cases arise from crimes committed in and around a city located on the banks of the Mississippi, I often find that the crimes have involved the legendary river in one way or another. Murder weapons have been thrown into its murky waters, some never to be recovered. Stolen cars have been driven into it, many disappearing forever into its muddy depths. Rapes, robberies, and assaults have taken place on its banks. Criminals have hidden underneath the bridge or have fled across it. But perhaps the most unusual local case featuring the mighty Mississippi was "The Case of the Considerate Leaper."

The incident began with a high-speed chase in Illinois one cold November evening. The Illinois State Police were pursuing two men fleeing from them on a stolen motorcycle. The thieves were heading in the direction of the bridge connecting Cape Girardeau to Illinois. Whether they would actually try to cross into Missouri remained to be seen. The Illinois officers radioed the Cape Girardeau Police Department for help as they chased the motorcycle toward the Mississippi River bridge.

The motorcyclist was Joey Marmaduke. Twenty-six years old, he already had a healthy start on an impressive criminal record with multiple convictions for stealing, assault, resisting arrest, and escape from prison. With his priors, he knew being caught in possession of a stolen motorcycle virtually guaranteed an extended stay in the penitentiary. He tried hard to elude the pursuing officers but found it impossible to shake them. His passenger was holding on for dear life.

As Joey Marmaduke roared closer and closer to the bridge over the Mississippi, Cape Girardeau police officers barricaded the Missouri side. If Marmaduke rode onto the bridge, he would be trapped, with Missouri lawmen blocking one end and Illinois State Police blocking the other. The bridge itself towered eighty feet over the river. Once on the bridge, Marmaduke would have nowhere to go. He would be trapped and forced to surrender.

Unaware that the police on the Missouri side had barricaded their end of the bridge, Joey Marmaduke drove onto it, optimistic he might reach the streets of Cape Girardeau and give the Illinois officers the slip. When he spotted the barricade ahead of him, he slid the motorcycle to a stop. As his passenger lay sprawled on the roadway in the middle of the bridge, Marmaduke dashed to the side of the bridge and climbed over the railing. He lowered himself to the top of one of the concrete pylons and stood in the darkness, assessing his situation.

Marmaduke stared down at the Father of Waters, its ripples glittering in the moonlight. The night was cold and dark. The Mississippi's treacherous current raced beneath him, its power a silent menace. Should he jump? If the fall did not kill him, the whirlpools would.

He glanced over his shoulder. The Illinois State Police had screeched their cars to a stop. Officers were leaping from the cars. They were already swarming his accomplice. The police were shining flashlights all around. They were looking for him. He knew they would spot him any moment. Joey Marmaduke took a deep breath. Without further thought, he jumped, hurtling into the darkness below. Before he could take another breath, he had sliced into the muddy water, feet first. It was shockingly cold.

Approaching officers heard the splash when Marmaduke hit the water. When they peered over the railing, though, all they saw was dark water. Joey Marmaduke had disappeared into the vast river like a tossed pebble.

Throughout the night and into the morning, police and firefighters commandeered every available boat. They combed the river, looking for Marmaduke's body. The search was still going strong when Sergeant Carl Eakins at the Cape Girardeau Police Department received a telephone call.

"This is Joey Marmaduke," the caller said. "I just thought you'd like to know I survived the jump. I made it. Don't waste any more time looking for me. But don't get your hopes up. I'm not turning myself in."

And he didn't. Although his underlying crime was not very serious, the audacity of his escape earned him a spot on Cape Girardeau County's list of ten most-wanted fugitives. He was not captured until almost a year later, when he was arrested in Charleston, West Virginia.

I always considered it laudable of Joey Marmaduke to make the call to the Cape Girardeau Police Department. The fictional Tom Sawyer aside, rarely had so many people spent so much time searching the Mississippi River for someone who was not really dead. It was courteous of him to let the police know they could quit wasting their time.

Years later, I met up with Joey Marmaduke in a courtroom. Dressed in a standard-issue orange jail uniform, he was on a court docket for a relatively minor drug offense. I struck up a conversation with him.

"What was it like jumping off that bridge?" I asked during a recess.

He seemed surprised I remembered. He was a bit reluctant to talk at first, but his eyes flickered with an interest in sharing the memory.

"It was cold. I hit the water and went down real deep. Going down, I thought I'd never make it to the surface, but I shot right back up. I swam to shore. The current carried me a long, long way downstream before I made it to the riverbank. It wasn't as bad as I thought it would be. You should try it sometime."

I smiled.

"It was good of you to call the police."

He grinned.

"My wife told me to. I'm not all bad."

After the incident on the bridge, Joey Marmaduke added more convictions to his rap sheet over the ensuing years, including a property damage offense, drug offenses, and more assault and resisting arrest charges. His lengthy criminal history includes twenty-one arrests and nine convictions. Nevertheless, I suspect Mark Twain would have liked Joey Marmaduke. I'm positive Huckleberry Finn would have.

Weeping Witness

> As a general thing, it is unwise for the cross-examiner to attempt to cope with a specialist in his own field of inquiry. Lengthy cross-examinations along the lines of the expert's theory are usually disastrous and should rarely be attempted.
>
> —Francis L. Wellman

Over the years, I have played mind games with myself to combat nervousness during a trial. When my trial experience was limited to less serious crimes, I would calm myself by thinking, *Well, at least this isn't a murder case. No reason to be so nervous!* I was able to use this technique ten times, before my eleventh jury trial, which was, in fact, a murder case. During that trial, I amended my mantra to the reminder that, *Well, at least this isn't a death-penalty case!* This procedure worked adequately until jury trial number thirty-two, my first death-penalty prosecution. From that point onward, I switched my approach to the one currently in use: *Hey, this isn't brain surgery. No one is lying on an operating table, facing immediate and irreversible death if I screw up!* I often wonder how neurosurgeons calm themselves as they prepare to poke around inside someone's brain.

Preparation and experience are the antidote to courtroom jitters. Eventually, a trial lawyer reaches the point where he or she has tried so many cases that the courtroom warrior knows the law of evidence backward and forward; can skillfully prepare opening statements, closing arguments, and cross-examinations; and has arrived at a level where an upcoming trial produces excitement but not nervousness. The Duke of Wellington once said: "No man fears to do that which he knows he does well." So it is with prosecutors.

I seldom needed to use the mantra by the time my seventy-second jury trial rolled around. It was a murder case that produced a cross-examination I hereby nominate, though with reservations, as a possible Perry Mason moment.

A true Perry Mason moment, of course, usually involves some shocking surprise dropped like a bombshell during the trial. That was not the case here. But I humbly suggest that when the prosecutor's cross-examination causes a murder defendant's expert witness to burst into tears right after leaving the witness stand, it is very possible that a Perry Mason moment has just taken place. That is what happened in "The Case of the Weeping Witness."

⚖

John Wes Selvy, sixteen, was on trial for murdering his girlfriend, Shekelia Johnson, fifteen. He had eventually admitted shooting her but claimed the gun accidentally discharged as he wrested it from her while trying to prevent her from committing suicide.

The prosecution's evidence pretty well refuted this bogus claim of accident. Selvy had lied to the police many times, first by denying he was even present when Shekelia was shot to death in an alley outside his home. His act of hiding his blood-splattered clothing was a tad suspicious. Also, the angle of the shot into her cheek was inconsistent with his story about an accidental discharge. Moreover, gunshot residue coated his hands, and not hers. Finally, friends of Shekelia had heard Selvy threaten that if he could not have her, nobody would. Some said he had vowed to kill her if she ever broke up with him.

To bolster its version of events, the defense was calling an expert witness named Dr. Ann Dinwiddie. She was both a lawyer and a psychologist. Public Defender Gary L. Robbins obviously expected her testimony to carry great weight with the jury. He was almost gleeful when he told me his expert would be presenting a "psychological autopsy" of Shekelia Johnson. This was supposedly a process by which a psychologist who never met the victim looks over some information about the deceased and feels qualified to render an opinion as to the dead person's mental condition while alive. In this case, Dr. Dinwiddie was going to claim that Shekelia was suicidal.

Cross-examining an expert witness is extremely difficult and requires a huge amount of preparation. The lawyer planning a cross-examination of an expert must not only know the law and the facts of his case, he must also learn enough about the expert's field to detect and expose any flaws in that expert's opinions. It is never easy. More often than not, the lawyer only succeeds in self-humiliation.

As I prepared to face off against Dr. Dinwiddie, I found some good ammunition to use against her. Most experts in the field of psychiatry felt that "psychological autopsies" were little more than speculation. The whole idea of a psychologist rendering a diagnosis of a person he or she has never met was not generally accepted in the scientific community. I tracked down articles and prior testimony by recognized experts. I read the 2,407–page treatise *Coping with Psychiatric and Psychological Testimony* by Jay Ziskin and David Faust. I spent hours refining my questions. By the time we were in the courtroom, I felt ready to tangle with her. I welcomed the shot of adrenaline when Gary Robbins announced, "Your Honor, we call Dr. Ann Dinwiddie."

We were in the huge courtroom at the Scott County courthouse in Benton, Missouri. It was an old-fashioned courtroom with tremendously high ceilings and a large balcony overlooking the theater of the courtroom. It always reminds me of the courtroom in the movie *To Kill a Mockingbird*. The seating area was packed with people, including friends and relatives of the dead girl, friends and relatives of the defendant, lawyers, courthouse personnel, reporters, and assorted curious spectators.

As Dr. Dinwiddie strode confidently to the witness stand, her husband entered the courtroom and slipped into one of the few empty seats in the spectators' section. He had tagged along to watch his well-credentialed wife in action. As both a psychologist and an attorney, she had reason to feel confident. Surely this hayseed of a prosecutor from southeast Missouri would not lay a glove on her.

I am in no way suggesting that my cross-examination of Dr. Dinwiddie was brilliant. It wasn't. Rather, it was only competent. Yet, as Professor Irving Younger always said, pitiful cross-examination is the norm in this day and age. Even a merely competent cross-examination is so rare today that when one is in progress, word of the big event will spread throughout the courthouse, and other lawyers will flock to the courtroom like kids to a circus tent to view the varmint themselves.

Dr. Dinwiddie testified that she was a licensed clinical psychologist with a practice in St. Louis and that she had both a doctorate in psychology and a law degree. She had worked in the field of psychology and psychological counseling for twenty-five years. After announcing that she had read the police reports in the case and had looked at some letters Shekelia had supposedly written to Selvy, she gave her opinion that Shekelia was experiencing difficulty in her relationship with Selvy and "from what I have been able to gather, there was a lot of conflict in this young woman about whether she wanted to live or whether she wanted to die. There's evidence in her writings to Wes that she wished that she was dead, that she wished that she was in Heaven."

When it was my turn, I charged into the fray.

"Dr. Dinwiddie, you said you got involved in this case about four months ago. Do you have any documents that would let you be exactly precise on the date?"

"I will try. I got some materials on March 10, so I believe it was about two weeks before that."

"So," I said, "if Shekelia died on August 10, you got involved in looking at her state of mind seven months *after* she was dead?"

"That's correct."

"When you are diagnosing a person as a clinical psychologist to see whether or not he or she has a mental disease, what do you *usually* do as far as the procedure that is involved in diagnosing that particular patient?"

"I didn't diagnose her, and I didn't say that she had a mental disease."

"Isn't it true that a person who would be thinking thoughts of killing themselves would be considered to be depressed?"

"Some people could be considered to be depressed, yes. Fifty percent of the suicides in our country today are depression related."

"Now," I said, "my question to you earlier was when you are diagnosing a patient to see whether he or she has a mental disease, can you describe what you *usually* do as far as procedure?"

"Sure, but I didn't diagnose Shekelia as having a mental disease."

Sometimes it is necessary to repeat the same question over and over to show the jury that the witness is avoiding it.

"My question is when you are diagnosing a person to see whether she or he has a mental disease, what do you *usually* do as far as procedure?"

"If you were to refer a live client to me and ask me to render a differential diagnosis about battered spouse syndrome, okay . . . "

I interrupted her.

"Say I am referring a live client to you, and this child has been drawing suicide notes and acting depressed, and I am bringing you this patient to look at. Describe to me the procedure you would do with that child?"

"What I would be interested in is obtaining information from a wide variety of sources. I would render tests. We would give psychological tests that would be appropriate for . . . "

"What type of tests would be appropriate for that age child?"

"In our hypothetical case?"

"Yes, ma'am."

"That doesn't have anything to do with this case," she sniffed.

I was not going to let her get away with that.

"That's for the judge and the jury to decide," I corrected her. "In the hypothetical case that I gave you, what series of tests would you give a live child about fourteen or fifteen, whose parents have brought her to you saying this child is having some emotional problems?"

Dr. Dinwiddie finally gave up quibbling and answered the question.

"The first thing I would probably do is talk to the adolescent herself, because sometimes adolescents will say things that they then retract. So one of the pieces I would look for is whether there is a consistent theme over a period of time. So have there been indications in the past that they felt particularly unhappy or blue about a particular situation? Was the emotion generalized? Is there any difficulty in other areas, so that we would engage in a dialogue to explore their view of the problem."

I nodded. I planned to show all of the things that would normally be done with a live patient and then drive home the point that none had been done here. That is precisely the weakness of a "psychological autopsy."

"In addition to meeting with the child personally," I said, "what other steps would be taken in doing a clinical examination of a child?"

"Then you look for writings. You look for suicide notes. You ask the parents if they have noticed anything different about the child. Are there any difficulties? Sometimes people start giving away things just prior to a suicide attempt or suicide act, and often this is the case with adolescents."

"So you would consult with the child's parents, that would be important?"

"Right."

"And other siblings?"

"Yes, and significant others."

"As far as psychological tests, what battery of psychological tests would you give a patient that was coming in that you were going to diagnose their mental condition?"

Dr. Dinwiddie explained that she would give at least five different psychological tests and track down the patient's medical records. I had her explain the purpose of each test.

I then asked, "The purpose of all these things is to be sure you have a comprehensive big picture of this child, isn't that right?"

"Your hypothetical started off with the task of the differential diagnosis."

"And the reason you want all that information is because you want to make as accurate a diagnosis as possible?"

"I would. You gave me the task of a differential diagnosis."

"And my question is the *reason* you want all that information is so you can make an accurate diagnosis, correct?"

"You want to make it within a reasonable degree of certainty. Not all diagnoses are perfect."

"And, in fact, the *less* information the person has, the less chances there are that your diagnosis is going to be perfect, isn't that right?"

"Correct."

"In diagnosing Shekelia Johnson, you never had a chance to talk to her at all, did you?"

"No. Your language is a little bit difficult, because I didn't *diagnose* her."

I wasn't going to let her off the hook.

"In *stating your opinion* to a reasonable degree of certainty to the jury *today* about Shekelia Johnson, you *never talked* to Shekelia Johnson in her life?"

"Correct."

"Not even for one second?"

"She died last August."

"Right! That was seven months *before* you got involved in looking at her and giving the jury this opinion about her, right?"

"No. I looked at the material she left behind."

"Seven months *after* she died."

"Correct."

"You *never* conducted any sort of tests on her such as the MMPI, the Millon, the Rorschach, projective drawings, sentence completion, academic tests, Wexler IQ, you never did *any* of these tests on her, did you?"

"That's correct."

"And you did not consult her pediatric records?"

"I was unable to get them."

"You did *not* get her grade transcripts?"

"I tried, but I was unable to."

"And you didn't get her academic performance in writing from *any* source, did you?"

"Right."

"She had a mother, Katie Johnson, who is here in the black dress, to whom she was very close. You *never once* had a conversation with Katie Johnson about her daughter, did you?"

"We did talk about pecan pie, but we didn't talk about Shekelia."

"*When* did you talk about pecan pie?"

"At the break."

"That was today?"

"Right."

"But you had already sent your opinion to Mr. Robbins before today, hadn't you?"

"What I had sent to Mr. Robbins was that it was possible to take a look at the writings that she left and it raised an issue as to whether or not there was suicidal ideation in her drawings."

"My question is you did *not* get any information from Katie Johnson about her daughter before you ventured to give an opinion about her daughter, did you?"

"I did not."

"Shekelia had *nineteen* siblings who are all mentioned in her obituary; you didn't talk personally with *any* of those individuals, did you?"

"No. I wasn't allowed to."

"Did you *call* Katie Johnson and ask?"

"We had requested information."

"But you did *not* personally *call* Katie Johnson and say, hey, I am trying to reach a *fair objective* opinion here. May I talk to you about your daughter?"

"No, I did not."

"Now, this sounds sort of obvious, but isn't it true that her mother and her siblings and her father and her grandmothers, they all know her *better* than you would, isn't that true?"

"No question about it."

"Shekelia didn't have an opportunity to explain or contradict anything in the stuff you relied on to reach your opinion?"

"That's correct."

"Now, you are not an M.D., correct?"

"Correct."

"You are a psychologist and not a psychiatrist?"

"Right."

"Now, you mentioned in direct that you testified in court before?"

"Yes."

"How many criminal cases have you testified in?"

"Three."

"And in each of those three cases, you were not giving the state of mind of a dead person, were you?"

"No."

"Now, isn't it true that this whole idea of looking at information about a person who is dead, that this science [of a psychological autopsy] was begun to try to determine why a person committed suicide, so you could prevent other suicides, rather than looking at a dead person to try to say whether this was a suicide or not?"

"No, it actually started with *wills*. When there was a contested will in an estate, they were wondering whether the state of mind of the person who wrote the will was okay, so this area, which is only like seven years old, actually started off in testamentary issues."

"Ma'am, you say this area is only seven years old; weren't there articles being written about it more than twenty years ago?"

"The idea that you could look at a person's state of mind goes back a long way, but the idea of a psychological autopsy, that's fairly recent."

"Now, are you familiar with Dr. George Murphy at Washington University Medical School?"

"No."

"Dr. George Murphy, this man you never heard of, wrote this article, "Some Clinical Considerations of the Prevention of Suicide Based on a Study of 134 Successful Suicides," and he is a pioneer in the field, but you never heard of him?"

"Are you talking about suicide or psychological autopsies?"

"Psychological autopsies. This is an article about psychological autopsies, and it was published July, 1959. Are you *certain* that this field of psychological autopsy has only been around seven years?"

"No. The original question was did this start off with suicide. My response was no, it started off looking at people who are contesting wills. Then you asked me whether or not Murphy's work was known to me, and I don't know his work."

"Is this the first psychological autopsy you have ever attempted to do? You need to answer yes or no."

"Yes."

"Obviously, then, you never testified in court before about a psychological autopsy?"

"That's correct."

"Have you ever heard of Dr. Harrison Pope, a psychiatrist who teaches at Harvard Medical School?"

"No."

(Yes, dear reader, this was the same Harrison Pope whom I cross-examined in the Pagano case, bless his heart! This time his pontifications supported my side!)

"Would you disagree with the statement he made, `It would be *pure speculation* for a psychiatrist to try to give a formal diagnosis of a dead person he has never met'?"

"I don't have any quarrel with that."

I had other questions I could have asked her, such as how much she was charging to testify and a few other things, but it is always a good idea to stop on a high note, and I had just hit a very high note.

"No further questions."

Gary Robbins floundered around with a few innocuous questions on redirect, but the damage had been done. When she left the witness stand, Dr. Dinwiddie rushed up the aisle and quickly disappeared into the hallway. Her husband bolted from the courtroom after her. Police officers outside later told me that she burst into tears once she left the courtroom and cried all the way to her car.

A better person than I, a more compassionate person, a more tolerant person, might feel a tad guilty about making a psychologist/attorney cry merely by asking her questions when she was under oath. But, truth be told, I do not feel even a twinge of remorse about it. Here was an expert witness being paid big bucks to try to feed a load of bunkum to a jury in order to help a cold-blooded killer get away with murder. Not only do I not feel bad about reducing her to tears, I hope I permanently cured her of any urge to accept money for conducting psychological autopsies of murder victims in homicide cases in the future.

The jury found John Wes Selvy guilty of second-degree murder and armed criminal action. He was sentenced to life plus fifty years in prison.

Another reason I nominate this cross-examination as a Perry Mason moment is that it was recognized as such by at least one experienced courtroom spectator. Fred Pennington, a cameraman with KFVS-TV, came up to me in the hallway afterward, and with absolutely no suggesting nor prompting on my part (I swear!) exclaimed, "Wow, good job, Perry Mason!" Fred has called me Perry Mason ever since. Needless to say, he is one of my favorite journalists and obviously a keen judge of legal talent.

Lead-Footed Physician

It's better to keep your mouth shut and appear stupid than to open it and remove all doubt.
—Mark Twain

Y ou would not expect a Perry Mason moment to unfold during a speeding trial. In fact, you do not anticipate a trial *at all* in a speeding case. Most of the thousands of people who get traffic tickets in Cape Girardeau County each year simply pay their fines by mail and get on with their lives. Those who opt for a trial usually choose a bench trial, which takes place in front of a judge rather than a jury. Nevertheless, Assistant Prosecuting Attorney Julie Hunter's first Perry Mason moment occurred in a speeding case.

Don't get the idea that Julie only does traffic cases. Far from it. She has handled dozens of jury trials, the majority dealing with sexual assault or child molestation. But you take your Perry Mason moments where you find them.

It was my fault the case went to trial. As the head of the office, I am the one who sets the policy, and our policy on speeding cases is simple. Unless a person convinces us that he is actually innocent, we never dismiss a speeding case, nor reduce the ticket to a slower speed or a nonmoving violation. No matter who calls and tries to convince us to give some leadfoot a break, we treat everyone the same, from the president of General Motors to a food stamp recipient. If you get nabbed speeding you take your choice of three penalties: (1) pay the ticket according to the standard fine schedule; (2) receive probation (for a first offense) and attend a driving improvement school; or (3) receive probation (for a first offense) and perform eight hours of community service. Those who get probation avoid getting points on their driving record.

My policy is apparently not the norm. Lawyers from other jurisdictions always profess shock when they discover they cannot get a better deal for their clients. They rant and rave and threaten to take the case to trial, but they rarely do. The reasons for that will become apparent.

A perfect example of why my policy is the correct approach involved the late Carrie D. Francke. She was a tremendous person. As an undergraduate at the University of Missouri–Columbia, she was the president of the student body. At law school, she excelled in appellate advocacy. As a young politician, she ran a statewide campaign for Senator John Danforth. As an assistant attorney general, she won a tremendous number of appellate arguments. By the age of thirty-four, she had returned to the university as a curator.

She was on the fast track.

She drove a Corvette.

Fast.

At 7:30 one weekday morning, she crashed and rolled her Corvette on I-70 in Montgomery County as she was rushing from Jefferson City to St. Louis for a court date. She died at the young age of thirty-four. In a speeding-ticket-plea-bargaining-expose, the *St. Louis Post-Dispatch* dug around and discovered that in the fifteen months leading up to her death, Carrie Francke had received *six* speeding tickets, and all but once, various local prosecuting attorneys had agreed to dismiss her case or to amend it to a nonmoving violation so she would not get points on her license. No driving school for her. No community-service hours. Three speeding convictions alone would have caused her license to be suspended. She had *six*. Perhaps if they had not been dismissed, the first and second tickets would have gotten her attention and slowed her down. Tough prosecutors doing their jobs might have saved her life.

I knew Carrie Francke in college. I admired her. But I was sorry I never got the chance to prosecute her for speeding. Had she received one of her tickets in my county, I would have treated her like everyone else. Getting a speeding conviction never killed anyone. But not getting one killed Carrie Francke.

I think of Carrie Francke every time someone whines and cries and criticizes my speeding policy. I *want* to make it inconvenient to get a speeding ticket. I want people to slow down.

Now, I fully recognize that a person who gets a speeding ticket is not a bad person. Take my wife, for instance. One fall afternoon we were driving back to Cape Girardeau from a training session for prosecutors at the Lake of the Ozarks in mid-Missouri. I was driving on Highway 54 between Jefferson City and Fulton in Calloway County. It was a flat stretch of roadway, where one could go a bit fast and still be fairly safe.

I, however, was poking along at the designated speed of fifty-five miles per hour, as I tend to do since I am cognizant of how humiliating it would be for a prosecutor to get a speeding ticket, especially one who refuses to make deals with speeders.

"Drive faster!" my wife suggested. "We're going to be late."

"I'm already driving the speed limit."

"Let me drive, then."

I pulled over, and we switched places. Not five minutes later, as she was booking along at seventy-one miles per hour, the red lights started flashing behind us. It was a state trooper. Tears welled in my wife's eyes. As she pulled to the shoulder of the road, her first thought was self-preservation.

"Tell him you're a prosecutor!"

"No way! We switched drivers *specifically* so you *could* speed. This was the most *premeditated* speeding case I've ever seen!"

I kept my face averted as my wife took her lumps. We paid the ticket by mail.

It turned out to be the best money I ever spent. From that time forward, I could quickly and efficiently conclude discussions with lawyers representing speeding defendants with a recitation of this story, which I always ended with the hard-to-argue-against conclusion: "If I wouldn't try to get my own *wife* a break, you don't think I'll do anything for your client, do you?"

Sometimes the critics get pretty ugly.

One vocabulary-challenged minister called me "evil" and "misguided" in the local newspaper after I charged a teenager with careless and imprudent driving when she crashed into a telephone pole going fifty-six in a thirty-five-miles-per-hour zone, killing one of her passengers (her eleven-year-old sister) and injuring two other kids in the car. One suspects that the befuddled pastor will be at a loss for good adjectives to criticize Lucifer or Hitler, since he used up all the good ones on me. The girl ultimately pled guilty to speeding and received probation. At my request, the judge ordered her to attend a hospital-sponsored driver-improvement school aimed at young adults and required her to perform several hours of community service work.

Even a fellow prosecutor got mad at me. He telephoned me when his secretary received a speeding ticket in my county. When I explained my policy, he argued that I should follow his example and change my policy. His was much better. He would routinely dismiss speeding tickets for buddies and colleagues, including secretaries of buddies and colleagues.

"Hell, the cops give people breaks out on the streets all the time," he argued. "I should be able to give someone a break, too! Besides, sometimes the tickets deserve to be dismissed."

I was unpersuaded.

"My cops know that if they write the ticket, it won't be dismissed," I said. "So they only write good tickets. My policy saves time on haggling with lawyers, too. They eventually learn we won't ever budge and quit calling."

"You need to change your policy," he repeated.

A few years later, a different prosecutor from the same part of the state got into trouble with the Missouri bar's disciplinary committee for dismissing a ticket for his own brother. I like my policy better. It smells better. It can, however, result in an occasional jury trial.

One nice thing about being the head guy is that after I make the tough policy, I can delegate someone else to actually spend an entire day trying the case. That's how Julie Hunter got "The Case of the Lead-Footed Physician."

⚖️

Dr. Linus DeSpeeda was on his way to work, cruising along I-55 at 102 miles per hour one brisk March day when he was caught on radar by alert State Trooper Jeremy L. Weadon. The posted speed limit was 70.

Dr. DeSpeeda was the only middle-aged white male on I-55 that morning driving a big red Ford Crown Victoria with oversized chrome wheels. He may have been the only person matching that description in the entire country.

Weadon was facing the opposite direction when he clocked him on the radar. By the time he turned around, he had lost sight of the Crown Victoria. He took off in the same direction, however, and eventually caught up with DeSpeeda.

Dr. DeSpeeda was courteous when pulled over. He was also admirably candid. Weadon noticed the green surgical scrubs the emergency-room doctor was wearing.

"Were you on your way to a medical emergency?"

"No. I was just running late for work."

The door of opportunity closed. Had it been a true medical emergency, the speeding would have been justified under the law, and Weadon would not have issued the ticket.

DeSpeeda accepted the ticket gracefully, and Weadon thought that would be the end of the matter. A speeder as polite as the doctor would show up in court (as all offenders going over ninety were required to do), plead guilty, and take his punishment like a man. That is not what happened.

DeSpeeda, who had recently testified as a witness in a child-abuse case handled by Assistant Prosecuting Attorney Scott Lipke, called Scott and tried to get him to dismiss the case. Scott exuded the expected level of sympathy for him, but explained my ironclad policy. No dice. The ticket was not going away. Eventually, after Scott told me the doctor could not understand why we would not dismiss his case, I wrote the doctor myself and explained why I allowed no exceptions to our policy.

Irate at the lack of special treatment, the doctor morphed into the stock-in-trade of a lucrative law practice—a rich guy who is in trouble or mad or both. He hired a lawyer and demanded his constitutional right of trial by jury. He was going to show us! *A jury trial! Oh, Heavens! Don't throw us into that briar patch!*

At trial, the defense attorney argued mistaken identity. The doctor claimed the trooper must have seen some *other* middle-aged white guy driving a big red Crown Victoria with oversized chrome wheels. He was unable to explain, though, why he had not raised that possibility with the trooper at the time Weadon was writing him the ticket.

Julie Hunter's Perry Mason moment came at the end of her cross-examination of the doctor.

It turned out he had been caught speeding four times in Ste. Genevieve County in the previous two years before Trooper Weadon's radar nailed him. The first time he had been going 91 in a 70-miles-per-hour zone, but the local prosecutor had allowed him to complete a driving school instead of getting points on his license. The next three times, the prosecutor had amended the speeding tickets to nonmoving violations, each time citing a loud muffler, thus preventing the doctor from getting points on his license. This was exactly the sort of plea-bargaining I would never allow.

Julie took the time to obtain certified copies of each conviction. Her cross-examination concluded on a very effective crescendo.

"Doctor, do you have any prior convictions of any sort, either criminal or traffic?"

"No," he lied. Or maybe he just forgot. He was a busy guy.

"No? Let me show you this certified copy of a conviction from Ste. Genevieve County, Missouri. Isn't it true you were convicted of having a loud muffler in that county just five months ago?"

"Well, yes. I suppose so."

"Is that your only conviction?"

"Yes, it is."

"Really? Let me show you this additional certified copy from the same court. Doesn't it show yet another conviction for having a loud muffler from three months earlier?"

"Yes."

"So, you just have these two?"

"That's right."

"Really? Let me show you this certified conviction. Isn't it true that you had yet a third conviction for loud muffler, this one from seven months earlier?"

"Yes."

"So, you've had *three* nonmoving violations for having a loud muffler in the past two years?"

"Yes."

Julie paused, then allowed herself a slight smile.

"Tell me, doctor, have you gotten that muffler fixed?"

The jury was snickering as she took her seat at the counsel table.

In her closing argument, Julie ended on another high note. Right before sitting down, she said to the jury:

> Dr. DeSpeeda was traveling at a speed of 102 miles per hour down the interstate at noon on a Wednesday. The potential for accident or injury is astounding at such a high rate of speed. He's an emergency room doctor! He sees and treats horrific injuries and accidents every day! He should be shaking the trooper's hand, saying, "Thank you. I screwed up, and it won't happen again. You may have saved a life." Dr. DeSpeeda hasn't thanked the officer, but the twelve of you can. Go back to that jury room and find the doctor guilty. Say thank you to Trooper Weadon for doing his job. Say thank you to Trooper Weadon for helping keep our roadways safe.

The jurors deliberated one hour before finding the lead-footed, badly mufflered doctor guilty of speeding. They set his fine at the maximum of $500. As the loser of the trial, he was also ordered to pay the court costs, which, because of jury expenses, totaled $481.40. Another kick to the wallet included his attorney fee, since his lawyer was not spending an entire day in the courtroom free of charge.

It is no wonder that most of these cases do not go to jury trial. Had he simply paid the standard fine it would have cost him the $500.00, plus only $57.50 in court costs.

⚖

My county is not the only one with a speeding case war story.

Tom Hoeh, the prosecuting attorney of Perry County, Missouri, a small county immediately to the north, runs a one-man office, personally handling every single case from speeding tickets to murder trials. He once prosecuted a case where an arrogant tax lawyer from St. Louis took his speeding case to jury trial, representing himself. Although the speeder might have been a tax expert, there were a few things this attorney did not know about criminal law. At the end of the trial, when the judge, prosecutor, and lawyer/defendant were putting together the jury instructions right before closing arguments, the tax lawyer noticed for the first time that the range of punishment for speeding included up to *one year* in the county jail.

His face blanched.

Nervously, he looked at Tom Hoeh.

"Exactly what punishment *are* you asking the jury for?"

Tom grinned at him. "I haven't decided yet."

Wisely, the pompous St. Louis tax lawyer decided not to give twelve residents of rural Perry County a shot at sticking him in their county jail. He pled guilty, paid his fine and court costs, and headed back to the big city.

Presumably driving the speed limit.

Titillating Tape

> [T]he Court [in obscenity cases] was faced with
> the task of trying to define what may be inde-
> finable . . . [U]nder the First and Fourteenth
> Amendments criminal laws in this area are con-
> stitutionally limited to hard-core pornography.
> I shall not today attempt to further define the
> kinds of material I understand to be embraced
> within that shorthand description; and perhaps I
> could never succeed in intelligibly doing so.
> But I know it when I see it.
>
> —Potter Stewart

> I had always contrived that a prosecutor was
> something more than a spineless warrant granter.
> One important aspect of his job was to protect
> people, sometimes even from themselves. The
> simple fact is that it frequently takes more guts
> on the part of a prosecutor to turn down
> a criminal warrant than to grant it.
>
> —Robert Traver

Over the years, zealous—I would say *overzealous*—prosecutors have ordered citizens arrested on obscenity crimes for distributing books like *Ulysses* by James Joyce, *An American Tragedy* by Theodore Dreiser, and *Lady Chatterley's Lover* by D. H. Lawrence. Some consider these books classics. Others call them obscene. Although they do not make my list of favorite books (the haunting murder scene in *An American Tragedy,* notwithstanding) it concerns me that prosecutors tried to prevent people from reading these works by prosecuting their distributors as criminals. Jailing someone for selling a book is a distinctly un-American concept.

Perhaps the most unique criminal offense on the books in the United States is pornography. It is the only crime for which "community standards" determine whether or not someone has committed a criminal offense.

Prosecuting obscenity cases is more difficult in many respects than prose-cuting murder, rape, or robbery cases—and properly so. The obstacle is our United States Constitution. The Constitution does not prohibit government from making it a crime to murder, rape, or rob; but it *does* state that govern-ment shall make no law "abridging the freedom of speech, or of the press." A responsible prosecutor must be especially careful not to violate a person's constitutional rights when dealing with a pornography complaint.

Not all pornography is illegal. The word *pornography* encompasses any material, such as a writing, painting, photograph, or film, containing a description or depiction of licentiousness or erotic behavior. What *is* illegal is pornography that also meets the legal definition of *obscenity,* as the word has come to be defined by the United States Supreme Court. That is where "community standards" have worked their way into the equation.

Under the applicable constitutional definition incorporated into the Mis-souri criminal statute, a book, magazine, or movie is obscene if: (1) applying contemporary community standards, its predominant appeal is to a prurient interest in sex; and (2) taken as a whole with the average person applying con-temporary community standards, it depicts or describes sexual conduct in a patently offensive way; and (3) taken as a whole, it lacks serious literary, artis-tic, political, or scientific value.

The three-part test is a mouthful, but it is the best definition the Supreme Court could come up with. The Court itself has seldom issued a unanimous opinion in an obscenity case. Over the years, the viewpoints of the justices have varied tremendously. Some have felt that the First Amendment bars the government from passing any law criminalizing words or pictures dealing with sexual content. For this reason, Justices William O. Douglas and Hugo Black refused to join the other justices in the conference room on "movie day" to watch X-rated films to determine whether or not they were illegal. To them, no matter what the skin flicks depicted, they were protected free speech. Other justices have felt the First Amendment did not protect obscene works, but they have struggled to come up with a foolproof test for deter-mining obscenity. Justice Potter Stewart voiced his frustration over attempting to devise a workable legal standard when he complained in a concurring opinion that it was nearly impossible to define obscenity, "but I know it when I see it."

Eventually, the Supreme Court, in *Miller v. California,* formulated the current three-step test to resolve the conflict between a person's First Amendment right of free speech to publish anything he wants versus the government's right to censor material it considers vile and repulsive. The Court's test was later incorporated into Missouri's pornography statute. The conflict between these opposing interests came to a head in my county in "The Case of the Titillating Tape."

⚖

It all began one February afternoon when a woman named Dora Melcher marched into the Cape Girardeau Police Department with an XXX-rated adult videotape.

"I want charges filed for this pornography," she declared.

Sergeant Brad Moore handled her complaint. Dora Melcher told him that she and her husband had rented the tape from a local video store. She said her husband rented adult movies on numerous occasions and things had reached the point where the couple "had to view them in order to have sex." She insisted that pornography charges be filed. She added that an organization called the American Family Association was "backing her up on this."

Brad Moore dutifully took her statement. He also interviewed the store owner, a fifty-eight-year-old woman, and the store clerk, a forty-two-year-old man. Both confirmed that the Melchers had rented the video from them after specifically asking for an adult video. They showed Moore how the pornographic tapes were kept in a separate room from other videos, well out of sight of anyone who did not want to see them.

The police report landed on my desk a few days later. I was not exactly thrilled. As an English major and occasional writer, I had always been keenly interested in the First Amendment. As a parent, though, I was concerned about the way moral values in the United States had been spiraling toward the gutter. As the prosecuting attorney of Cape Girardeau County, it was my job to decide how to handle this complaint.

First of all, no matter what the offense, the decision whether to charge someone with a crime should not be made lightly. In this case I wanted to make sure a crime had in fact been committed before I charged the store clerk or store owner with a criminal offense. I did not want someone arrested on my say-so for something that would ultimately prove to be constitutionally protected free speech. On the other hand, as an elected official, I did not relish the idea of getting into a public spat with any organization including the words "American Family" in its title.

Needless to say, the first thing I was required to do was to watch the movie. I was not a First Amendment absolutist like Justices Douglas and Black. The content might make a difference. I suspected that, like Justice Potter Stewart, I would know obscenity when I saw it.

I have forgotten its title, but the film had little or no plot and featured lots of explicit sex scenes between consenting adults. I could easily see where it would offend many people, but I was not particularly bothered by it, nor was I sure that my community would want someone prosecuted criminally for renting this particular tape to an adult. I especially was not convinced that a jury of twelve people would make a unanimous finding that a person I would charge with a crime should be criminally punished for providing it to another adult.

But how was I supposed to decipher Cape Girardeau County's contemporary community standards in regard to dirty movies? One option would be to just slap the store owner and clerk with criminal charges, jail them, and take the case to trial to see if I could get a conviction. It would be like throwing mud on the courthouse wall to see if anything would stick. But it did not seem right to charge the store owner and clerk with crimes, force them to hire expensive lawyers, and then take their cases all the way to trial before even knowing if I was upholding the community's standards. Nor did it seem right to play God, or at least to play bully, by threatening the store owner with criminal prosecution if she did not remove this tape from her shelves. If the movie was constitutionally protected speech, I had no right ordering citizens to remove it from their stores. And, of course, the way our free-market system works, if no one in Cape Girardeau wanted to watch the tape, no one would rent it, and the store owner would eventually remove it from the shelf due to lack of interest.

Another key concern was that I had no desire to assume the mantle of "Community Censoring Czar for Cape Girardeau County," undertaking the daunting chore of watching every movie in every store to tell store owners which would be considered obscene and which would not. I had too many pending murder, rape, robbery, assault, stealing, and DWI cases to spend my time watching dirty movies.

I finally hit upon an idea. I would do a survey of the local community to determine its standards. I would use the results to help me decide whether a charge should be filed. The results could even constitute evidence in court if I *did* file the charge.

It was easy to come up with a pool of people. Two hundred and thirty-seven citizens had just finished a three-month stint of jury service. Their names had been pulled at random from a master list of county residents, which was compiled from driver's license records and registered voter lists. This group would be representative of exactly the sort of people who would end up sitting on a jury should a criminal charge be filed.

I put together a questionnaire for them and sent it out, along with a brief cover letter and a postage-paid return envelope. I was pleased when 59 percent of them promptly responded to the survey. The results themselves were pretty explicit:

1. Do you feel that adults should be prosecuted for watching, in their homes, a sexually explicit movie of an adult man and woman having sexual intercourse? YES 7% NO 92%

1A. Do you feel an adult should be prohibited by the government from renting or buying this movie? YES 21% NO 76%

1B. Do you feel a sales clerk, working for a video store, should be convicted of a crime (one day to one year in jail or a fine of up to $1,000) for renting this movie to an adult? YES 14% NO 86%

1C. Do you feel the owner of the video store that carried this movie, if he knew they carried it, should be convicted of a crime (one day to one year in jail or a fine of up to $1,000) if it were rented to an adult? YES 24% NO 75%

2. Do you feel that adults should be prosecuted for watching, in their homes, a sexually explicit movie of an adult man and woman having oral sex (genitals of one person to mouth of another)? YES 10% NO 88%

2A. Do you feel an adult should be prohibited by the government from renting or buying this movie? YES 25% NO 74%

2B. Do you feel a sales clerk, working for a video store, should be convicted of a crime (one day to one year in jail or a fine of up to $1,000) for renting this movie to an adult? YES 14% NO 83%

2C. Do you feel the owner of the video store that carried this movie, if he knew they carried it, should be convicted of a crime (one day to one year in jail or a fine of up to $1,000) if it were rented to an adult? YES 26% NO 73%

All together, my questionnaire covered six areas, each with multiple questions. One question asked, "Do you feel we currently have a problem with pornography in Cape Girardeau County?" Sixty-nine percent answered no. The last question asked, "Would you like to see the prosecutor and the police do more to investigate and prosecute people who sell sexually explicit tapes and magazines than they are currently doing?" Sixty-one percent said no.

In addition to tabulating the survey results, I read all United States Supreme Court cases dealing with obscenity, and I studied all Missouri cases on the topic. I also read Attorney General Edwin Meese's voluminous report on pornography in the United States. When the survey results arrived, I drafted my office's policy on pornography, which incorporated my community's standards.

Under my written guidelines, our office prosecutes only people who possess or sell pornography that unquestionably violates the legal definition of obscenity. In general, as long as sexually explicit material portrays only consenting adults and is being purchased or rented by consenting adults, any doubt whether to file a case will be resolved in favor of the private citizen, and the charge will not be filed. Conversely, if children are depicted in the material, or if the material is furnished to children, or if it is displayed so that children may see it, any doubt whether to file the case will be resolved in favor of the government, and the charge will be filed.

Applying my newly minted policy on pornography, I declined to file the criminal charge requested by Dora Melcher. At the same time, my office did file a charge in a different case against a man who showed an obscene movie to two young boys, ages twelve and thirteen.

Dora Melcher was not a happy camper. She had envisioned herself as the heroine who single-handedly forced the local prosecutor to rid the county of all sexually explicit movies. She was determined to get her way.

The next thing I knew, my office was being picketed by the American Family Association. This only amounted to six people, some of whom did not even live in my county, carrying signs; still, it is insulting to be picketed for anything. Besides, it looked like more than six people on TV. Being picketed reminded me of Abraham Lincoln's joke about what it felt like to be president. He quoted a remark made by a man who was tarred and feathered and carried out of town tied to a rail: "If it weren't for the honor of the thing, I'd have much rather walked."

The editor of our local newspaper, the *Southeast Missourian,* had a brainstorm and asked me to write an opinion column explaining my position in not filing charges. He wanted to juxtapose it with an opposing viewpoint from Dora Melcher, plus one from a local minister, and yet another from a newspaper columnist fresh out of college. I was all *for* this idea. *Free speech in action! Give me my pen!* I promptly submitted my piece.

Needless to say, my prose was flawlessly written. The other columns, in my not-so-humble opinion, were sad specimens. Once I unhorsed my opponents in the journalistic joust, "The Case of the Titillating Tape" appeared to be over.

My policy on pornography proved workable. Over the years, my office has successfully prosecuted many cases where adults provided sexually explicit movies or photographs to children. We have prevented the public display of adult material. At the same time, the government in our county has stayed out of the private lives of the people of our community regarding what consenting adults watch in the privacy of their own homes and regarding what they can rent from local video stores or buy in local bookstores. I was in for a surprise, however, a few months after the opinion pieces appeared in the local paper.

One October afternoon, a brown paper package arrived in the mail at my office. When I opened it, I found two issues of *Adult Video News* magazine together with a cover letter. The letter read:

Dear Mr. Swingle,

Our clipping service has kept us more or less informed about the ruckus surrounding your polling of county residents on their viewing habits, and I just wanted to take a moment to write a letter of congratulations on your taking such a pro–First Amendment stand—a position which I can see, especially from the articles in the *Southeast Missourian,* has brought you a lot of heat from the censorship groups.

I enclose a copy of our September issue, where an article on your poll appears on page 30, and an advance printing of an article which will appear in our November issue. I only wish I could have quoted more extensively from your Aug. 31 article, but our space is often limited. However, rest assured that among the adult entertainment community (most of whom read our magazine), you will be considered a true American hero in these dark days of religious repression.

> Yours truly,
> Mark Kernes
> Managing Editor

With growing curiosity, I opened the September issue to the page mentioning my policy on pornography:

> What A Novel Idea!
> Ask The Public!

Cape Girardeau, MO—If we had a Good Guy of the Month Award, Cape Girardeau County Prosecuting Attorney Morley Swingle would be the winner. Faced with a complaint from a woman who said she'd rented a "dirty" movie at a local video store—claiming that her husband was "addicted" to pornography in the process—and another charge against a man who allegedly showed a sexually explicit tape to some minors, Swingle set about to do what any prosecuting attorney stuck with *Miller* guidelines should at least attempt: He surveyed local residents to establish what the local "community standard" was.

Swingle got the names of 237 locals from the just-concluded panel of residents who served as jurors, and asked them several questions concerning whether adults should be prosecuted for watching or renting sexually explicit tapes, and whether store owners or clerks should be prosecuted for making them available.

Swingle was little prepared for the results. Over 70 percent of those responding (139 out of the 237) felt that Americans should be able to watch whatever they want to, sexually speaking, in their own homes, and stores should be free to provide the material.

Of course, within days, the American Family Association castigated Swingle in the press for daring to actually ask the people what their tastes were—and lo and behold, it turned out that the lady who'd rented the explicit tape and wanted the store that rented it prosecuted was none other than an officer of the local chapter of the AFA!

The local newspapers were kind enough to print responses from several of those surveyed, and in almost every case, the opinion was that nobody has to look at "pornography" if he/she doesn't want to, but those that have the urge should be able to obtain it—and most bristled at the idea the censors have more of a handle on public tastes than the public itself.

Swingle was also criticized for expending tax money to conduct the survey. The total bill came to $137.46, a few bucks less than the $25,000 it can cost for a full-scale pornography prosecution.

Feeling rather pleased, I then turned to the November issue. Once again, they had kind things to say about me:

Missouri Prosecuting Attorney Maintains
Pro-Speech Stance
American Family Assn. and Clergy
Step Up Attacks

Cape Girardeau County, MO—Morley Swingle, the youthful Prosecuting Attorney who actually surveyed county residents to find out what the community standards were before agreeing to prosecute a local video store (see September *News-Line*), was the subject of an attack by would-be censors in the *Southeast Missourian,* a daily newspaper. Swingle, however, ably defended himself from the often irrational and irrelevant statements made by his attackers, and explained in clear language the legal restraints on censorship-by-prosecution and his reasons for not acting on the American Family Association's complaints.

Dora Melcher, President of the local AFA chapter and reportedly the renter of the XXX tape in question, wrote a lengthy diatribe alleging that she had received poor treatment by Swingle (whom, interestingly, she never mentions by name) and his staff and that Swingle was somehow delinquent in performing his duties.

Melcher consistently refers to "illegal pornography," a sure clue that she doesn't understand the legal distinction between "obscenity" (unlawful) and "pornography" (lawful). However, she admits that she rented the tape in question for the sole purpose of turning it over to Swingle for "review" and eventual prosecution; she never watched it herself. Later she writes, "All I've ever asked was to rid Cape Co. of all pornography, not prosecute anyone or harm any business"—which is akin to saying, "Sure I let go of the hammer; I didn't know it was going to fall."

Melcher also denies that she ever claimed she or her husband were "addicted" to pornography, but early news reports of the incident contained that very claim as Melcher's reason for wanting the tape prosecuted in the first place. After being "informed" of her earlier statement, she writes, "I then realized that I was on trial and not pornography."

Joining Melcher in her denunciation of Swingle is Pastor Joe Twichell, who views society as having "taken a shift from encouraging moral behavior to espousing an amoral attitude where absolutely nothing should be considered wrong (despite how vile it may have seemed a decade ago). Those who still 'dare' to believe in moral absolutes are accused of being extremists, radicals and even fascists."

Twichell's view is that individuals make their lives more perfectly moral by physically opposing ideas and materials which they believe are "immoral." He writes, "Pornography undermines the moral teachings children and youth receive from their parents, teachers, churches and synagogues." What Twichell doesn't seem to understand is that in a free society, everyone is welcome to his/her beliefs—but one person or group forcing their beliefs on others in the same society is indeed censorship—and morally wrong.

Swingle writes an excellent rebuttal to Melcher and Twichell. . . . He briefly reviews the Melcher incident, correcting her stated version of the events, then distinguishes her case from another recent one, where an adult showed a sexually explicit tape to two minor boys.

Writes Swingle, "In the real world where I work, the prosecutor is not playing Monopoly or Moot Court. The actions of the prosecutor have serious and real consequences. If I file a charge against Jane Doe for renting a tape to an undercover officer, she faces the possibility of going to jail and being fined. I am not going to abuse my position by filing charges against someone because I do not like the book or tape that person is selling." And later, "In general, what a person reads or watches in his home is his own business, and my office will not prosecute him." How refreshing to hear such rational words from a prosecutor! Is it too early to run this guy for Congress?

I put the magazine down. There it was. What a bittersweet development. One of the nicest compliments I had ever received was emblazoned upon the editorial page of a publication in which I'd be embarrassed to have anyone see my name. Praise from *Adult Video News* was not exactly a tribute one would trumpet in a campaign brochure.

Still, I had followed the law. In the process of doing my sworn duty to uphold the Constitution, I had helped educate the public about a complicated legal issue. I had protected the rights of private citizens from overzealous censorship by refusing to be pressured into turning from prosecutor to persecutor. I was proud of myself. But not proud enough to share the *Adult Video News* articles with very many people.

Until now.

Perforated Patrol Car

> All courtroom proceedings seem more like
> prize-ring combat than a calm, dignified
> effort to find out the truth.
>
> —Clarence Darrow

David Allen Smith was perhaps the craftiest criminal I ever prosecuted. It is an assessment he would undoubtedly share. He was thirty-three years old when I prosecuted him for attempted escape from the city jail at the Cape Girardeau Police Department. By that time, he had acquired thousands of dollars from his life of crime. The problem for him was that he was in jail and could not spend it. It must be extremely frustrating to have made your fortune only to find yourself locked away from it.

A bank robbery allegedly netted him approximately $50,000. The money was never recovered. A buddy of his successfully robbed an armored car of 1.7 million dollars. Likewise, that money was floating around somewhere. If David Allen Smith could just get out of jail, he would be on Easy Street. Instead, he found himself in the "Iron Bar Hotel."

Lord knows he had tried to escape. In fact, that was why he was at the Cape Girardeau Police Department. He was a federal prisoner, awaiting trial in federal court for an attempted escape from a federal prison in Memphis. His female accomplice had hijacked a helicopter and tried to fly it inside the prison grounds to pluck him out. The copter crashed and the plan was foiled. By the time I prosecuted him, he was already serving twenty-five years for a Memphis bank robbery, plus ten years for two assaults committed during the robbery.

David Allen Smith had assessed the situation and concluded that his best chance of escaping was to find a way out of the comparatively small jail at the

189

Cape Girardeau Police Department while he was awaiting his trial in federal court. He sweet-talked a love-smitten female prisoner into smuggling a gun to him once she got out of jail. Sure enough, the gun arrived, disassembled, hidden inside a box of candy. Many of the chocolate-covered peanuts were actually chocolate-covered .25-caliber bullets. The woman also smuggled him hacksaw blades concealed inside baby powder containers. It is still unclear to me what plausible explanation was given as to why a prisoner needed baby powder. Once his tools arrived, he worked feverishly on his plan over a four-day time frame.

He was housed in the maximum-security unit. It consisted of four cells in a row, facing a blank wall, with a four-foot-wide corridor between the front bars of the cells and the wall. To get out, he would need to cut through the bars of his cell, get through the locked door at the end of the corridor, and then find a way through another locked door at the sallyport separating the jail from the rest of the police department. It was a daunting task. He came up with a better solution.

The wall directly across from his cell was an exterior wall. It was made of concrete blocks, with a veneer of regular bricks slapped onto the outside of the concrete blocks. Instead of going through the locked doors, he decided to cut through the wall.

First, he used the hacksaw blades to cut nine-inch-long removable sections from two of the metal bars of his cell. When he was done, he refitted them so he could remove them in an instant. Now he could slip in and out of his cell at will. More important, he had access to the exterior wall.

He was one of the few prisoners never allowed to leave his cell. Two others in the maximum security area *were* allowed to come and go from their cells at times. They would sometimes sit on a mattress in front of his cell and play cards with him. The mattress was lying in the hallway. It made for a nice bit of camouflage.

David Allen Smith began the laborious process of cutting out two concrete blocks, making a hole big enough to slip through. Once the hole was eventually made, the drop to the ground outside would be only eight to ten feet.

The jailers checked the maximum security area once an hour, so he had about forty minutes to chip away at the mortar surrounding the concrete blocks. He would then slip back inside his cell, reposition the bars, and act like nothing was going on. Between digging sessions, he leaned the mattress against the wall to cover the hole he was making in the concrete blocks.

Finally, he had cut out one whole block. He flushed part of it down his toilet and hid the other parts in his cell. He knew that once he got just one more block out, only the three-inch-thick bricks would separate him from freedom. "Three inches!" he wrote in a note to a fellow inmate. "It's so close I can taste it!"

One day in May, his carefully laid plans fell apart. One of the jailers, Chet Going, was taking medications to a prisoner in the maximum security area at about 10:40 P.M. Chet noticed the mattress leaning against the wall. He glanced behind it. He spotted the hole in the wall and stood gaping at it for a moment.

"What's going on here?" He turned toward David Allen Smith's cell.

He froze. Smith was pointing a gun at him.

"Sit down!" Smith ordered.

Chet Going sat on the floor. At this point, Chet felt he was going to be held at gunpoint as a hostage, but he did not expect Smith to be able to get out of his cell. Chet did not even have Smith's cell key with him.

"Can you help me get out of here?" Smith asked.

"David, I can't help you. I don't have a key."

"Okay. Lie down."

Chet Going lay face down on the floor.

Much to his surprise, within seconds, Smith was out of his cell.

Secretly, Chet hit a panic alarm he carried. It would alert the dispatchers that a jailbreak was in progress.

David Allen Smith tied his gun to his hand with a plastic garbage bag. He made Chet get up, put one arm around Chet's neck, and pressed the gun to the back of Chet's head.

"You're not going to get out," Chet said, with more bravado than he felt.

"If I don't get out, you don't get out," Smith vowed.

Chet did not expect them to make it past the sallyport. It was a six-foot square enclosed buffer zone between the jail door and the rest of the department. The jailer himself never carried a key to the sallyport. It had to be opened by the dispatchers, who were down on the first floor. When a jailer wanted out, he would stand in front of the video monitor and ask that the door be unlocked. The dispatcher was trained not to open the door without checking the monitor and making sure everything was okay.

Chet Going realized a good chance existed that he might be shot to death in the sallyport when David Allen Smith realized he was going to get no further. He accepted his fate.

"Well, that's the chance I took when I hired on here," he thought to himself.

When Chet and David Allen Smith came through the door from the jail into the sallyport, Chet spun and tried to slam the door between him and Smith. Smith managed to force his shoulder and foot inside the door. With a powerful shove, Smith pushed it open and rammed the gun into Chet's chest. He hissed, "Don't try that again!"

Rick Price, a uniformed patrolman, saw them coming through the jail door. His casual greeting to Chet froze on his lips when he saw the gun in Smith's hand. Price quickly drew his Smith and Wesson service revolver, pulled the hammer back, and pointed it at Smith.

"Drop the gun!" he ordered.

"Put your gun back in the holster," Smith yelled, burying his gun in Chet Going's ribs.

Price backed up, lowering his gun a bit.

"If you don't put down your gun I'll kill Chet!"

Price lowered his gun, stepped into a doorway out of the range of fire, and spoke into his portable walkie-talkie: "Headquarters, we have a jailbreak in process!"

"Get on the phone and tell them to let you out!" Smith ordered, moving the gun to Chet's head.

Chet complied. Much to his shock, the locked door opened. It should not have happened, but the dispatcher had not followed protocol.

Downstairs in the dispatch room, things were in a state of confusion. In the two years the dispatcher had worked at the department, the panic alarm had never sounded. The dispatcher was responsible for recognizing more than two hundred possible alarms. Not immediately identifying it, the dispatcher pulled a manual and was trying to find out what alarm number 508 meant. Meanwhile, Chet's request to open the door came at the exact same time Rick Price was broadcasting the jailbreak in progress. Without looking at the monitor, the dispatcher hit the button unlocking the door. Almost simultaneously, the other dispatcher yelled, "He's got a gun to Chet's head!"

With a shift change coming up at 11:00 P.M., more officers than usual were in the building. The six just getting off a shift had been joined by the six coming onto the midnight shift. Price's radio broadcast alerted them to the crisis: a jailbreak in their midst.

Lieutenant Steve Strong issued a command to the officers in the station: "Do *not* let him off the premises. Shoot if necessary."

The officers fanned out. Some took positions at the bottom of the steps inside the building. Others took positions on the parking lot outside near the back door. Others covered the front door. David Allen Smith could not get out of the building without encountering armed officers.

Smith, his gun still pressed to Chet's head, positioned Chet in front of him as a human shield. He made his way down the stairway toward the back door of the station. His gun was still tied to his hand, loaded and ready to fire.

Steve Strong waited near the bottom of the steps. He heard the footsteps as David Allen Smith and his reluctant human shield came down the concrete stairs. He pointed his .357 Magnum Smith and Wesson revolver at Smith as the robber and his hostage came into view. Chet's face was pale.

"Do you know the count?" Strong mouthed to Chet. The jailer nodded.

On his second day at work Chet Going had been trained that if he were ever taken hostage, the officer trying to rescue him would tell the bad guy that he was going to count to three before shooting. In reality, the officer would shoot at two. The hostage had to know to drop to the floor *before* waiting for the word *three*. Dropping at *two* was very important if one did not want to be directly in the line of fire.

"You're not leaving!" Strong yelled to Smith.

"Yes, I am!"

"If you don't drop your gun by the time I count three, I'll shoot!" Strong warned. "One!"

Strong aimed his gun at Smith. Chet was in his way. Smith was still pointing his gun at his hostage. Chet had two guns pointed at him. Things did not look good.

"Two!"

Chet dropped toward the floor. As he went down, he reached out and grabbed the door handle, throwing open the back door of the station and falling through it.

Strong fired.

Smith lunged through the open door, pointing his gun at Chet and jerking his arm as if firing.

Officer Brad Moore, positioned near Steve Strong, also fired at Smith as the federal prisoner disappeared through the door.

Chet and Strong both thought Smith was shooting Chet. The jailer was down.

Once in the parking lot, Smith dashed to a nearby patrol car. He crouched between it and another car, bobbing as officers opened fire upon him. After several seconds of thunderous gunfire, Smith staggered and went down on the pavement of the parking lot.

"Cease firing!" Brad Moore yelled. "He's been hit. Call an ambulance."

"Drop your weapon!" officers yelled at Smith.

"I can't," he said. It was tied to his hand.

Patrolman Fred Holzum raced forward and kicked the gun from his fingers.

Rick Price and Steve Shields approached Smith. They tended to him as they awaited the ambulance. Smith had been hit one time in the center of his chest. The bullet actually nicked his heart. Eleven shots had been fired at him. Most drilled holes into the side of the patrol car behind him.

Captain Howard Boyd recovered the .25-caliber semiautomatic handgun that had been tied to Smith's hand. It was loaded, a shell still in its chamber. The shell's primer was dented, indicating that the firing pin had struck the primer, suggesting that Smith had indeed pulled the trigger when he pointed the gun at Chet. Fortunately for Chet, the gun had misfired. Boyd later test-fired the gun, and found that it misfired about 30 percent of the time.

Smith recovered from his wound and lived to face prosecution. I charged him with attempted escape, kidnapping, and armed criminal action. His case began its trek through the court system.

Meanwhile, each officer who fired a shot at David Allen Smith awaited the ballistics results with bated breath. Eleven shots fired and only one hit! The pitiful marksmanship was rather embarrassing for the department. But everyone was curious. Whose shot hit him? Which officer was the only one who actually shot Smith, rather than the patrol car? Many Miss America finalists have endured the wait for contest results with less anxious anticipation.

Andy Wagoner of the Southeast Missouri Regional Crime Laboratory compared the slug taken from David Allen Smith's chest to slugs fired from each officer's weapon. There were sufficient markings for him to make a conclusive match.

The winning contestant was Steve Strong.

The numerous officers who only succeeded in killing a patrol car endured significant ribbing for months. Most of them will remain nameless, but they know who they are.

⚖

David Allen Smith took his case to trial. He decided to claim that Chet Going had been a willing participant in the escape attempt. In this scenario, David Allen Smith had not committed any kidnapping, because his victim was consenting to the whole thing.

It should be noted that Chet Going was completely cleared by investigations into the jailbreak by both the Cape Girardeau Police Department and the United States Marshals Service. One of the other jailers, however, flunked a polygraph test and was fired but never faced criminal charges because of a lack of solid evidence. The woman who smuggled David Allen Smith the gun pled guilty and received a ten-year prison sentence for her part in the crime. Neither side called her to testify at Smith's trial.

With his shoulder-length blond hair and his wire-rimmed glasses, David Allen Smith looked something like John Lennon of the Beatles. He was smarter than the average criminal, and I took that into account when I prepared my cross-examination.

In *The Art of Cross-Examination,* Francis L. Wellman, who served as a prosecutor and trial lawyer in New York City in the 1880s and 1890s, wrote of the importance of tailoring a cross-examination to the intelligence of the witness. He gives one unforgettable example from a case where he was defending the Metropolitan Street Railway after two of its trolley cars had collided, injuring a man:

> The plaintiff, a laboring man, had been thrown to the street pavement from the platform of the car by the force of the collision, and had dislocated his shoulder. He had testified in his own behalf that he had been permanently injured in so far as he had not been able to follow his usual employment for the reason that he could not raise his arm above a point parallel with his shoulder. Upon cross-examination, while acting for the railroad, I asked the witness a few sympathetic questions about his sufferings, and upon getting on a friendly basis with him suggested that he be good enough to show the jury the extreme limit to which he could raise his arm since the accident. The plaintiff slowly and with considerable difficulty raised his arm to the parallel of his shoulder. "Now, using the same arm, show the jury how high you could get it up before the accident," was the next quiet suggestion; whereupon the witness extended his arm to its full height above his head, amid peals of laughter from the court and jury.

It was unlikely that I would be able to completely trip up a clever witness like David Allen Smith, but I felt I could probably show him to be what he was—a liar. I was armed with a note found in the toilet of Smith's jail cell. It had been torn to shreds, but evidence technicians reassembled it.

After he took the stand and claimed that Chet Going was to be paid $50,000 for helping him escape, it was my turn. I decided to ask him other questions before confronting him with the note.

"Mr. Smith, isn't it true that your plan for getting out of jail was using a woman named Mary Chatterly, whom you had met in the Cape City jail?"

"Yes."

"You had met her and, in fact, when she got out of jail, you had some of those other people make calls to her and you kept up contact with her while she was out of jail?"

"Yes."

"You wrote numerous letters to her while she was out of jail?"

"Yes."

"In fact, she agreed that she was going to get the hacksaw blades in to you, and she was the one who brought the hacksaw blades in the baby powder to the jail to give to [the other jailer] to give to you?"

"She was going to have them, not smuggled in by him, but as a way to get around him."

"Your position is he didn't know they were in there, but she had given them to him, and he didn't find them and give them to you?"

"Correct."

"And the same thing as to the gun. She is going to steal one of her husband's guns, get it in the box of candy at your direction, and actually put the bullets inside pieces of candy and get it smuggled in to you?"

"Correct."

"What benefits did you promise Mary Chatterly for helping you get the hacksaw blades and gun?

"For us to be together."

"The original plan was to go out the hole and not even involve the jailer?"

"Yes, that was the original idea."

"Now, you testified in direct that you never intended to use that gun. My question is, why carry a *loaded* gun if you don't intend to use it?"

"Because I didn't want to shoot anybody."

"Why not have an *unloaded* gun?"

He shrugged.

"You shrugged your shoulders. You indicate you don't know the answer to that?"

"A gun's a gun."

"A *loaded* gun is a gun capable of killing. An *unloaded* gun is not capable of killing. You chose to have a *loaded* gun, isn't that right?"

"Yes."

From letters found in other inmates' cells, it was clear that someone named "Reb" was planning to help Smith once he got out. I held up the reassembled note.

"In this note, when you say Reb is supposed to get on a bus, and Mary is supposed to pick him up, and he is bringing the stuff, who's Reb?"

"It's a name I use for another person."

"Who is that other person?"

"That person doesn't want to volunteer."

"That person isn't in the courtroom. *You,* here in the courtroom, are refusing to answer the question. Who's Reb that you are referring to as the person who is supposed to get on a bus and bring the stuff?"

"Just a friend."

"What is his name?"

"He doesn't wish to be disclosed. I am *not* a snitch."

"So you're *not* going to tell us his name?"

"No."

"Now, in this other note it says here, `I have my tie strings ready in case I have to get the drop on Chester.' You mean the tie strings to tie the gun in your hand, or what?"

"No, no."

"How would tie strings help a person get a *drop* on somebody?"

"I don't understand."

"Well, most of us have never had occasion to get *the drop* on anybody. When you say `I have my tie strings ready in case I have to get the drop on Chester,' what are the tie strings and how is that going to help someone get the drop on somebody?"

"Oh, tying somebody to the bars or whatever."

⚖

In closing argument, lawyers are allowed to use stories, analogies, metaphors, and other literary devices to make their points. I began with a story about the late Federal District Judge Kenneth Wangelin.

About a year ago, a federal judge in Cape Girardeau named Kenneth Wangelin, who was from Poplar Bluff, passed away. One time when he was in the courtroom sentencing of a criminal defendant in a drug case, the defendant said to him something that many defendants say, "Judge, don't send me to prison. I'm not the kind of person who could survive in prison. You might as well give me the death penalty as send me to prison." Judge Wangelin took off his glasses, leaned over the bench, and looked straight at the defendant and said, "Son, I'd like to give you the death penalty, but it's not within the range of punishment. Ten years!" That's the kind of case we have here. If the death penalty were allowed here in Missouri for the kind of case where a person escapes with a gun, holding it at the head of a jailer, I would like to ask for a death penalty. What we have here are two crimes, attempted escape and kidnapping, that carry a possible range of punishment of 10 to 30 years or life in prison; plus a third charge, armed criminal action, that carries a term of years of three years or more. I've seen juries come back with 100 years for armed criminal action. What I am asking the jury to do in this case is to send a message to this defendant, and to other manipulating convicts in prison who are calculating ways to escape from jail, who are calculating ways to have guns smuggled in, to have files smuggled in, so they can use them to put the jailer and the public in danger by having a gunfight situation. I am asking you to send a message to him and other prisoners that: "You use a weapon to try to escape, you will be put away so you will not be seen out on the streets again."

Later, I addressed his claim that Chet Going was involved.

You know, this whole show that Chet was involved was just a vindictive act of a dangerous con man. He's mad. He's upset that it didn't work, that he got shot. He's mad that Chet turned out to be a stronger person than he was. He's mad at Chet, and he's trying to take Chet down with him because Chet, more than anybody, behaved heroically and stopped this thing. So he's mad at Chet and he's trying to cause problems for Chet at the same time. What about his refusal to tell us Reb's identity? He said he won't tell us because "I'm not a snitch." If he's not a snitch and if Chet Going were really involved, what is he doing to Chet Going? He's snitching as much as he can! He's a liar, that's what he is. Chet Going is the one who resisted, even though this man was pointing a gun at him. I submit to you there are two heroes in this case. One is Chet Going, and the other is Steve Strong, who took the responsibility of giving the order to shoot to kill. "Do not let this man get to the public. Do not let him get off police department premises. Shoot to kill." And he did shoot to kill. Both of them behaved heroically.

I believed it then. I believe it now. Both are heroes.

The jury found David Allen Smith guilty of all three counts and recommended two life sentences plus one hundred years in prison. Judge Anthony Heckemeyer ultimately ran all three sentences consecutively.

Yes, David Allen Smith was a smart guy. Somewhere the money he stole awaits him when he gets out of prison. It is off in the distance, always out of reach, like the pot of gold at the end of a rainbow. It will be a long, long time before he gets a chance to spend it, thanks to Chet Going and Steve Strong.

I never learned how much it cost to repair the perforated patrol car. It was not something the chief of police liked to discuss. Being a considerate person, I avoided the topic.

All officers of the department continued to receive frequent marksmanship training. It seemed to me they were spending a bit more time at the firing range.

Steve Strong was later promoted to chief of police.

Battered Bride

But love is blind, and lovers cannot see
The pretty follies that themselves commit.
                    —William Shakespeare

Love is blind, but marriage restores its sight.
                    —Georg Christoph Lichtenberg

Nora Rice had a secret when she married Clem Rice. Lots of brides have secrets, some significant and some silly. But hers was rather more extraordinary than most and would come back to haunt her sooner than she expected. Really good secrets are hard to keep.

Nora's wedding was normal in many ways. She was thirty-five years old, a good marrying age since one should know what one seeks in a spouse by that time. She had been dating her fiancé for a while, which is always prudent. She had even moved in with him for a trial run at cohabitation, a practice no longer universally condemned and in some circles even recommended. In short, on that Monday afternoon in March she was much like many other blushing brides.

One difference, however, was immediately noticeable. Her husband-to-be was not clad in black. Nor did he even wear a suit. Instead, he was decked out completely in orange.

He was not a reject from a Fruit of the Loom advertisement. He was, in fact, a prisoner at the Cape Girardeau County jail. Nora's wedding was taking place in the courtroom of Associate Circuit Judge Gary A. Kamp at the Jackson courthouse. Kamp, freshly elected as the newest judge in the county, had taken office just nine weeks earlier. By Missouri statute, judges may perform marriage ceremonies. This was to be one of the first conducted by Judge Kamp.

Lots of things rush through a woman's mind on her wedding day. Most probably feel incomparable surges of love for the men they are marrying. Many might experience bittersweet sadness while taking this final step toward leaving the loving home of their parents. Some may wonder if they are doing the right thing. Others are totally frazzled and stressed-out by the complications of a big wedding. Only a mind-reader could know precisely what Nora Rice was thinking on that eventful day as she stood in the division III courtroom with her husband-to-be in front of the black-robed Judge Kamp. One thing she was undoubtedly thinking was both functionally practical and the *main* reason for the urgency of the ceremony: *By marrying him I won't have to testify against him!*

Missouri is one of only four states in the country where the law still allows a woman to refuse to testify against her husband in a domestic violence case. Prosecutors have tried unsuccessfully for years to persuade the legislature to change this antiquated law because of the unwanted message it sends about spouse abuse: *Yo, forty-six progressive states! Send us your wife-beaters, your woman-haters and your thugs-who-like-to-give-the-old-lady-an-old-fashioned-thumping-now-and-then! The public policy of our state is that if the abuser can coax, cajole, threaten or intimidate his victim into refusing to testify, no one can force her to do it.* How wonderful it is to live in an enlightened state like Missouri!

But I have editorialized. Sorry.

Clem Rice was in jail for a domestic assault upon Nora. His transgressions included hitting her on the nose and chin, choking her, throwing her to the ground, kicking her in the ribs, pushing her against a wall, throwing a shot glass at her head, and otherwise behaving in a manner inconsistent with the profile of a high draft pick in the marriage lottery. Most women would find his method of courtship rather unappealing. Some would decide it was high time to return the engagement ring. Some would cut off his gonads while he was sleeping. Nora was a pacifist, though, and her trip to the emergency room had not lessened her adoration for this man. In her written statement to the police describing in detail what he did to her, she concluded: "He hurts me all the time. Please don't hurt him. I love him." She drew a picture of a heart next to her words.

This would probably be the proper place to say that domestic violence cases are among the hardest and most heartbreaking cases for a prosecutor to handle. Much too often, you find yourself watching helplessly as a battered victim goes back to her abuser, no matter how much effort you expended trying to prevent further abuse from occurring. Sometimes jail helps. Sometimes counseling helps. All too often, nothing helps. In Nora's case, she was marrying her abuser as a preemptive strike against the prosecution to ruin the state's case against the man who had left her black and blue.

There she was, standing in the courtroom, looking at the groom all decked out in his jail-issue jumpsuit. Perhaps Nora thought Clem looked good in orange. Maybe this was her idea of a romantic wedding. Whatever was going on in her mind, she did not back out of the courthouse ceremony.

The nuptial event itself was rather understated. You had your judge, the only one who really dressed for the occasion. He wore his black judicial robe, still practically brand new. You had your bride, wearing one of her nicer outfits; after all, the sign on the door made it clear that shorts were not allowed in the courtroom. You had your groom, unmistakable with the rather tacky and informal "CAPE GIRARDEAU COUNTY JAIL" emblazoned on the back of his jumpsuit. Two division III court clerks served as official witnesses to the ceremony. Also accepting kind invitations to the wedding were two burly bailiffs from the sheriff's department. They were assigned the duty of transporting the prisoner across the street to the courthouse. Perhaps one served as best man and the other as a bridesmaid. Those details will forever remain fuzzy, however, since neither will admit to being a bridesmaid, even for the laudable purpose of historical accuracy.

As for photography, Nora had not opted for a professional studio. She would simply make do with his and hers mug shots: his for assault; hers for a recent shoplifting offense.

No rings were exchanged, but the groom was not completely unadorned by precious metal. He wore shiny handcuffs and shackles, accoutrements not uncommon in a marriage, but usually invisible to the naked eye.

When the ceremony was over, the bride set off for her honeymoon night. The groom, on the other hand, trudged back to the county jail. Consummation of the marriage would be forced to wait for the intercession of one of three things: an inexpensive bailbondsman; the serving of the groom's jail sentence; or a stroke of luck rendering a conviction unlikely, such as a key witness suddenly becoming legally entitled to invoke the spousal privilege when the case came up for trial. Nora undoubtedly had a hunch this marriage was going to be consummated in the very near future. She was probably all smiles as she left the courthouse. She and the defendant had outfoxed the prosecutor!

Even though I had not been invited to the wedding, I eventually heard about it. As Clem Rice's prosecutor in his domestic violence case, I was not especially pleased to hear about the nuptials. This particular assault case was not one I could still win without the cooperation of the victim. There were no other witnesses to the assault besides Nora. The defendant had not confessed. Her statement to the police would not be admissible in court since it constituted hearsay. Once Nora informed my office that her recent wedded bliss would prevent her from testifying about a trivial bit of brutality in the home environment, the case went down the tubes.

Clem Rice was released shortly thereafter, free to return to Nora's loving embrace. But the story was not over. Not quite yet. There was still the matter of Nora's little secret. Some beans were about to be spilled as a result of a rather extraordinary coincidence.

The bailiffs at the Cape Girardeau County Sheriff's Department perform a variety of functions. They transport prisoners to and from the courthouse. They provide courtroom security during hearings and trials. They serve subpoenas on witnesses and civil summonses on parties to civil lawsuits. It is a hectic job. Lots of prisoners come and go. Many pieces of legal paper are served upon literally thousands of litigants and witnesses each year.

Yet, in spite of all the water under the bridge, the bailiff who acted as either the best man or maid of honor at the wedding of Nora Rice (again, he refuses to be clear upon this one point in an otherwise forthright discussion of the matter) remembered Nora quite well when some civil papers to be served landed in his hands. These were from a civil suit in St. Louis.

"Why," he said, astounded. "This is the same woman who just got married in Judge Kamp's courtroom a couple of weeks ago!"

He called me.

"You remember that case you had on Clem Rice, the one you had to dismiss because he married Nora, the witness against him?"

"Yes."

"Well, I've got some interesting news for you."

"Okay."

"I just got some papers from a court in St. Louis to serve on Nora in a civil case."

"So?"

"It's the *type* of lawsuit that's so interesting."

"Frankly, nothing much interests me anymore about Clem and Nora Rice."

"You're going to eat those words. This particular document is the divorce petition from Nora's husband in St. Louis. Her *real* husband. It seems she was already married to one husband when she married Clem Rice. Isn't there a law against that?"

"Bigamy," I said.

"I know it's big of you to take my call when you're so busy," I could almost hear him smiling over the telephone, "but I just thought you'd want to know about this. Isn't it a crime to marry someone when you already have a spouse?"

"Bigamy is a class D felony," I said. "It carries up to four years in prison."

"There you go," he said. "And quit calling me a bridesmaid!"

Fate had dumped on Nora Rice like a cloud of diarrhea-stricken starlings on a Civil War statue. The exact same bailiff who acted as one of the few witnesses at her tiny courthouse wedding had been assigned the duty of serving her with the divorce papers from her previous marriage.

What were the odds of that?

⚖

I must confess, I did not end up filing the bigamy charge against Nora Rice. For one thing, by the time the bigamy case fell into my lap, she had already picked up felony charges for fraudulently attempting to obtain prescription drugs. I could get a sufficient pound of her flesh without tacking on the additional bigamy charge. Furthermore, to win the bigamy case, I would need to bring her other husband from St. Louis to testify in my case. Having already met one of the men Nora had selected as husband material, I was not enthusiastic about meeting another. It would be just our community's luck if he liked our town and decided to stay. Besides, he was now muddying the water by claiming she *possibly* thought she was already divorced because he had told her years earlier he *planned* to divorce her. As Thomas Jefferson liked to say, the game did not seem to be worth the candle.

Finally, I had the feeling that being married to Clem Rice would prove to be punishment enough for Nora. The initial glow of seeing that devilishly handsome man in that natty orange jail outfit would eventually fade, and she would ultimately see his true colors. Sure enough, within a year he assaulted her again. This time she was willing to testify. Love had blinded her, but marriage restored her sight.

Shootout at the Super 8 Motel

Have you ever wondered why police officers wear
a shield on their left side? This is a direct,
intentional, overt reference to the knights of
old. There really were knights. They woke up
every day and donned armor. They hung a weapon
on their hip and a shield on their left side.
And they went forth and did good deeds and
administered justice in the land. . . . Today in
both the military and law enforcement communities, we have warriors who don armor every day,
take up their shields, strap on their weapons,
and go forth to do good deeds. . . . These new
knights are real and are embodying the spirit of
the ancient model of the knight paladin, the
champion of the weak and the oppressed, dedicated to righteousness and justice.
——Lieutenant Colonel Dave Grossman
and Loren W. Christensen

Every law enforcement officer in the United States has spent a significant amount of time carefully considering, fearing, fretting over, or
fantasizing about being involved in a shootout with some gun-toting
desperado. Some have thought about it since childhood days playing cops and
robbers. What else crosses one's mind while standing at a firing range, plug-
ging away at targets shaped like human bodies? Getting caught in a gunfight
is a very real risk of the job of being a police officer. As Lieutenant Colonel

Dave Grossman likes to say during training he provides law enforcement officers, most sane people run away from the sound of gunfire. The duty of the
police officer is to run toward it.

Although shootouts between lawmen and outlaws are no longer as common as in the days of Wyatt Earp and Wild Bill Hickok, they remain a fact of
life (or death) faced by the men and women who enforce the criminal laws of
our country. During my career as a prosecutor, cops in my jurisdiction have
been involved in more than one gunfight. From my bird's-eye view as a prosecuting attorney, I have learned that Hollywood has given us several mistaken
impressions about shootouts.

For one thing, when a person is shot, his body does not go flying backward to slam into the wall behind him nor crash through a nearby storefront
window. Rather, the perforated body keeps moving in the direction it had
been going. The impact of the slug doesn't knock it in a different direction.
Even if the bullet hit the subject's brain and killed him instantly, the gunshot
victim would simply drop, his momentum carrying him in the same direction
he had been moving before he ceased to care where he went or fell.

Which brings up another point. The first shot, or even repeated shots, seldom kills the adversary instantly. It is not unheard of for a person shot through
the heart to run fifty yards before collapsing. That is half the distance of a football field. This is possible because even though the heart has quit pumping
blood, the brain is still functioning on the blood it had previously been supplied. The brain doesn't quit operating until it runs out of fresh oxygen. It can
still control the function of the feet. And the trigger finger.

This is an extremely important factor to keep in mind in regard to gun-
fights, because it means that even if you shoot the other guy first, he may not
go down; he may return fire and kill you, too. The winner of a gunfight is not
always the fastest draw, like in the movies, but the shooter who successfully
incapacitates the other shooter first. The victor of a shootout is usually the first
person who puts a bullet into his opponent's brain or spinal cord.

Police officers go to the firing range regularly to keep their firearms skills
sharp. Officers of the Cape Girardeau Police Department are required to qual-
ify with their firearms twice a year. Certified firearms instructors work with
them to improve their accuracy and instincts. Shootouts with paintball guns
have been incorporated into the training programs of most police depart-
ments. The goal is to be so well trained you will react automatically during a
gunfight, with accurate and deadly shooting skills. When a police officer
loses a gunfight, the officer has not only lost his or her life, he may have failed

to prevent the killer from murdering other people as well. That is why officers are trained to shoot to kill when they decide they must shoot at all.

An officer never knows when a gunfight will take place. Certainly, Keith May and Brad Moore had no idea they were on their way to a gunfight when they were dispatched to the Super 8 Motel at 8:30 P.M. one chilly Saturday in February. It was supposed to be a routine case about drugs in a motel room.

⚖

Keith May is a friend of mine. We have worked closely over the years when he served in the detective division and during his seven years working undercover drug cases. He helped me haul the furniture when my office moved from one building to another. He is intelligent and professional and adept at finding the humor in any situation. On the night he was sent to the Super 8 Motel, he had been a police officer for sixteen years.

Brad Moore is a respected veteran of the patrol division. As one of its sergeants, he commands a group of patrol officers during his shift. He typically supervises six officers. His wife is a probation and parole officer for the Missouri Board of Probation and Parole. A few years ago, when I noticed that his daughter had become a National Merit Scholar, I congratulated him. He smiled and said, "She gets it from her mother." When he accompanied Keith May to the Super 8 Motel, he had been a police officer for twenty-four years.

Brad was one of the two firearms instructors at the Cape Girardeau Police Department. The other was Keith May. They knew a thing or two about guns.

⚖

Keith May and Brad Moore had not been involved in the drug investigation culminating in their visit to the Super 8 Motel. The preliminary work had all been done by other officers.

It had started much earlier in the day when an employee of the motel noticed suspicious behavior. The occupants of room 120, a man and a woman, were seen carrying cans of ether and bottles of butane back and forth from the room. The alert motel clerk suspected they might be getting ready to cook up a batch of methamphetamine. He called the police. Drug investigators began working the case but were not able to develop enough evidence of probable cause to ask the prosecutor to try for a search warrant.

"Swing by and do a 'knock-and-talk,'" the narcotics officer requested.

Keith May had spent seven years as a narcotics officer himself, so this was routine work for him. As Brad Moore said later, Keith was the "knock-and-talk" man. A "knock-and-talk" occurs when the police do not yet have sufficient evidence of criminal activity to take to a judge to get a search warrant, so they decide instead to simply knock on the door, identify themselves as police officers, and request permission to come inside. Once inside the door, they explain what's going on and request permission to search. It is surprising how many people will consent to the search, even when practically sitting on drugs or other illegal contraband. The officers in my jurisdiction have been aggressive in using "knock-and-talk" searches. I even wrote an article about this particular type of search for a law journal. With a nod to the poet Ogden Nash, I titled it: "Knock and Talk Consent Searches: If Called by a Panther, Don't Anther."

So, on that chilly evening in February, Keith May and Brad Moore went to the Super 8 Motel in Cape Girardeau to do a routine "knock-and-talk." They wanted to snoop around room 120 for a meth lab. No one had any particular reason to think the occupants of the room would be especially dangerous.

⚖

Keith knocked on the door. After a few minutes, the woman opened it a crack. Her name was Jenna McGillicutty. She was twenty-seven years old.

"I'd like to talk to you," Keith said. "We've had a report about some drug activity going on in this room. Would you talk to us?"

"Sure," she said. "I'll need to put on some clothes, though."

She closed the door.

As she closed it, Brad Moore noticed that she was already wearing clothing, specifically a white shirt and a pair of denim shorts. Why would she lie about her reason for closing the door? Perhaps her real reason for the delay was to hide something. He mentioned it to Keith May.

Nevertheless, moments later she was back at the door. She opened it, but still did not invite them in.

"Are you the only one in the room?" Keith asked.

"No. My husband's with me. We were just doing the nasty."

"Is he dressed?"

"Not yet."

"Well, we're all boys," Keith joked. "We're not easily embarrassed. May we come in?"

She closed the door for a couple of minutes, but finally opened it. She invited them inside.

Keith was surprised to see that in spite of the woman's quip about doing "the nasty," the man was fully clothed. He wore a black sleeveless tank top, gray sweatpants, white socks, and brown boots, which he had laced up. He was lying on the double bed closest to the door in the standard-sized motel room. He was a big guy, 6' 2", 220 pounds. His hair was cut short over his ears. It was blond with dark roots. He sported a moustache and goatee. A large tattoo of a jester grinned at the officers from the man's right shoulder.

His name was Matthew Stephen Marsh. He was twenty. Originally from Indiana, he had been living with McGillicutty for a couple of months in nearby Scott City, Missouri.

"What's your name?" Keith asked.

Marsh gave the name and social security number of McGillicutty's husband, which he had memorized. Keith May wrote the information on his clipboard. At that point he had no way of knowing the man was lying.

"You're not in any trouble," Keith assured him. "We just had a report about drugs in your room. May we look around?"

"No problem," Marsh said.

Keith noticed a smell of ether, a telltale sign of methamphetamine, but as he and Brad Moore searched the room, they did not immediately find anything. In fact, they were just about to leave when Brad Moore lifted a bit of clothing on the dresser and found a glass jar with white residue on it and a butter knife in it.

"What's this?" Brad Moore asked.

"I don't know. It's not mine," Marsh said.

Marsh was still lying on the bed closest to the door, his back propped against the headboard. Jenna McGillicutty had moved to a position on the other bed. Keith May stood at the foot of Marsh's bed, facing Marsh. Brad Moore was on the other side of the room, looking down at the jar coated with white residue.

Marsh stood up.

"Sit down," Keith May said.

Suddenly, Marsh stuck a hand underneath a pillow on the bed.

"What are you doing?" Keith asked.

Marsh came up with a gun. Without a word, he pointed it at Brad Moore.

"Gun!" Keith yelled. "Drop it, man!"

The guns of Keith May and Brad Moore were both holstered. This is standard procedure in a "knock-and-talk" because it would be next to impossible for a prosecutor to convince a judge that consent to a search had been voluntary if the officers asking for permission to search had been brandishing guns as they made the request.

Keith May drew his .40-caliber Glock semiautomatic handgun as Marsh fired at Brad Moore. Keith drew fast, but Marsh's gun had already been aimed at Brad before Keith had time to react.

Brad Moore felt the shot strike him in his left shoulder. It hit the socket of his arm, rendering it useless. The pain was excruciating.

Jenna McGillicutty screamed and curled into the fetal position near the headboard of her bed.

In terrible pain, Brad Moore drew his Glock with his right hand.

Keith May fired at Marsh at about the same time Marsh turned his gun upon May. They were no farther apart than the length of a bed.

Marsh's shot hit Keith on the right side of his abdomen, just an inch below his bulletproof vest. It passed completely through his body, although Keith could not tell at first where he had been hit.

Keith kept firing at Marsh.

Brad Moore started firing at Marsh.

Marsh dropped to his knees but still gripped his gun in his hand. Down but not out, he was not giving up. He lunged forward.

The lawmen continued firing. A fusillade of bullets slammed into Marsh.

Marsh finally fell face-first to the carpet, motionless. His gun rested just a foot from his hand.

By that time, Brad Moore was on his knees, his left arm dangling limply.

"I can't get his gun," Brad said. "I can't move my arm."

"I'll get it," Jenna McGillicutty volunteered.

"*No!* Stay away from it!" Keith May ordered.

Keith opened the motel room door and slumped to the floor.

He spoke into his radio.

"Headquarters! We need assistance. We've got two officers down, two officers down."

Brad Moore, convinced he was bleeding to death, ordered Jenna McGillicutty to get him a towel from the bathroom. She did so, bringing him a used, wet one. He pressed it to his wound.

She approached Keith May.

"Don't touch me," he said.

⚖️

Three minutes later, Trooper Todd Turlington of the Missouri Highway Patrol dashed into the motel, gun drawn. He had been on patrol nearby when he heard May's urgent broadcast. He ran to the first-floor room where two officers were down.

Keith May was lying on the floor, half in and half out of the motel room. Brad Moore was leaning against the foot of one of the double beds, clutching his arm. Jenna McGillicutty was kneeling beside him, yelling for help. Marsh lay on his face between the beds, a .380 Lorcin semiautomatic handgun lying inches from his hand. Turlington grabbed the gun, took out its magazine, ejected the shell from the chamber, and slipped the pistol into the waistband of his pants.

Other officers and ambulances arrived within minutes. McGillicutty was handcuffed. May and Moore were rushed to the hospital. The coroner was summoned for Marsh. The body was autopsied the next day.

Marsh's body bore nine gunshot wounds. A shot to the right side of his face had knocked out six teeth and broken his jaw. Two shots had plowed through his neck. One had struck his right chest and gone through his liver. Four had entered his shoulder and driven through his body, leaving "multiple perforations" of his right lung and heart. Another shot had hit his upper left arm.

The autopsy revealed that he had been under the influence of methamphetamine at the time he pulled the gun on the officers. Methamphetamine causes restlessness, confusion, anxiety, hallucinations, paranoid psychosis, and violent and irrational behavior. It can even cause cardiac arrest. In Marsh's case, it undoubtedly contributed to his foolish decision to shoot two police officers, thereby drastically shortening his life expectancy.

Marsh's pants contained thirteen live .380-caliber rounds in the right front pocket and seven live rounds in the left front pocket. Had he not been riddled with bullets, he could have continued the gunfight for quite a while.

⚖

I was on call that Saturday night, meaning I was to be paged if the police needed a prosecutor. The calls usually involve search-and-seizure questions, or requests for search warrants. I was with my wife and children at our favorite Mexican restaurant, *El Torrero*. Our dinner was interrupted by the call that two of my colleagues had been shot. It was not clear whether they would live or die. I hurried first to the motel room, where the acrid odor of gun smoke still clung to the air, and spoke to officers at the scene. I then rushed to the hospital, where off-duty officers and their wives had begun a vigil for their fallen friends. At the time, most of the fear was for Keith May, since the shot to his gut seemed much worse than Brad's shot to the upper arm. Keith was undergoing surgery. Everyone hoped and prayed that no vital organs had been hit.

From the hospital I went to the police station, where investigators were questioning Jenna McGillicutty about the identity of the shooter and how the two of them had come to be at the Super 8 Motel with a gun. She gave written consent for further searches of the motel room and her car. I prepared search warrants for her mobile home in Scott City and for samples of her blood and urine. Police found four baggies of methamphetamine in the nightstand in the motel room, plus a meth lab in her car. The meth lab consisted of the normal items: a mason jar with residue, some ephedrine pills, a bottle of Liquid Fire drain cleaner, two cans of butane, coffee filters, propane fuel, two cans of Sterno, starting fluid, a cooking pan, and glassware.

It was a huge relief when we heard the news that both officers would live. To everyone's surprise, it turned out that Brad Moore's injuries were the more severe; it was unlikely his arm socket could ever be fully repaired.

⚖

Within hours, the public was abuzz about the shooting. A twenty-year-old man had been shot to death by the police. Two officers were wounded in a shootout at a local motel. Would the officers live? Would they be charged with the man's death?

Once again, the local prosecutor was thrust center stage. Some important decisions would need to be made. This time, the coroner and I used what is known as a coroner's inquest to answer the questions.

Coroner's inquests have existed since the Middle Ages. Under early common law, the office of coroner was second only to that of sheriff. In past centuries, knighthood was a prerequisite for the job. The coroner's powers were both judicial and ministerial. He was responsible for determining the cause and manner of death of any person whose life came to a violent or sudden end in his jurisdiction. In the old days, the coroner would often summon his jury while the body was still warm, and an inquiry into the cause and manner of death would begin immediately, right next to the body.

In modern times, the coroner (no longer required to be a knight) and the prosecutor work together and conduct the coroner's inquest in a courtroom. As litigation goes, the procedure is somewhat akin to shooting fish in a barrel, since pesky things like defense attorneys and judges are not present. It is purely and simply a chance for the evidence to be presented in a public forum to a jury charged with the responsibility of determining whether the death came as a result of foul play. Coroner's inquests can be particularly therapeutic for the community when, as in a case like this, the public needs to hear all of the facts in order to be able to rest assured that a particular killing was justified and that nothing is being swept under the rug.

Seven weeks after the shooting, once the lab reports were completed and the officers were physically able to come to the courtroom to testify, Coroner Michael H. Hurst convened an inquest to hear testimony about the shootout. As prosecutor, I was required to call the witnesses and examine them in open court, in front of anyone who cared to attend.

The courtroom was packed, filled to capacity with members of the media, with friends and family of Brad Moore and Keith May, with curious spectators, and with family members of Matthew Stephen Marsh. His family had heard a rumor that he had been shot eighteen times by overzealous police officers. Nevertheless, his violent death did not come as a complete surprise to them, since he had told at least one family member that if the cops ever tried to arrest him, they would have a shootout on their hands.

The six members of the coroner's jury heard both Keith May and Brad Moore describe what had happened. They heard Detective Trevor Pulley describe the crime scene. Phil Gregory, an investigator from the Missouri Highway Patrol, played them Jenna McGillicutty's taped statement. State Trooper Brenda Cone, a member of the Southeast Missouri Drug Task Force, told them about the drug investigation leading up to the shootout. The coroner took the stand to describe the bullet wounds to the body of Matthew Stephen Marsh. He provided the jury with a copy of the autopsy report prepared by Dr. Russell D. Deidiker. Not surprisingly, the coroner's jury ruled the shooting a case of justifiable self-defense.

In her statement, Jenna McGillicutty told how Marsh had been acting in an abnormally violent manner while bingeing on methamphetamine. Just the day before, in a violent rage, he had shot out the windshield of her car while she and her seventeen-year-old stepdaughter were cowering inside it. He had put the gun to McGillicutty's head during his rampage. She had not known he brought the gun to the motel, she claimed. She had specifically asked him to leave it at home and thought he had done so. He "freaked"

when the officers knocked at the motel room door. He quickly hid the drugs and told her to put on her shoes.

She accepted responsibility for the meth lab found in her car and pled guilty. I charged her with possession of a controlled substance. When the time came for her sentencing, I urged the judge to send her to prison for seven years, the maximum sentence possible for a first offense of possession of a controlled substance. It seemed to me that a drug possession culminating in a fatal shootout with the police was a bit worse than your typical drug-possession case. I made my argument to the judge:

> As you know, Jenna M. McGillicutty is the person who rented the motel room where she and Matthew Marsh were "getting high" and "making methamphetamine." She and Marsh had a history of methamphetamine usage. When police officers Keith May and Brad Moore responded to the motel room door after a tip that methamphetamine-related items had been carried into the room, McGillicutty is the one who let them into the room and then watched as Marsh pulled a gun on the officers and opened fire upon them. No case in Cape Girardeau County this year better illustrates the dangers involved in use of methamphetamine. In most cases the danger comes from the destruction the drug does to the user's body. In this case the danger came from the lengths to which users will sometimes go to avoid apprehension, putting them and the police and the public in danger. Other meth users need to see her get a prison sentence. The public needs to see her get a prison sentence. Her family needs to see her get a prison sentence. Keith May and Brad Moore need to see her get a prison sentence. Please give Jenna McGillicutty a sentence of seven years in this case.

One of the most frustrating parts of a prosecutor's job occurs when a judge simply does not view things the way the prosecutor does. Honest and honorable people can see fact situations in different ways. The judge in Jenna McGillicutty's case, who had run for his judgeship on a platform that he would be "tough on crime," chose to view her case as that of a routine first offender. He gave her probation as if this were merely a run-of-the-mill drug case. I was frustrated and exasperated. Fortunately, my condition did not last long. Jenna McGillicutty gave me another crack at her six months later when she was caught with another meth lab. This time I charged her with manufacture of methamphetamine, possession of methamphetamine, and possession of drug paraphernalia. Her probation was revoked and she was sent to prison for seven years.

⚖️

The shootout at the Super 8 Motel lasted about twenty seconds from the first shot until the last. It took place in a tiny motel room, the shooters less than twelve feet apart. Marsh fired twice, hitting both officers. Between them, May and Moore fired a total of fourteen shots, nine striking Marsh. Moore hit him five times. May four times. Both fired shots that would have proven fatal.

Keith May and Brad Moore each knew beforehand that if they were ever involved in a gunfight, it would not be like those portrayed by Hollywood. Even so, both were surprised at how fast and unexpectedly it happened, and how quickly it was over.

It is impossible to know what Matthew Stephen Marsh expected. What he undoubtedly learned during those split seconds is that it is not a good idea to engage in a gunfight with two firearms instructors, even when you get the drop on them and even when you shoot them first. If he had it to do over again, he might think twice, too, about getting hooked on methamphetamine in the first place. Stephen Matthew Marsh fought the law, and the law won.

⚖️

Prior to the shootout at the Super 8 Motel, the last time a Cape Girardeau police officer had shot and killed a suspect was sixteen years earlier, when a reserve officer named Winford Griffith shot Ricky Dean Burton, twenty-nine, twice in the chest as Burton was flourishing a knife in the emergency room at Southeast Hospital. A coroner's jury also ruled that killing justified by self-defense.

Several months after the shooting of Ricky Dean Burton, Ed Barker, a veteran police officer, pulled over a car for speeding. He was in the process of writing the ticket when the speeder said, "I'm Ricky Burton's brother."

Now, we have all had it happen. You know you *should* recognize a face or a name, but it just doesn't come to you why it should ring a bell. So it went for Ed Barker. He didn't remember the name, but he got the distinct impression that the driver expected him to recognize it. He decided that instead of admitting the truth, he would say something vague and hope to figure out from the context of the conversation why the name sounded so familiar.

His strategy worked, but not exactly as planned.

"How is Ricky, anyway?" was the vague statement he chose to make.

The driver was first stunned, then furious.

"You killed him, you [blankety-blanks]!"

Barker tore up the ticket. This speeder had been punished enough.

Venomous Voice

There is no character, howsoever good and fine,
but it can be destroyed by ridicule, howsoever
poor and witless. Observe the ass, for instance:
his character is about perfect, he is the
choicest spirit among all the humbler animals,
yet see what ridicule has brought him to.
Instead of feeling complimented when we are
called an ass, we are left in doubt.

—Mark Twain

The mice living in a few little holes of an
immense building do not know if the building
is eternal, who is the architect, or why the
architect built it. They try to preserve their
lives, to people their holes, and to escape the
destructive animals which pursue them. We are
the mice; and the divine architect who built
this universe has not yet, so far as I know,
told His secret to any of us.

—Voltaire

So, I am sitting at that dinner table with Mark Twain, and I work up
the courage to say what I am thinking.

"You know, you owe me one."

His bushy eyebrows lower over his glittering green eyes. His hair still has
its auburn color; it has not yet turned white.

217

"How do you calculate *that,* Mr. Prosecutor? We've never met until this evening."

"I did you something of a favor one time."

"If you refer to naming your oldest daughter, Olivia, after my wife, I already know *all* about it. Where I hang out these days, they've got more birth and death records than you can shake a stick at. It was nice of you to name her after Livy. We both appreciate it. Most people don't realize the contribution that wonderful woman made to my books by serving as my first reader and editor."

"No, Mr. Clemens. My daughter's name wasn't what I had in mind. I'm thinking of something else. But before I get to that, now that you mention *where* you came from to get to this dinner, well, that brings up rather more important questions."

Twain winks.

"I'll wager it does."

"For instance," I continue, "I always liked what you wrote in the flyleaf of your Saint-Simon book: 'So much blood has been shed by the Church because of an omission from the Gospel: Ye shall be indifferent as to what your neighbor's religion is. Not merely tolerant of it, but *indifferent* to it. Divinity is claimed for many religions, but no religion is great enough or divine enough to add that new law to its code.'"

I study his eyes.

"Your words seem both profound and controversial to me. Do you still believe them? Is evangelism an overrated, perhaps even negative, aspect of religion?"

"You got any cigars around here?" He makes a show of surveying the tabletop.

"What about the note you wrote in Conway's *Sacred Anthology:* 'Religion. The easy confidence with which I know another man's religion is folly teaches me to suspect that my own is also.' By now you must know the answers to all the great questions about religion. You can imagine what I'm feeling as I sit here with you. I have the opportunity of a lifetime to hear the truth!"

"Hang it, I'm not finding a single cigar! What kind of uncivilized establishment do you run here?"

"This room is a nonsmoking room."

"What!"

"Smoking is not allowed in most public places."

"Since when?"

"Oh, some time in the 1990s. I think you're avoiding my question."

He leans back in his chair.

"Well, so much for my majestic vice. Yes, young man, I *am* avoiding your question. You wouldn't believe the confidentiality agreements I had to sign in order to attend this little shindig. Had I known you wouldn't have any cigars, I might not have come. Certainly, we'll at least share some strong drink?"

"I've got beer in the cooler here."

"Excellent." His tone softens. "Look, Mr. Prosecutor, it's like this. If I tell you the secrets of the afterworld, you'll have no choice but to become a prophet. You'll be driven to share your knowledge. Being a prophet is a hard life. People won't believe you really know what you're talking about. They'll accuse you of being a fraud or a charlatan. Two thousand years ago you'd have been crucified. In later times you'd have been burned at the stake. Nowadays, you'd be labeled a kook. Those particular religions with some of their facts a bit wrong will call you a heretic. The best you could hope for would be a small cult following and an ambivalent profile of yourself on some television newsmagazine."

He makes his way to the cooler and extracts a can of *Coors Light*. He studies it for a moment.

"How do you open this blamed thing?"

"Pull up that little tab on the top."

He pops the top and takes a long drink straight from the can.

"Oh, that's good," he sighs. "That's something I miss."

He settles back into his chair.

"Do you like your job, Mr. Prosecutor?"

"Very much. I enjoy trying cases. I love studying the law."

"Well, well, a regular Pudd'nhead Wilson. Look, don't put yourself in a position where you become a prophet. Don't even tell a soul I was able to come back and dine with you. I'm not here to interfere with anyone's religion, either to strengthen it or weaken it. When I was alive I found it difficult to believe that one's religion could affect his hereafter one way or the other, no matter which religion. But I always felt that a man's religious beliefs were a great comfort to him during his life on earth and hence a valuable possession to him. So, let's steer away from these religion questions. The fine print in those confidentiality agreements could cause me no end of problems should I say too much. Besides, as Voltaire said, a human being's capacity to understand the hereafter is much like a barn mouse's capacity to comprehend the world outside his barn."

"I respect that," I say. "I'll drop the subject."

"So, what did you mean I owe you one?" he asks.

I tell him about "The Case of the Venomous Voice."

⚖

Audrey Morton was a drug dealer, but you would not have known it from looking at her. She was forty-five years old but looked much older. She was a heavyset, dark-haired, matronly white woman, prematurely aged by a hard life. If you were casting someone from Hollywood to play her role, you could not go wrong taking Roseanne Barr on one of her rough days.

Audrey Morton was making good money selling marijuana to kids half her age. They would come to her small white-frame house on Hickory Street to buy their weed. She was nabbed by the police when one of her buyers, a twenty-year-old boy, found himself in trouble and agreed to wear a wire and go into her house to make a tape-recorded buy from her. Detective Curt Casteel and other officers provided him with the buy money and the tape recorder and sent him in. The tape turned out to be priceless. At one point, the young informant asked her if she would get out her scales and weigh the marijuana in front of him, so he could make sure he was getting his twenty dollars' worth. She bristled. "I don't weigh them every damn time somebody comes in. Either they take my word or they don't. You don't want it, you don't have to buy it. There's the shitting door. It's weighed or I wouldn't sell it. . . . If you wanted a hundred dollars' worth, two hundred dollars' worth, I can see digging the shitting things out, but you have to let me know ahead of time to do that. The shit's weighed, but I'm not going to dig the shitting scales out!" Her voice was nasally and high-pitched and loaded with southeast Missouri twang. It dripped venom as she berated him for his temerity. Once he made the buy, he returned to the lurking police and provided them with the marijuana. He made a second buy from her the next day, also tape-recorded.

I charged her with two counts of selling marijuana. After her arrest, she claimed she had not been the person in the house who made the sales. The informant was the only witness who could confirm her identity, so it looked like the case would rest completely upon his credibility. The police had not seen the drug buys take place. They had merely sent the kid inside and listened to the transmissions over the wire. I heard her speak at her arraignment, though. I listened to the tapes. Her voice was a dead ringer for the nasally twang on the tapes.

I had an idea. As I am wont to do, I hit the law books.

I discovered that although Missouri appellate courts had never decided a case exactly on point, other states had allowed a prosecutor to ask the judge to order a criminal defendant to read something aloud for the jury, so the jurors could hear a sample of her voice. Defendants often claimed this was unconstitutional on the theory it compelled a defendant to testify against herself. The courts held, though, that a voice sample was not testimonial. A defendant in that situation was not testifying, because the content of what she was saying was unimportant. It simply amounted to letting the jury hear her voice, in the same way a witness could be compelled to raise a shirtsleeve to reveal a scar or tattoo or to walk across the courtroom to show a limp. The sound of the voice was merely a physical characteristic, like the color of one's hair or the size of one's nose.

The subject matter to be read, though, had to be innocuous. You could not, for example, require the witness to read a tract about the dangers of illegal drug use or verses from the Bible containing the Ten Commandments. In a New York case the judge had ordered the defendant to read a page from *People* magazine.

I prepared a trial brief on the issue. Defense attorney Donald Rhodes and I argued the matter at length before Circuit Judge Stanley A. Grimm during the pretrial conference. After reading the cases, Judge Grimm agreed with me and issued an order specifying that after the tapes were played, Audrey Morton was to read something innocuous to the jury so they could compare her voice to the voice on the tapes.

It worked like a charm. After the tapes were played, while the sound of that venomous voice still rang in the jurors' ears, I called Audrey Morton to the stand and handed her Mark Twain's *Life on the Mississippi*. Judge Grimm instructed her to read the first page to the jury.

"The Mississippi is well worth reading about," she read. "It is not a commonplace river, but on the contrary is in all ways remarkable. Considering the Missouri its main branch, it is the longest river in the world—four thousand three hundred miles. It seems safe to say that it is also the crookedest river in the world, since in one part of its journey it uses up one thousand three hundred miles to cover the same ground that the crow would fly over in six hundred and seventy-five."

As she continued reading Mark Twain's words, many thoughts filled my mind. First and foremost, of course, was the fact that her voice was undoubtedly the same voice on the tapes: high-pitched, nasal, and shrill, with a pronounced southeast Missouri accent. It would have been difficult to imitate that voice, or even to disguise it. The case was certainly won. In fact, it amounted to something of a Perry Mason moment.

My second thought was that the choice of reading material was satisfying and appropriate. Our criminal case had originated in Cape Girardeau, Missouri, a town nestled on the banks of the mighty Mississippi. In fact, her drug-dealing took place just nine blocks from the river. Mark Twain had visited Cape Girardeau numerous times, his feet touching the cobblestones of our levee at least two to four times per month during his three years as a riverboat pilot. When he guided steamboats over the great river between St. Louis and New Orleans, he stopped at Cape Girardeau both on the way downriver and on the way back. Somehow, it all seemed perfect.

It was not so perfect for Audrey Morton. The jury found her guilty and whopped her with a prison sentence of ten years on each of the two counts, with the sentences to run concurrently. She appealed her conviction. Forcing her to read from *Life on the Mississippi* became the central issue on appeal. In a unanimous decision authored by Judge George Flanagan, the court of appeals held that Missouri would follow the lead of other states and allow a trial judge to force a criminal defendant to read something to the jury in order to provide them with a voice sample. The scholarly opinion concluded:

> The defendant [claims] that the trial court erred in granting over defendant's objection the prosecutor's request that the defendant read to the jury, at the close of the presentation of the state's case, an excerpt from Mark Twain's *Life on the Mississippi.* . . . Although the record does not disclose the words read by the defendant, the state's brief sets forth the language contained on page 1 of a 1927 edition of *Life on the Mississippi.* There the inimitable author describes the river itself. Neither in the trial court nor in this court does defendant claim that the language was offensive or obnoxious, nor does defendant deny the accuracy of the state's brief's account of what was read. The object of the demonstration was not the language used but a voice, a physical characteristic which, like a limp or gesture, defies accurate verbal description. . . . The reading was brief and the text was innocuous. This court holds that procedures utilized here did not deprive defendant of a fair trial.

The case was published in the hardcover law books and assumed its role as an important legal precedent. Mark Twain had become a part of Missouri criminal law exactly seventy-five years after his death.

I thought Mark Twain would get a kick out of that.

Wherever he was.

Pernicious Protestors

I have not devoted eight years of my life
to the administration of justice because I take
pleasure in prosecuting and convicting. Rather,
I think of them as eight years spent in one of
the laboratories which tests the qualities of
government and its ability to make right those
things that are wrong.

—Thomas E. Dewey

One sad September day, Jeremy R. Shank, an eighteen-year-old corporal in the United States Army, was killed in a gun battle in Iraq. He was from Jackson, Missouri. The brave young man's funeral was scheduled for a Sunday afternoon in his hometown, at the First Baptist Church just a few blocks from my office in the courthouse. The visitation would be at the local McCombs Funeral Home. A great public outpouring of sympathy for his family suggested that both events would be well attended.

On the Wednesday before the funeral, there began an intense legal skirmish that evolved into an example of how a prosecutor can have an impact upon his community simply by doing some fast research and brief-writing and by standing up against those who would misuse the right to free speech to hurt other people. It all began that morning with a fax I received from a lawyer in Kansas.

In a two-page, single-spaced letter, the attorney informed me that she represented a church that planned to come to Jackson to protest at the soldier's funeral. I had never heard of it, but Jackson police officers told me that the group had become known for its practice of going around the country to the funerals of soldiers and holding up signs with slogans like "Thank God for

224

Dead Soldiers" and "Soldiers Die God Laughs." They also targeted funerals of homosexuals, again displaying various messages of hate, their favorite being "God Hates Fags." In fact, their Web site bore the same slogan. Her letter to me proclaimed that her clients were coming to Jackson to protest at the local boy's funeral because they wanted to get out the message that the "mores-of-sin" of the United States had "incurred the condign wrath of God, which wrath manifest [sic] by the death of these soldiers." She demanded to know my interpretation of one of Missouri's new laws, which made it a crime to protest "in front of" or "around" the location of a funeral from an hour before to an hour after the service. Her clients were coming to my county to raise a ruckus, but first they wanted assurance they would not be arrested and so they wanted to be positive my interpretation of the statute agreed with theirs. Her inquiry showed a certain lack of courage in their convictions on the part of her clients.

I had no desire to dispense free legal advice. Less than an hour later, I sent her a letter by return fax. My message was short and to the point. I told her that the law barring protesters from funerals would "be vigorously enforced in Cape Girardeau County" and that violators "would be prosecuted to the maximum extent possible under the law." I added, "I decline your invitation to debate specific clauses of the law with you prior to the arrests and prosecutions of any persons who violate this law. I have attached for you a copy of the law. Your clients will violate it at their peril."

I thought that might be the end of it. I was wrong.

An hour later I got a voice mail from Anthony E. Rothert, a lawyer with the American Civil Liberties Union in St. Louis. He also requested my interpretation of Missouri's statute criminalizing funeral protests. He warned that the ACLU planned to sue me in federal court the next day if I intended to enforce the statute. He claimed the statute was so vague that would-be protesters did "not know where they can safely hold their protest without facing arrest." I responded that the statute would be strictly enforced and that I was available for an appearance in federal court at any time on Thursday.

I had mixed feelings about the potential lawsuit. On the one hand, the good and honorable part of me preferred that the protesters simply give up the idea of coming to Cape Girardeau County to disrupt the funeral. It would be better if they would allow the friends and family of the slain soldier to grieve in peace. On the other hand, I enjoy a good legal fight on an important and novel issue. Threatening to sue me in an attempt to dissuade me from doing my job was like threatening to throw a pig into the mud. I would be in my element. I liked the idea of slugging it out with them in court, and I relished the thought of giving them a good legal thrashing. Still, I tried my best not to hope that they would sue me.

In the meantime, I prepared for a fight. I stayed up until midnight that night, reading all the major cases dealing with the constitutionality of restricting freedom of speech. It turned out that although the Constitution prohibits the government from abridging free speech, it allows regulation of the time and place of that speech. A leading case, involving abortion protesters who had targeted a doctor's home for around-the-clock demonstrations, upheld the prohibition of picketing "in front of or around" a person's home. Another important line of cases held that the federal court should generally abstain from getting involved until a criminal prosecution had run its course in state court, allowing the state judiciary to address the constitutionality of a state criminal statute like Missouri's funeral-protest law. In other words, the federal court should not stick its nose into the middle of a state court criminal case.

My computerized legal research into cases involving this barnstorming "church" also revealed that the Kansas lawyer who wrote me the letter had been briefly suspended in 1989. Her license to practice law had been yanked for making false statements about federal judges. Apparently, dishonesty is a temporary condition in Kansas, however. Her suspension lasted only one year.

When I went to bed, I still thought the hate group was probably bluffing about suing me. But I was ready just in case they weren't.

When I got to work the next morning, another fax awaited me from the American Civil Liberties Union. They were going to request a temporary restraining order against me on behalf of one of the Kansas protestors. The petition would be filed at 2:00 that afternoon at the federal courthouse in St. Louis and would name me as a defendant. They invited me to appear in court to oppose them if I so chose. *Oh, yeah,* I thought, *I'll be there.*

I quickly wrote an eleven-page brief on the constitutionality of the statute and then headed for St. Louis. During the two-hour drive I rehearsed the points to make during oral argument, and I mentally crossed my fingers, hoping to draw a favorable judge.

I knew there was no way to predict who would hear the petition. Temporary restraining orders always involve urgency. A suit seeking one is assigned to a judge available that day. It could be given to any of the eleven federal district judges with offices in the courthouse. The lawyers cannot pick the judge. It is completely the luck of the draw.

On the way to the courthouse, I thought about the federal judges in St. Louis. My first choice would clearly be Senior District Judge Stephen N.

Limbaugh, Sr. He was the father of Missouri Supreme Court Judge Stephen Limbaugh (who, early in his judicial career, when he was a circuit court judge, presided over my Delores Luton trial). Both were former elected prosecutors for Cape Girardeau County. The senior Judge Limbaugh was a legal scholar and a past-president of the Missouri Bar Association. He had a healthy respect for precedent, and I suspected that he would follow the rulings of the cases I had found. My second choice was District Judge Henry E. Autrey, a former state trial judge who had presided over one of my hazing trials. He was a former assistant prosecutor for the City of St. Louis. I had a huge amount of respect for both Autrey and Limbaugh, and I liked my chances on this particular legal issue in front of either of them. I did not know enough about the other nine judges to even hazard a guess how they might view the matter.

I arrived early at the federal courthouse and made my way to the clerk's office. At precisely 2:00, the lawyer for the American Civil Liberties Union arrived and filed the lawsuit. Sheriff John Jordan and Jackson Chief of Police James Humphreys were also named as defendants. I immediately filed my response on behalf of all three of us. The clerks disappeared for a moment to do whatever machinations they employ to decide which judge will get the case.

Eventually, one of them returned and announced, "The judge will be Judge Limbaugh."

I nodded, concealing my elation. So far so good.

"He's out of the building at the moment," she said, "but he should be back at 3:00. Would you rather wait for him to return or would the two of you agree to go to the next judge on the list?"

I did not wait for Rothert's thoughts. "I'll wait for Judge Limbaugh," I said.

It turned out that Judge Limbaugh was on vacation that week but had come in that day to deal with a few urgent matters. Providence had smiled on Cape Girardeau County in the designation of the judge. Now it was up to me to win the case on its merits.

An hour later, Judge Limbaugh welcomed us into his chambers and invited us to argue the case. He let the lawyer for the American Civil Liberties Union go first. Rothert, a passionate advocate for free speech, who zealously argues for its protection at virtually any place and any time, asserted that the law enforcement officers and I should be barred from enforcing "this unconstitutionally vague" criminal statute. He argued that his clients would suffer irreparable harm if they were arrested and prosecuted in Cape Girardeau County for protesting at the funeral. When it was my turn, I countered that the criminal statute merely banned them from protesting "in front of" or "around" the location of the funeral within an hour before or after the service. They were free to protest the war almost anyplace else in the world on that particular day, including Jackson's public parks or the Cape Girardeau riverfront, but they had to stay away from the funeral. I pointed out that at least thirteen other states had enacted similar laws. The legislative history showed that these laws were intended to allow families to grieve in peace at the funerals of their loved ones and to prevent others from inflicting emotional distress upon them. I reminded Judge Limbaugh that the words "in front of" and "around" were words of common usage and that a reasonably intelligent person could understand what they meant. I added that the cases starting with *Younger v. Harris* in 1971 had discouraged federal courts from interfering with a state court criminal prosecution, absent a strong showing of irreparable harm. I cited cases holding that undergoing a criminal prosecution is not generally considered irreparable harm.

At the end of the hearing, Judge Limbaugh held that the ACLU had not shown that the protestors would suffer irreparable harm if they were arrested for protesting in front of or around the funeral, and he declined to issue the temporary restraining order. He added that if he were asked to address the constitutionality of the statute based on what he had heard up to that point, he would find it constitutional. The case was over. The lawsuit against me had lasted slightly less than two hours. I was free to prosecute the jayhawking hatemongers if they decided to come to Cape Girardeau County to protest at Jeremy Shank's funeral. It had been a good day's work.

As the ACLU lawyer and I left the courthouse, I offered to get him a map of the route the funeral procession would be taking from the visitation at the funeral home (scheduled for noon on Sunday) to the church (where the funeral was scheduled to begin at 2:00 P.M.). I warned him that protestors outside either place would risk prosecution. He told me I need not send him the map.

"In light of Judge Limbaugh's ruling, they won't be coming," he said.

It was good news, and I relayed it by telephone to Lt. Bob Bonney at the Jackson Police Department, but law enforcement officials in Cape Girardeau County did not take the surrender at face value. They prepared just in case. Eighty-three officers from eight different law enforcement agencies volunteered to help Chief of Police James Humphreys enforce security at the funeral. Chief Humphreys held a planning session for all officers and told them that starting an hour before the funeral, anyone protesting within sight of the church was to be arrested. The same applied to the visitation at the funeral home. Judge Gary A. Kamp was the judge who happened to be on call for the weekend. Of all the judges in the circuit, he had a reputation for setting the highest bonds. If the protestors showed up in Jackson to make a spectacle of Jeremy Shank's funeral, they would find it far easier to get into Cape Girardeau County than to get out of it.

I was the prosecutor on call that weekend. I spent Sunday morning at my office in the courthouse, typing charges for various miscreants arrested on Saturday night for routine things like domestic violence and drunk driving. I was ready to type arrest warrants for the prospective visitors from Kansas. In fact, I planned to do so enthusiastically. I was decked out in my Mizzou black-and-gold, in honor of the traditional rivalry between the University of Missouri Tigers and the University of Kansas Jayhawks. If given a chance, I was going to bag some real-life Jayhawkers. Two of my secretaries had volunteered to come in and help me type charges if there were more than I could type by myself in one afternoon. They were at their homes, awaiting my call.

As it turned out, the hatemongers were all talk. They never showed up. The funeral went smoothly. Jeremy Shank, a fine young man, was given a fond farewell by his family, friends, and hundreds of sympathetic community members. His father, Jim Shank, delivered a moving eulogy, noting that his son had specifically requested that his father speak at his funeral if he did not make it home.

At the end of the day, I was glad the protestors stayed home. I was proud that the Cape Girardeau County prosecuting attorney had helped prevent the pernicious protestors from raising a ruckus at the funeral of a local hero. I had not alerted the media to the story about my successful legal battle to keep them out of town, though. While I usually don't shun good media coverage, I felt that publicity was just what those zealots wanted. They weren't going to get any from me.

Two weeks later, *USA Today* and the *St. Louis Post-Dispatch* reported that the same group of Kansans had traveled to Kentucky and convinced a federal judge to issue a temporary restraining order barring enforcement of Kentucky's state statute prohibiting protests outside funerals. The headline of the *USA Today* article proclaimed, "Law Limiting Funeral Protests Tossed Out." The *Post-Dispatch* article four days later was headlined, "Demonstrators Hit at Soldier's Funeral." The story reported that the demonstrators had surrounded the funeral home and squared off and exchanged shouts with mourners for more than an hour outside the funeral of Sgt. Charles Jason Jones in London,

Kentucky. Reading it, I realized Cape Girardeau County had had a narrow escape. I had made a big difference in what had happened in my community on that particular Sunday afternoon.

I felt a renewed sense of pride over what Judge Limbaugh and I had prevented from occurring in our community. Make no mistake about it. It makes a difference who holds the job of prosecuting attorney in a jurisdiction. It makes a difference who sits on the bench as a federal or state judge. Prosecutors and judges are sworn to follow the law. But they must be sufficiently competent to find and learn the law in order to follow it. They must be sufficiently humble and harbor a genuine respect for the law to follow its precedents and avoid basing their interpretation of the law upon their personal whims.

I sent the Kentucky prosecutor a copy of my brief and wished him luck with any future cases in his jurisdiction. I also sent my brief to Missouri prosecutors across the state. The training coordinator for Missouri prosecutors forwarded it to the National District Attorney's Association, making it available to prosecutors throughout the country. I felt I had a shot at becoming a real thorn in the foot of that Kansas hate group. I hoped I would. Sometimes a good enemy can provide you with more entertainment and enjoyment than your friends.

Published Prosecutor

> There are three infallible ways of pleasing an author, and the three form a rising scale of compliment: 1—to tell him you have read one of his books; 2—to tell him you have read all of his books; 3—to ask him to let you read the manuscript of his forth-coming book. No. 1 admits you to his respect; No. 2 admits you to his admiration; No. 3 carries you clear into his heart.
>
> —Mark Twain

As a college undergraduate, I majored in English. It proved to be good preparation for law school because so much of being a lawyer, at least of being a trial lawyer, involves writing and storytelling. Also, since English classes were my favorites, I tended to make good grades in them, and good grades are a prerequisite to getting accepted into law school. The English background served me especially well during the first semester of law school, when the grade for each class was based solely upon a final essay test. The following year, students who had majored in accounting and business gained ground on me when we hit classes like Income Taxation and Business Organization.

Even after I began working as a lawyer and prosecutor I kept up my interest in reading and writing. I published several articles in law journals and contributed a book chapter here and there to law books. But my real passion remained writing fiction.

It is hard to describe my excitement when my historical novel, *The Gold of Cape Girardeau*, was finally published. I had labored over it during evenings, weekends, and vacations for many years, so it was literally a dream come true when it finally hit the bookstores. It received favorable reviews, and its first printing of three thousand copies sold out quickly. Its second printing of three thousand also sold out. Now in later printings, sales are still chugging along.

Dr. Susan Swartwout, the publisher of the Southeast Missouri State University Press, told me when the book came out one October that she had given a copy to a reviewer named Harper Barnes at the *St. Louis Post-Dispatch*. Excited at the prospect of seeing my book reviewed in the very same paper that had landed in my yard daily for over twenty years, I began monitoring its book page as if I were on a stakeout.

Christmas came and went with no review of my book. I called the *Post-Dispatch* and asked for the book editor. She turned out to be a crisply polite woman named Jane Henderson. I told her who I was and why I was calling.

"The book never reached my desk," she said.

"The University Press gave a copy to Harper Barnes," I said.

"Well, maybe they did. But it never got to me. A book has to cross my desk before it gets reviewed in our newspaper. Have the publisher send me another copy if you'd like."

Later the same day, Dr. Swartwout mailed another copy of *The Gold of Cape Girardeau* directly to the attention of Jane Henderson.

I resumed my book-page surveillance but resisted calling until sometime in March. This time, the book had arrived but was buried somewhere in a stack in Jane Henderson's office.

"Look," she patiently explained, "as the book editor at the *St. Louis Post-Dispatch,* I personally get two hundred books *per week* from publishers and authors hoping we'll do a story or a review about their book. You need to understand. Statistically, the odds are not in your favor."

Glumly, I hung up, figuring that was the end of it.

In late May, I got a call from Jane Henderson.

"Hey, I read your book. I loved it. We're going to do a story about it next Wednesday. Will you have the University Press email me a color photograph of you along with the cover of the book?"

"Done!"

On Big Wednesday I leaped out of bed about 5:00 A.M. and grabbed the morning paper shortly after it hit the turf. Sure enough, the story about my novel was on the front page of the Everyday section, along with a color photograph of the first-time author, with my name in bold letters right under the picture.

Now, I had been in the newspaper many times over the years through my job as a prosecutor, but this was something entirely different. This was a moment I had dreamed about since my freshman year of college. In fact, I had wanted to be a published novelist longer than I had thought of being a lawyer. Oh, how sweet it was.

Hey, wait a minute! I realized I would need extra copies!

I hurriedly dressed and drove to a convenience store (formerly a 7-Eleven in a previous life) and plopped a half dozen copies of that morning's *St. Louis Post-Dispatch* onto the counter. The young man at the cash register did a double-take when he saw me. He looked to be in his twenties, with a smooth, handsome face and clean-cut dark hair.

"You look familiar," he said.

No doubt that my head puffed up visibly. Well, well, I thought. He must have read this morning's *St. Louis Post-Dispatch*. I'll have a little fun with this.

I opened the newspaper to the Everyday section and pointed to my picture on its front page. My name was still underneath the photo. Yes, indeed it was. "Funny you should say that on today of all days," I smiled. "There I am, right there."

He leaned over and studied the picture. Suddenly, his head jerked up.

"Morley Swingle!" he exclaimed. "You're the one who gave me my *felony* conviction!"

Ooof. It was not exactly the reaction I had been anticipating. To make matters worse, I did not remember him. As far as I knew, I had never seen him before in my life.

"Well," I said lamely, "things seem to be going better for you now."

His eyes narrowed.

"You don't remember me, do you?"

"Not really."

He was insulted.

"Don't you remember? I first got put on probation for assaulting my girl-friend, but after I kept sending her threatening letters, my probation got revoked and I was sent to prison."

I racked my brain. It just did not ring a bell.

"You have to remember," I said, "my office prosecutes over two thousand cases per year. Maybe it's a *good* thing the prosecutor doesn't recall you personally."

I quickly paid for the newspapers and fled the scene. Once I got to the office, I looked up the clerk's case. It turned out that although I had filed the charge, Assistant Prosecuting Attorney Angel M. Woodruff had handled most of the court appearances. At least I was not losing my mind.

In the end, the incident provided me with a much-needed dose of humility. The *St. Louis Post-Dispatch* boasts a circulation of some 300,000. As excited as I had been about having my book featured prominently upon its pages, I gradually came to realize that despite the newspaper's large readership, this felon was probably the only person in Cape Girardeau who actually saw the story about my book.

⚖

The convenience-store fiasco, however, was not my most bizarre encounter triggered by being a published prosecutor. That honor is reserved for an incident occurring a year after the publication of *The Gold of Cape Girardeau.*

I was handling a death-penalty murder trial in New Madrid, Missouri, down near Missouri's bootheel, right on top of the New Madrid fault. The case was particularly horrible. Two killers had discovered that Ralph E. Lape, Jr., a divorced man who lived alone, maintained a large bank account. They decided to kidnap him and steal his ATM card and PIN number. After jumping him and beating him and binding him with duct tape, they drove him the seventy-nine miles to New Madrid County and dug his grave while he was still alive. When the hole in the ground was big enough, they dragged him to it, and one of them fired a shot into his brain. No one will ever know which kidnapper actually pulled the trigger. Although they admitted working together in plotting the crime, pulling off the abduction, and digging the grave for the hog-tied victim, each claimed the other was the triggerman.

Mark Anthony Gill was the first to go to trial. The case went smoothly. We submitted it to the jury after only a week. While the jury began deliberating Gill's fate, I waited at the counsel table in the open courtroom. Gill called out to me from the defense's table, "Mr. Swingle, there's something I'd like to say to you."

I had just given an impassioned closing argument asking the jury to put him to death, so my curiosity was piqued.

"I'm not allowed to talk to you without your lawyers being present, but as soon as they come back in the courtroom, I'd be glad to hear what you have to say."

A few minutes later, David Kenyon and Sharon Turlington of the Missouri Public Defender's "death squad" rejoined him at the counsel table. I approached them.

"While you were out of the room, your client told me he wanted to say something to me," I said.

Mark Anthony Gill, the man for whom I was seeking the death penalty, then said to me, quietly, with apparent sincerity, "I just wanted to say that I sure would like to have a copy of your book."

Zap! I felt like I was in a scene from *The Twilight Zone*. For several moments I could think of absolutely nothing to say.

"I imagine that can be arranged," I finally said.

The jury eventually returned a verdict of death.

When I got home, I thought a lot about Gill's request for a copy of my book. Was he sincere? Did he really want to read it? Or was he instinctively familiar with Mark Twain's observation that the surest method of weaseling your way into a writer's good graces is to say something complimentary about his book. Perhaps he simply detected my vanity. Did it show so plainly?

I decided that through his attorneys I would send Gill a copy of *The Gold of Cape Girardeau*. I would pay for it out of my own pocket. It seemed like the least I could do, since the man was heading to death row because of my charging decision, my hard work at trial, and my incomparable courtroom eloquence. The tremendous job by the police who investigated the case had a little something to do with it, too, of course. Not to mention the heinousness of his crime.

Then I faced the problem of the inscription. Normally, when someone buys a copy of my book and I am anywhere in the vicinity, I will enthusiastically autograph it for him or her. Being a tolerably clever person, I often think of something witty to say. Oh, boy. This one was hard. You can imagine the tasteless quips that went through my mind. My first thought was something like, "You're on Death Row. Read fast!" Upon further reflection, I found that inscription too insensitive, even for me. Besides, it was not literally true. Most inmates awaiting execution languish six to ten years. He would not need to be a speed-reader by anyone's standards. Several other similar comments were summarily rejected once I decided against trying to be clever.

I considered writing something for this condemned man that might help him deal with the guilt he must certainly be feeling. In my wallet I carried two quotations from Dr. Harold Bloomfield's wonderful book *Making Peace with Your Past*. Many times over the years I had shared them with crime victims and criminal defendants. One read: "How can this terrible experience make me stronger, wiser, more compassionate, more tolerant, or more grateful for each moment from now on?" The other was a prayer spoken by Jews on the High

Holy Day of Yom Kippur: "Purify me, revive me, uplift me. Forgive my past and lead me into the future." I almost inscribed Gill's book with the Yom Kippur prayer, but then I recalled how the lawyers handling his appeal would undoubtedly be searching for any possible issue to get his conviction reversed, no matter how bogus. I pictured some inscription I had penned playing a lead role in a published appellate decision.

Better to say nothing, I decided. I ended up mailing the book unsigned.

But I do sincerely hope that God has forgiven Mark Anthony Gill and is leading him into the future. I hope that Gill is wiser, stronger, more compassionate, more tolerant, and more grateful for each moment in his life. I also hope that his eventual death by lethal injection might save the lives of other kidnap victims whose kidnappers make the right choice when deciding whether their hostages will live or die.

Motivational Message

The thousandth time you try a case, you will be
as terrified as you were the first time you
tried a case. But you turn it to advantage
through a physiological process which I cannot
explain, but which every trial lawyer experiences and after a while comes to master. That
terror produces a flow of adrenaline that is
beyond belief. I am positive when I try a case
that if a madman came running up with a .38
revolver and from six inches away pulled the
trigger twice, the bullets would bounce off. If
a locomotive came through the back wall of the
courtroom, with one hand I could stop it. That
is why every trial lawyer does things in the
courtroom on his feet when on trial that he is
not smart enough to do in the office. You hear
yourself saying things and, my God, that's
clever! Am I really saying that? It's as if
somebody else has taken over, and it is somebody else. It's you with adrenaline running
through your bloodstream. What you are able to
do after a while is put a cap on it. You make
the adrenaline work for you.

—Irving Younger

Vince Lombardi was famous for his galvanizing speeches to the Green Bay Packers. General George Patton also knew a thing or two about inspiring his troops. But not all stimulating speakers are so well known. In fact, one of the most motivational messages I ever received came from a coward who chose to remain anonymous.

It all began with the birth of my first child. I had every intention of being with my wife at the hospital throughout the entire adventure. Fully trained by Lamaze classes for my limited role in the production, I was ready to supervise my well-educated and sensible wife to make sure she did not forget to breathe during any key moment of the proceedings.

Most important, I managed to avoid having any of my cases set for jury trial within either a week before or a week after the baby's due date of August 6. Well, I take that back. One jury trial did slip through. It was scheduled for Monday, August 11. But what were the chances that the baby would miss the due date and arrive precisely five days late?

The case was the prosecution of Keith Drinkard. It was to be my twenty-eighth jury trial. I was at the time an assistant prosecutor for Larry H. Ferrell, a mentor I truly liked and admired.

The case was an important one. Drinkard, a Detroit drug dealer, had been nabbed by officers of the federal Drug Enforcement Administration (DEA). He had sold several sheets of LSD to a street-level dealer from southeast Missouri, knowing that the man from Missouri planned to return to Cape Girardeau to sell it to local customers. After the local dealer was caught and agreed to testify against Drinkard, the DEA brought me the case to prosecute. I charged Drinkard with conspiracy to sell LSD.

An interesting quirk about the case was that Drinkard had never set foot in Missouri. Conspiracy laws, however, allow a prosecution to take place either where the agreement to commit a crime occurred or where an overt act toward committing it occurred. Since Drinkard sold the LSD to his buyer in Detroit knowing the buyer was planning to return to Cape Girardeau to resell it, he could be prosecuted in the state courts of Missouri or Michigan, or in federal court. Prosecutors and police could make a choice where to prosecute him. Frankly, I was flattered the DEA brought the case to me.

Needless to say, Drinkard was stunned when he was arrested in Michigan on my charge and extradited to Missouri to stand trial at a small courthouse in southeast Missouri. He hired Richard Ochs, a talented trial lawyer from St. Louis, to represent him. I fended off a motion to dismiss the case for alleged lack of jurisdiction and prepared diligently for the August 11 trial date.

My wife's due date came and went. I did not become alarmed. Again, what were the chances the baby would arrive on the day of this one particular trial?

I was meeting with DEA Agent Rick Coleman at my house on the Sunday afternoon before the trial, doing some last-minute preparation, when my very pregnant wife interrupted our very important meeting.

"I'm having labor pains," she said.

What did she know? This was her first baby, after all!

"Not now!" I said. "The trial is tomorrow. Maybe it's gas pains. Why don't you go lie down and see if they go away?"

Dutifully, she disappeared into the bedroom, but Coleman and I both suspected that I was soon going to face a bit of a scheduling problem.

An hour or so later she reappeared.

"The labor pains are four minutes apart."

Though a poor Lamaze student, I realized this meant it was a good thing we only lived two blocks from the hospital. I thrust the box of police reports and exhibits into Coleman's hands.

"I'll see you at the courthouse in the morning," I said.

My wife and I arrived at the hospital about 7:00 P.M. on the eve of my trial.

It was unthinkable that the jury trial would be postponed. This was not just a local case involving local witnesses. The defendant lived in Detroit. He had been brought to Cape Girardeau from Michigan. The DEA chemist had already made the trip from Chicago. Forty jurors had already received notices requiring them to appear at the courthouse in the morning. The case was definitely going to trial. I did not even consider asking the judge for a continuance.

I did, however, call my boss, Larry Ferrell. Larry was familiar with the facts of the case. He was a veteran trial lawyer. He had tried dozens of drug cases. He was my friend. As I expected, he volunteered to try the case should it turn out the baby had not arrived by the time the trial started at 8:00 A.M. The trial was to be held in rural Bollinger County, Missouri, about thirty miles from the hospital.

Meanwhile, at Southeast Hospital, my wife and I did the normal things a couple does when having their first child. While she was occupied with real work, I donned surgical scrubs, tried to stay out of the way, and offered ineffectual, and mostly unappreciated breathing tips.

Our baby was born at 3:02 on that momentous Monday morning. The hours between 7:00 P.M. and 3:00 A.M. flew by for me. I believe they moved a bit slower for my wife.

We had not known the sex of our child before she was born. We did know, though, that if she was a girl she would be named Olivia.

The thrill of holding your child in your hands just seconds after her birth is one of those moments you never forget, but I did not have long to savor it. Once mother and daughter were resting comfortably, I dashed home, assured the confused dog that everything was okay, and leaped into the shower. Minutes later, I donned my navy blue "jury trial" suit, ran back to the car, and drove off to Bollinger County. I had a case to try.

Ironically, I was prosecuting a drug dealer while sky-high myself, but my drug was adrenaline. I could not have taped an eyelid closed, even had I stayed home.

It felt good when Circuit Judge A. J. Seier announced to a courtroom filled with jurors, witnesses, lawyers, and, of course, the drug dealer, that the prosecutor had become a father for the first time during the night. Not only was this unusual birth announcement enjoyable to hear, but I hoped it might give me a slight edge with the jurors. *What a guy! His child was born just hours ago but he still shows up for the trial!* Of such stuff are legends born.

The case was essentially a simple one. I presented the testimony of the local drug dealer who went up to Detroit and bought the LSD from Drinkard, the testimony of a local customer who bought some of it from the dealer when he returned from Detroit, the testimony of Rick Coleman, the DEA agent who made the case, and the testimony of the chemist who analyzed the LSD. I had rested the state's case by 2:30 P.M. We had a verdict by 5:00 P.M. The jury gave Drinkard ten years. The judge set a sentencing date and allowed the defendant to remain free on bond pending sentencing.

After packing my files, I headed back toward the hospital on the winding, blacktop roads of Bollinger County. With a new child born and another jury verdict under my belt, I had much on my mind. At that point I had been awake for approximately thirty-six consecutive hours.

Studies show that a person deprived of sleep for twenty-four hours is in an equivalent physiological and psychological condition to a person legally drunk. I don't know about that. I am certainly making no admissions here. What I do know is that as I drove over the hilly roads of Bollinger County, I was eagerly anticipating holding my newborn daughter. I was wondering about my wife's postchildbirth condition. I was feeling a bit cocky about winning a jury trial on the very day my first child was born. As the rural landscape shot by, my mind was filled with a million thoughts. Very few had anything to do with safe driving.

At the tricky intersection of Route 34 and Highway 72, I rear-ended a car that had first stopped at the stop sign, pulled out, but then suddenly stopped again. Fortunately, nobody was hurt. Lonnie Moore, a deputy with the sheriff's department, responded to work the scene. It is hard to blame a traffic accident on the other guy when you have rear-ended him. I didn't even try. With the front end of my car crumpled like a prizefighter's broken nose, I eventually resumed my drive to the hospital.

I made it to the hospital by 8:00 P.M. It had been more than thirty-eight hours since I'd had any sleep, but I still was not a bit tired. I was an adrenaline junkie, wired on the childbirth megadose, coupled with an extra shot from the jury trial. What a day! A child born, a jury trial victory, and a car wreck, all in one long day. I finally had time to settle down and visit with my wife and brand-new daughter. Although I did not know it, my motivational message was soon to come. At least it did not interrupt us that night.

⚖️

Three days later the *Southeast Missourian* carried Olivia's birth announcement. True to form, the newspaper listed the occupations of the new parents. Later that night, at 2:00 A.M., I was in the process of acquiring some new-parent experience, rocking a colicky baby, when the telephone rang. Colic, by the way, takes a tad of the fun out of the business of parenting. If you don't know what it is, I am not going to tell you. I want you to remain open to the idea of reproduction.

So, there I was, rocking my crying baby girl, when I picked up the ringing telephone. I figured it would be the police needing a search warrant. They are usually at the other end of my late-night phone calls.

A deep male voice said, "I hope your baby dies you [blankety-blank] so you can share the grief you cause other people."

The line went dead.

I felt a white-hot anger.

What a horrible thing to say.

What a coward.

Olivia quieted down, and I looked into her eyes. Whatever the caller had hoped to accomplish, the effect upon me was instantaneous and profound and affects me to this day. It drilled home to me the sad reality that there are truly evil people in the world. Those in law enforcement who are good at their jobs—whether as police officers or prosecutors—are making the community a safer place for everyone else. I knew when I hung up the telephone that it was unlikely I would ever go back to private practice.

So, whoever made that call, thank you for the motivational message. You galvanized me and helped give direction and focus to my life. I did not recognize your voice, but it seems probable that I had prosecuted you. I hope you profited from your stay in the hoosegow. I wish you many more days and nights of free lodging in the penal institutions of the great state of Missouri or elsewhere. But, during your travels through the calabooses of our country, take some advice from Tim Allen, the star of the television show *Home Improvement,* who served a stint in prison for a drug sale made during his reckless youth. The title of his wonderfully candid autobiography is instructive: *Don't Stand Too Close to a Naked Man.*

To the rest of my esteemed readers, I say thank you for letting me entertain you for a few hours and for allowing me to give you a glimpse of what it is like to be a prosecutor in America. I am grateful for the opportunity to hold one of the best jobs in the world. There is never a dull moment. Plus, you run across an entertaining story now and then.

The state rests.

Afterword and Acknowledgments . . .

During his prosecutor days, former Chief Justice Earl Warren wrote in a preface to a proposed manual that the district attorney "has become the most powerful officer in local government." He noted that the prosecutor "declares and determines the law enforcement standards of his county" and decides who shall be prosecuted and who "shall not be subjected to our criminal procedure." Warren thought it strange "that no one had ever bothered to write a book about the business of being a district attorney." I have tried to do so.

To make it more readable, I eliminated several footnotes cluttering up the first draft. Those who want to do further reading can find my references here.

For law students and others who might want to read the published appellate decisions generated by the cases described in this book, their citations are as follows: "The Case of the Perry Mason Moment" was *State v. Luton,* 795 S.W.2d 468 (Mo. App. E.D. 1990); "The Case of the Cross-Eyed Juror" was *State v. Allen,* 905 S.W.2d 874 (Mo. banc 1995); "The Case of the Fool for a Client" was *State v. McGee,* 781 S.W.2d 161 (Mo. App. E.D. 1989); "The Case of the Millionaire Murderer" was *State v. Pagano,* 882 S.W.2d 326 (Mo. App. S.D. 1994); "The Case of the Homicidal Energizer Bunny" was *State v. Bucklew,* 973 S.W.2d 83 (Mo. banc 1998); "The Case of the Weeping Witness" was *State v. Selvy,* 921 S.W.2d 114 (Mo. App. S.D. 1996); "The Case of the Venomous Voice" was *State v. Morton,* 684 S.W.2d 601 (Mo. App. S.D. 1985); "The Case of the Published Prosecutor" was *State v. Gill,* 167 S.W.3d 184 (Mo. banc 2005); and "The Case of the Motivational Message" was *State v. Drinkard,* 750 S.W.2d 630 (Mo. App. S.D. 1988). The visit to the *Oprah Winfrey Show* described in "The Case of the *Oprah* Appearance" aired on April 9, 1997, as "Dangerous Initiation Rituals."

For those interested in reading good biographies of prosecutors or others in the legal profession, I can recommend several. Anything written by former Los Angeles prosecutor Vincent Bugliosi is worth reading. My Bugliosi quotes came from *And the Sea Will Tell* and *Outrage: The Five Reasons Why O. J. Simpson Got Away with Murder,* published by W. W. Norton and Company in 1991 and 1996, respectively. I use *Outrage* as a teaching tool for young lawyers at my office. The best book ever written about life as a prosecutor is Robert Traver's *Small Town D. A.*, published by E. P. Dutton in 1954. Clarence Darrow's *The Story of My Life,* published by Charles Scribner's Sons in 1932, is one of my favorite legal autobiographies. I used several quotes from it. The posthumously completed autobiography of Thomas E. Dewey, *Twenty against the Underworld,* edited by Rodney Campbell and published by Doubleday in 1974, is told mainly in Dewey's own words, some of which I borrowed. The quote from Frank Hogan, a celebrated New York prosecutor, also came from the Dewey book. The Earl Warren quotes beginning both this section and "The Case of the Prancing Mare" are from John D. Weaver's excellent biography, *Warren: The Man, the Court, the Era,* published by Little, Brown and Company in 1967. My favorite Warren biography, though, is *Super Chief: Earl Warren and His Supreme Court,* by Bernard Schwartz, published by New York University Press in 1983. The best biography of Robert H. Jackson is Eugene C. Gerhart's *America's Advocate: Robert H. Jackson,* published by the Bobbs-Merrill Company in 1958. I used several quotes from it. Jackson's great speech to prosecutors about the importance of their job was reprinted as an essay: "The Federal Prosecutor," *Journal of American Judicature Society* 24 (1940): 18. It can also be found in the book *Ethical Issues in Prosecution* by John Jay Douglas, published by the National College of District Attorneys. Christopher Darden tells what it was like to suffer one of the most public losses ever by a prosecutor in *In Contempt,* written with Jess Walter and published by ReganBooks in 1996. Chief Justice Charles Evans Hughes's quip that God made Sundays so a man could work one day a week without being interrupted by phone calls came from Robert J. Steamer's *Chief Justice: Leadership and the Supreme Court,* published by the University of South Carolina Press in 1986. The inside tidbit that Supreme Court justices watched X-rated movies on "movie day" came from *The Brethren: Inside the Supreme Court,* by Bob Woodward and Scott Armstrong, published by Simon and Schuster in 1979. Jerry Seinfeld's humorous definition of a lawyer is from *SeinLanguage,* published by Bantam Books in 1993.

I quoted from several sources about practicing law as a prosecutor or trial lawyer. The best book ever written about cross-examination is probably Francis L. Wellman's *The Art of Cross-Examination,* published in 1903. It is now available in paperback through Touchstone Books. The late Irving Younger's tremendous lectures about trial practice are available on tapes and videotapes from the Professional Education Group, Inc., Minnetonka, Minnesota. My Irving Younger quotes came from their videotape of his lecture *Credibility and*

Cross-Examination. The classic observation by John Henry Wigmore that cross-examination is the greatest engine ever invented for the discovery of truth came from his treatise *Evidence in Trials at Common Law,* Sec. 1367 (Chadbourn Rev. 1974). Any lawyer preparing to cross-examine a mental health expert should consult *Coping with Psychiatric and Psychological Testimony,* by Jay Ziskin and David Faust, published by Law and Psychology Press in 1995.

Supreme Court cases mentioned in this book include *Berger v. United States,* 295 U.S. 78 (1935), the source of the great quote from Justice George Sutherland about the role of the prosecutor being to strike hard blows but fair ones; *Faretta v. California,* 422 U.S. 806 (1975), offering Justice Harry A. Blackmun's observation that a person who acts as his own lawyer has a fool for a client; *Michigan State Police v. Sitz,* 496 U.S. 444 (1990), containing Chief Justice Rehnquist's description of the immensity of the problem of driving while intoxicated; *Santobello v. New York,* 404 U.S. 257 (1971), supplying Chief Justice Warren E. Burger's quote about plea bargaining; *Tennessee v. Garner,* 471 U.S. 1 (1985), setting out when a police officer may use deadly force; *Jacobellis v. Ohio,* 378 U.S. 184 (1964), giving Potter Stewart's quip about knowing obscenity when he sees it; and *Brady v. Maryland,* 373 U.S. 83 (1963), the source of the "Brady Rule" requiring prosecutors to turn over to the defense any exculpatory evidence.

True-crime books can be a fertile source of closing argument material for a prosecutor. They often quote large sections from successful closing arguments. For my own summations, I have often borrowed bits from Vincent Bugliosi's closing argument set out in his book *Till Death Do Us Part,* published by W. W. Norton and Company in 1978. I learned about the Texas criminal defense lawyer photographing homes of jurors in Gary Cartwright's *Blood Will Tell,* published by Harcourt Brace Jovanovich in 1979. Joseph Wambaugh's *The Blooding,* published by William Morrow and Company in 1989, is a wonderful true-crime book dealing with the first murder case solved by DNA analysis. F. Lee Bailey's *The Defense Never Rests,* published by Stein and Day in 1971, is one of the books that inspired me to go to law school.

Other quotes in this book came from a variety of sources. Joan E. Jacoby wrote an authoritative series of articles about the historical context of prosecutors in America, published in *The Prosecutor,* the journal of the National District Attorneys Association. These were published in 1997 and republished in 2005. Along with her book *The American Prosecutor: A Search for Identity,* published by Lexington Books, D. C. Heath and Company in 1980, these are probably the most comprehensive writings on the subject. *National*

Prosecution Standards, Second Edition is a manual for prosecutors published by the National District Attorneys Association in 1991. It is must reading for all prosecutors. Likewise, every prosecutor should read *Prosecutorial Misconduct,* by Bennett L. Gershman. An updated version is issued each year by Thomson/West. It provides a list of things a prosecutor should never do. As the saying goes, an ounce of prevention is worth a pound of cure. One of my quotes about prosecutorial discretion came from *The Invisible Justice System: Discretion and the Law,* by Burton Atkins and Mark Pogrebin, published by the Anderson Publishing Company in 1982. The quote about plea bargaining being a fish market needing to be hosed down was from Ralph Adam Fine's *Escape of the Guilty,* published by Dodd Mead in 1986. The excerpt from the Carl Sandburg poem about the hearse horse snickering when hauling a lawyer away is taken from "The Lawyers Know Too Much," published in the book *Smoke and Steel* by Harcourt, Brace and Howe in 1920. The Richard Nixon and Monica Lewinsky pontifications about perjury came from articles about the Clinton scandal in the February 2, 1998, issue of *Time* magazine. The quote about police officers' badges being shaped like shields came from *On Combat: The Psychology and Physiology of Deadly Conflict in War and Peace,* by Lt. Col. Dave Grossman and Loren W. Christensen, published by PPCT Research Publications in 2004. This excellent book is the authoritative source on the effects upon a human being of being in a gunfight or other close combat. Senator George Graham Vest's famous speech about the dog being man's best friend has been reprinted in numerous works, including volume 3 of Robert C. Byrd's *The Senate, 1789–1989: Classic Speeches, 1830–1993,* published in Washington, D.C., by the Government Printing Office in 1994.

Those who enjoy reading fiction portraying a lawyer or prosecutor as a main character would probably share my enthusiasm for some of my favorite law-related novels. These include *To Kill a Mockingbird,* by Harper Lee; *Anatomy of a Murder,* by Robert Traver; *Rumpole of the Bailey* and the later books in the series, by John Mortimer; *Presumed Innocent,* by Scott Turow; *The Bonfire of the Vanities,* by Tom Wolfe; and *A Time to Kill,* by John Grisham. Ironically, the Perry Mason novels by Erle Stanley Gardner never struck me as being anywhere near as good as the television show and the movies. I understood why when I read a biography of Gardner and learned that the lawyer-turned-novelist dictated many of his novels for a secretary to type.

Last but not least, I am indebted to many people who helped me with this book. The law enforcement officers and members of my staff who lived these stories with me will occupy special places in my heart forever. Professor

Stephen D. Easton, a former federal prosecutor, read the manuscript with a critical eye and offered many valuable suggestions. Professor Edward H. Hunvald also read it. His helpful criticism was much kinder than his classroom grilling of me in the past. Sara Davis, editor at the University of Missouri Press, worked long hours as we differentiated the right words from the almost right words. As usual, my wife, daughters, and mother served as my initial readers and improved the book with their comments and suggestions.

I hope I never see you in court, dear reader. If I do, it means you have probably become either a crime victim or a criminal. Neither role is much fun. If one must be in a courtroom in a criminal case, the best place to be is at the counsel table for the prosecution. It is the best seat in the house.

Index . . .

Index

Morley Swingle has been Prosecuting Attorney for Cape Girardeau County for more than twenty years, and he has taught at seminars around the country. Some of the thousands of cases Swingle has prosecuted have been featured on the *Oprah Winfrey Show, Dateline,* and Court TV. He is the author of a novel, *The Gold of Cape Girardeau, and* a member of the Mystery Writers of America.